THE DYNAMICS
OF FOREIGN POLICYMAKING

Westview Replica Editions

The concept of Westview Replica Editions is a response to the continuing crisis in academic and informational publishing. Library budgets for books have been severely curtailed. Ever larger portions of general library budgets are being diverted from the purchase of books and used for data banks, computers, micromedia, and other methods of information retrieval. Interlibrary loan structures further reduce the edition sizes required to satisfy the needs of the scholarly community. Economic pressures on the university presses and the few private scholarly publishing companies have severely limited the capacity of the industry to properly serve the academic and research communities. As a result, many manuscripts dealing with important subjects, often representing the highest level of scholarship, are no longer economically viable publishing projects—or, if accepted for publication, are typically subject to lead times ranging from one to three years.

Westview Replica Editions are our practical solution to the problem. We accept a manuscript in camera-ready form, typed according to our specifications, and move it immediately into the production process. As always, the selection criteria include the importance of the subject, the work's contribution to scholarship, and its insight, originality of thought, and excellence of exposition. The responsibility for editing and proofreading lies with the author or sponsoring institution. We prepare chapter headings and display pages, file for copyright, and obtain Library of Congress Cataloging in Publication Data. A detailed manual contains simple instructions for preparing the final typescript, and our editorial staff is always available to answer questions.

The end result is a book printed on acid-free paper and bound in sturdy library-quality soft covers. We manufacture these books ourselves using equipment that does not require a lengthy make-ready process and that allows us to publish first editions of 300 to 600 copies and to reprint even smaller quantities as needed. Thus, we can produce Replica Editions quickly and can keep even very specialized books in print as long as there is a demand for them.

About the Book and Authors

The Dynamics of Foreign Policymaking:
The President, the Congress, and the Panama Canal Treaties
William L. Furlong
and Margaret E. Scranton

Negotiations and ratification of the 1977 Panama Canal Treaties were major events in the making and conduct of U.S. foreign policy. Beginning in 1973, the negotiations spanned three administrations, and the ratification process dominated the first year and a half of the Carter presidency.

This book explains the making of the Canal Treaties, looking at the interaction of executive and congressional policymaking, the domestic politics of the ratification campaign, and the international dynamics of superpower–small power relations. After presenting a brief history of the Canal and U.S.-Panama negotiations, the authors consider the executive branch's impact on the conduct of the treaty negotiations, comparing the administrations of Presidents Nixon, Ford, and Carter according to their opportunities for action, their initiatives and pressure toward resolution, their relationships with the bureaucracy (the Defense and State departments) and Congress, and their commitment to conclude the negotiations. Drs. Furlong and Scranton then turn to the ratification process and discuss how innovative action taken by the Senate will likely affect future treaty approval. Particularly important in their treatment of foreign policymaking is the central, but seldom analyzed, role of the House of Representatives.

William L. Furlong is associate professor of political science at Utah State University. **Margaret E. Scranton** is associate professor of political science at the University of Arkansas at Little Rock.

THE DYNAMICS OF FOREIGN POLICYMAKING

The President, the Congress, and the Panama Canal Treaties

William L. Furlong
and Margaret E. Scranton

Westview Press / Boulder and London

Copyright © 1984 by Westview Press, Inc.

Published in 1984 in the United States of America by Westview Press, Inc., 5500 Central Avenue, Boulder, Colorado 80301; Frederick A. Praeger, Publisher

Library of Congress Catalog Card Number 84-50032
ISBN 0-86531-804-2

Composition for this book was provided by the authors
Printed and bound in the United States of America

10   9   8   7   6   5   4   3   2   1

TABLE OF CONTENTS

LIST OF MAPS, TABLES, CHARTS AND FIGURES

PREFACE

The 1980s appear to be a decade of conflict and confrontation in U.S. foreign affairs, especially in our relations with Latin America. The process of resolution and a legacy of decades of popular grievances in Central America dominate the news, and the relative merits of conciliatory or confrontational approaches to the region are the subject of lively debate among scholars and policymakers. Thus current and successive administrations face the task of redefining U.S. national interests in an uncertain and increasingly unmalleable environment. In this context, the 1977 Panama Canal treaties stand out as an example of successful bilateral problem-solving and the use of negotiations as an instrument of U.S. foreign policy. Moreover, these negotiations, undertaken in the absence of a severe crisis or violences, proved to be a successful application of preventive rather than reactive diplomacy.

This book is about the politics and processes of negotiating and ratifying the 1977 Panama Canal treaties. Our focus is on the two principal institutions involved in U.S. foreign policymaking: the executive and the legislative. We trace the evolution of the 1977 treaties from their initiation in 1973 through their implementation as of late 1983.

We found the Panama Canal treaties to provide a valuable vantage point for exploring the dynamics of U.S. foreign policy. The interests of the United States in Panama and the Canal have always been related to broader foreign policy goals and doctrines. Moreover, Canal policy has traditionally been related to trends at home and abroad that either promoted or, more often, precluded an accommodative response to Panama's grievances. Since our analysis of Canal policy spans a decade, 1973–1983, our study relates these broader trends and developments to U.S. objectives and actions on this single issue.

The politics of changing foreign policy is a major theme of our analysis. As an issue, Panama Canal policy represents a symbolically charged and highly controversial problem for the United States to resolve. Like other divisible issues which open the policy process to unusually high levels of public attention, Canal policy fully taxed the capacities of the executive and the Congress to exercise their constitutional powers and to respond concurrently to legitimate Panamanian grievances and contradictory domestic pressures and preferences. Moreover, both branches had to manage the divisive effects of advocacy and resistance to change in Canal policy at the same time that they were engaged in the broader talks of redefining the meaning of national security in a changing world. The years 1973–1983 were marked by rapid and significant changes abroad. By focusing on policymaking for one issue throughout this decade, our study demonstrates the political challenges that face any administration that attempts to make fundamental changes in a well-established external relationship. These challenges have been compounded by developments at home, including internal reforms in Congress, the rise of the New Right as an influence on foreign policy, and the emergence of a fragmented consensus, with elite opinion divided over the merits of cold war doctrine versus détente. These challenges are aptly illustrated by the case of the 1977 Panama Canal treaties, which narrowly missed defeat by the Senate in one of the longest and most difficult ratification processes in U.S. history.

Another major theme of our study concerns the negotiations process and conditions that facilitate or frustrate the use of bargaining to resolve bilateral conflicts. As a product of fourteen years of negotiations, the 1977 Canal treaties represent a substantial diplomatic achievement for the United States and Panama. Our analysis of the negotiations held between 1974 and 1977 explores how the U.S. negotiating team overcame organizational resistance to bargaining with Panama as well as constraints posed by election year politics. We also analyze negotiating strategy, largely from a U.S. perspective, and how different issues on the bilateral agenda were resolved.

A third major theme of our study is methodological. We developed an eclectic model to analyze and provide an integrated explanation for U.S. Canal policymaking. Our analytical approach combines several concepts and theories in the field of foreign policymaking, and we willingly acknowledge our intellectual debts to the theorists cited in Chapter 1. We also want to give special recognition to three scholars whose ideas have been particularly significant for our study: to Robert Wendzel for his work on bargaining, to I. William Zartman for his work on the negotiating process, and to Charles O. Jones for his work on the public policy process. The authors of this study collaborated closely with each other in developing the analytical framework presented in the introduction and in drawing their conclusions. Any faults found in these areas are ours alone, not the theorists'. Other chapters were primarily written by one of the authors.

William L. Furlong, a specialist in Latin American politics as well as U.S. foreign policy, had the arduous task of developing an overview of U.S.-Panamanian relations and the history of Canal policy beginning with the idea of building an interoceanic canal, through the 1903 Hay-Bunau-Varilla treaty, and up to the 1977 treaties. This historical overview is provided for the reader unfamiliar with U.S.-Latin American relations and with the issue of Canal policy. Professor Furlong is also primarily responsible for the chapters on Congress, its role in ratification and passage of implementation legislation for the 1977 treaties, and the evaluation of treaty implementation. He was in Panama during the summer of 1977, when the Panamanian government upset the negotiations by introducing unexpectedly large financial demands. Professor Furlong was also in Panama during April 1978, when the final vote on the resolution for ratification was cast in the U.S. Senate. In addition to his expertise on the region and Panama, Professor Furlong conducted over thirty interviews with participants in the White House, Congress, and the Departments of State and Defense. His confidential interviews, conducted in Washington, D.C..during 1978 to 1983, also included participants in the negotiations and the treaty implementation processes.

Margaret E. Scranton, a specialist in U.S. foreign policymaking, has researched two decades of U.S.-Panamanian relations and Canal policy. Her dissertation, ''Changing United States Foreign Policy: Negotiating New Panama Canal Treaties, 1958–1978,'' received the American Political Science Association's Helen Dwight Reid Award in 1981. Professor Scranton is primarily responsible for the third chapter, analyzing the evolution of U.S. Canal policy objectives and the merits and risks of changing Canal policy, and for the chapter on the 1974–1977 negotiations and analysis of executive impact. She interviewed over twenty-five participants in the negotiations and ratification process during 1977–1978 while she held a Foreign Policy Studies Research Fellowship at The Brookings Institution. Professor Scranton was in Washington researching Canal policymaking through the ratification process.

In addition to confidential interviews, both authors consulted the vast public record of hearings and other government documents related to the 1977 treaties. We have taken careful precautions to verify and cross-check our interview and documentary evidence. As with all studies of this kind, however, we realize the limitations of available data and accept full responsibility for errors of interpretation.

This study is indebted to the support of many sources. The International Programs Office at Utah State University provided grant funding for a forum on the Panama Canal treaties that produced much of the impetus for this study. The USU Department of Political Science provided generous material and moral support, as well as financial resources for typing and editing of the manuscript's several drafts. The department's Milton R. Merrill Chair Fund also provided financial support for partial editing and publication-related expenses. We are also indebted to many people who have supported our study. Numerous present and former officials and advisers gave generously of their time and insight during our interviews. We owe heartfelt thanks to all of those unnamed interview sources. Additional thanks are due to the people at Utah State University, especially Cindy Nielsen, Craig L. Albiston, Linda Speth and Carmen Bullock for the tireless efforts in typing and editing, and to Boyd Wennergren for USU's International Programs' support. Special recognition is due to the editors of Westview Press for their patience and understanding as the text evolved and overcame terrible obstacles of space and time. Finally, very special thanks are due to our families, who now know more than they ever wanted to about Panama Canal policy.

William L. Furlong
Margaret E. Scranton

CHRONOLOGY

1846	Bidlack-Mallarino Treaty with Colombia is agreed to (ratified by the U.S. in 1848)
1850	Clayton-Bulwer Treaty between the U.S. and Great Britain is ratified
1850 May	Transisthmian Railroad construction begun
1855 Jan	Transisthmian Railroad is completed
1901 Nov	Hay-Pauncefote Treaty between U.S. and Great Britain is negotiated and second one is ratified with Senate suggested changes
1902	Hepburn Bill and Spooner Amendment recommending that the U.S. construct an isthmian canal in Panama is passed by Congress
1903	Hay-Herran Treaty with Colombia for a concession in the province of Panama is drafted, but rejected by Colombia in August
1903 Nov	Panama declares independence from Colombia
1903 Nov	Hay-Bunau-Varilla Treaty signed in November, ratified in Panama in December, U.S. ratification in February 1904
1907	Root-Cortes-Ardsemena Treaties drafted but never ratified by Colombia
1912 Apr	Panama Canal Act establishes government in Canal Zone, etc.
1914 Apr	Thompson-Urrutia Treaty with Colombia, U.S. ratification delayed until April 1921 and implemented until March 1922
1926 Jul	Kellogg-Alfaro Treaty with Panama agreed to but later withdrawn by Panama and never submitted to U.S. Senate
1936 Mar	Hull-Alfaro Treaty (General Treaty of Friendship and Cooperation) modifying Hay-Bunau-Varilla Treaty is ratified
1939	Implementation Legislation is passed for Hull-Alfaro Treaty
1955 Jan	Treaty of Mutual Understanding and Cooperation modifying Hay-Bunau-Varilla Treaty is ratified
1957	Implementation Legislation is passed for 1955 treaty

1959 Nov	Flag demonstrations and U.S. reaffirmation of Panama's "titular sovereignty"
1960	New U.S. flags policy implemented, allowing the Panamanian flag to be flown at one site in the Canal Zone
1961	Kennedy administration Task Force on Latin America reviews canal policy
1962 Jun	President Kennedy meets with President Chiari in Washington to discuss canal treaty matters; U.S.-Panamanian discussions begin on Panama's grievances against existing canal treaties
1964 Jan	Flag incidents and riots
1965 Sep	Johnson-Robles Guidelines for negotiations on a new treaty
1967	Three new treaties negotiated but never submitted to Panamanian National Assembly or to U.S. Senate
1968 Oct	Colonel Omar Torrijos assumes leadership of Panama after ousting President Arnulfo Arias in a successful coup
1970 Dec	Atlantic-Pacific Interoceanic Canal Study Commission completes final report
1971 Jan	Negotiations on new treaty resume
1972	Panama rejects U.S. draft treaty offer and implements diplomatic strategy to internationalize the canal treaty issue
1973 Mar	U.N. Security Council meets in Panama and the U.S. is forced to veto a resolution dealing with the Canal
Jun	Nixon administration completes its review of canal policy
Jul	Panama invites the U.S. to resume negotiations in Panama to be based upon the Kissinger-Tack Agreement
Sep	Ambassador-at-large Ellsworth Bunker confirmed as new chief Panama Canal negotiator
1974 Feb	Secretary of State Henry Kissinger and Foreign Minister Juan Antonio Tack sign the Kissinger-Tack Agreement
Jun	Formal negotiations begin at Contadora Island, Panama, and continue until March, 1975. Three conceptual agreements and a status of forces agreement are drafted
Jun	Panama Canal Company increases canal toll fees for the first time in history

Jul	House Panama Canal Subcommittee of the Merchant Marine and Fisheries Committee begins hearings
Aug	Panama accepts U.S. proposal for economic benefits; agreement is reached on "lands and waters" issues; negotiating teams announce, on 10 August, that two draft treaties have been concluded
Aug 10	Negotiators announce agreement on all major issues
Sept 6	Treaty texts are initialled by U.S. and Panamanian negotiators
Sep 7	Treaties signed in Washington, D.C., in elaborate ceremony.
Sep 8	The House International Relations Committee begins hearings
Sep 16	The Senate Intelligence Committee begins investigating allegations of wiretapping and blackmail during negotiations
Sep 26	The Senate Foreign Relations Committee begins hearings
Oct 3	Fifty-one members of the House of Representatives take case to court, challenging the constitutionality of executive disposition of U.S. property without the consent of the House.
Oct 14	President Carter and General Torrijos issue Statement of Understanding
Oct 20	House Armed Services Committee begins hearings
Oct 23	Plebiscite in Panama ratifies treaty by a 2 to 1 margin
Nov 9	Senate Majority Leader Robert Byrd and six other senators tour Panama, the first of over forty-two senators and representatives to visit Panama before U.S. ratification
1978 Jan 24	Senate Armed Services Committee begins hearings
Jan 30	Treaties reported out of Senate Foreign Relations Committee by a vote of 14 to 1
Feb 1	President Carter gives nationally televised "fireside chat" on treaties
Feb 8	Debate on treaties begins on Senate floor
Mar 16	Senate approves Neutrality Treaty by a vote of 68 to 32

Apr 16	U.S. Court of Appeals for District of Columbia rules by a 2 to 1 decision that U.S. property can be transferred by a treaty without House of Representatives consideration
Apr 18	Senate approves Panama Canal Treaty by a vote of 68 to 32
May 15	Supreme Court allows April 16 Court of Appeals decision to stand
Jun 16	Ratification instruments exchanged in Panama between President Carter and General Torrijos
1979 Jan 15	Implementation legislation introduced into House of Representatives
Feb 14–20	The Panama Canal Subcommittee of the House Merchant and Fisheries Committee, which has major responsibility for the bill, holds hearings
Mar 29	House votes to eliminate arms sales credits to Panama
Apr 5	House votes to cut off nearly all economic and technical assistance to Panama
Apr 11	Implementation legislation is reported out of the four committees. Two separate implementing bills (HR 1716 and HR 111) are reported out of Merchant Marine Committee
Apr 26	House Rules Committee grants rule to HR 111 (Murphy Bill) and kills administration bill
May 1	Senate cuts economic aid to Panama
May 17–21	House floor debate on implementation legislation
May 17	Administration and House Speaker Thomas P. O'Neill postpone detailed consideration of HR111 until proponents can improve position
Jun 26–27	Senate Armed Services Committee holds hearing on implementation bill by a vote
Jul 17	Senate Armed Services Committee reports compromise bill combining administration bill and HR 111 by partisan vote of 9 to 8
Jul 26	Senate approves implementation by a vote of 64 to 30
Sep 20	House rejects conference report
Sep 26	New conference report finally approved by a vote of 232 to 188

Oct 1	Implementation takes effect and treaties begin to be implemented and part of Canal Zone turned over to Panama
1980 Apr	Senate confirms nominations to New Panama Canal Commission
Jun	The Advisory Board to the Canal Commission is approved and holds its first meeting
1981 Jul 31	General Omar Torrijos is killed in an airplane accident
1982 Mar 31	The jurisdiction of all police, legal, and juridical functions in the old Canal Zone and many functions regarding Canal employees are transferred to Panama
Oct	Trans-Panamanian oil pipeline commences operation

MAP OF PANAMA

UNITED STATES

MEXICO

SOUTH AMERICA

CARIBBEAN SEA

COSTA RICA

COLON

PANAMA CITY

COLOMBIA

PACIFIC OCEAN

Panama Canal Locks

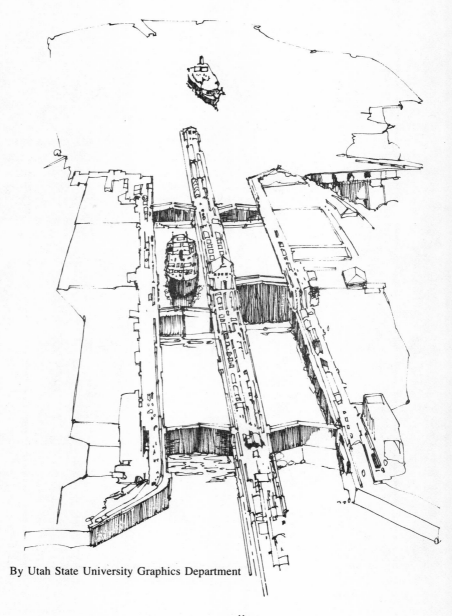

By Utah State University Graphics Department

CHAPTER 1
INTRODUCTION AND ANALYSIS

Few foreign policy issues, outside of wars and treaties of peace after war, have involved the executive, the Congress, the public, interest groups, and the Departments of Defense and State as did the 1977 Panama Canal Treaties. This issue produced one of the heaviest letterwriting campaigns to Congress in American history, as large segments of the public continually and consistently opposed the treaties. The Senate's hearings and debates on the issue were among the longest and most extensive in that chamber's history. The House of Representatives tried repeatedly but unsuccessfully to prevent negotiations, ratification, and implementation. In this context, the Carter administration remained on the defensive and came the closest that any administration has come to a treaty fiasco since the Treaty of Versailles was rejected in 1919. At the same time, the Departments of Defense and State demonstrated an unusual degree of cooperation and unity in order to negotiate successfully with Panama and win approval of the Senate for the treaties.

This issue generated intense and sustained public interest, catching the attention of young and old, liberal and conservative. It became one of the most talked about campaign issues in the 1976 presidential election, and four years later, Ronald Reagan's earlier stand against ''negotiating away'' the Panama Canal helped catapult him into the presidency.

In Panama, on the other hand, the treaties were a welcome replacement to the onerous and hated 1903 Hay-Bunau-Varilla Treaty, despite opposition from either those who did not want the United States to leave or those who wanted them out immediately. In a free and open election, monitored for fairness by foreign observers, a majority in excess of 2 to 1 voted in favor of the treaties.

One reason for the extraordinary degree of interest the treaties generated in both countries was the symbolic value and nationalist sentiments aroused by the Canal itself. Another reason lay in the fact that negotiations to replace the 1903 treaty had been underway for fourteen years. Following the riots of 1964, which claimed the lives of twenty-four Panamanians and four U. S. soldiers and left over two hundred Panamanians wounded, the United States agreed to consider Panama's grievances at the negotiating table. In 1965, guidelines were set and by 1967 three new treaties were drafted. However, political conditions in Panama and the United States were not favorable, and neither government submitted them to their respective legislative branches.

1

Serious negotiations began again in 1973 and were finally completed in August 1977. This process was long and difficult, but the signing of the treaties in September 1977 did not end the struggle for a new partnership. Instead, it was two more years before the treaties were finally ratified and implementation begun.

Unlike most foreign policy issues, during approval and ratification of the Panama Canal Treaties, the public and Congress played a central and continuing role in the whole policymaking process. Usually foreign policy in the United States is made by the president and his key advisors and cabinet. Therefore, the president traditionally has had a wide latitude in making foreign policy, and executive dominance has been a constitutionally sanctioned and accepted norm. Other major actors in domestic policy, such as the Congress, interest groups, political parties, and the public, have played a much lesser role with regard to most foreign policy decisions. The president and his advisors have occupied the center of the decision-making process while Congress and public opinion remained on the periphery.

When treaties are negotiated, however, the president must seek approbation from the Senate whose constitutional responsibility is to give their advise and consent by approving or rejecting all treaties. Treaty approval requires a two-thirds majority vote. Politically, public and interest group support may also be necessary to gain the sixty-seven votes needed for Senate approval. Therefore the ratification of a treaty presents the president with a special foreign policy problem. He cannot — with only his advisors, the State Department, and the Armed Services — make policy that ignores public pressure or congressional sentiment.

Because the eventual approval of the Senate is necessary, input from these other sources may be solicited by the executive branch while negotiations are underway. At this early stage, an aware president must take into account various groups and their power, accommodating their views where possible to defuse some opposition and avert outright rejection at the approval stage. Thus, Congress, interest groups, the electorate, public agencies, and even public opinion can have important influence and exert considerable pressure throughout the negotiations.

After a treaty has been negotiated, signed, and delivered to the Senate for its consideration, the activities of these groups can increase considerably. Pressures and influence from these groups can change foreign policy through forcing the Senate to alter, redefine, or reject a carefully and delicately formulated policy that has been negotiated between two or more nations. Many of these groups do not understand the complexities and intricacies of foreign policy, or the consequences of altering a signed treaty, including the possibility of creating an international crisis, but this prospect does not inhibit their entry into the process. Thus the relative

2

openness of foreign policy attendant to treaty negotiations and ratification makes the process quite similar to policymaking in the domestic arena.

Figure 1.1 shows this condition of influence and pressure in the process of the making foreign policy. The president is one of several competing power centers capable of exerting influence over foreign policy. This competitive situation does not always prevail; contrasting periods of executive dominance in foreign affairs are associated with crisis conditions and severe threats in the geopolitical setting. A related condition that promotes executive dominance is strong and widespread agreement that is a strong consensus on beliefs and objectives underlying U. S. foreign policy. From the 1940s to the mid-1960s, due to a consensus on major foreign policy issues and a bipartisan approach by the major branches of government, conflict between and among these groups was not frequently evident. The president and his key advisors were correctly perceived and accepted as the focus of most foreign policy formulation. Since the 1960s, however, conditions have changed and for many situations the competition-for-influence model is now a more accurate description of how foreign policy is made.

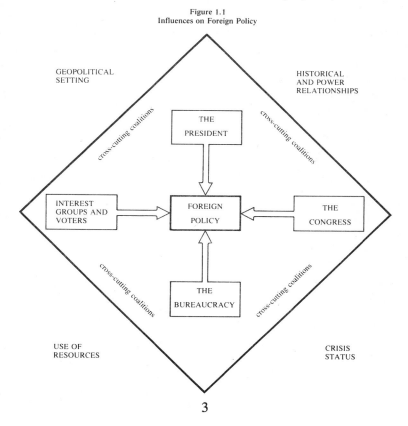

Figure 1.1
Influences on Foreign Policy

Analysis and the Treaties

In analyzing U.S. foreign policy, a number of perspectives can be utilized.[1] Three major perspectives are important to this analysis of the Panama Canal Treaties. The first is an organizational perspective that concentrates attention on the bureaucratic or organizational processes and structures of the government and the activities of organized groups and interests outside the government. The second is a bargaining perspective that looks mainly at the timing of bargaining within geopolitical constraints and its relationship to crisis avoidance. Windows of opportunity and possibility, arising from developments in the global and regional environments, are of key importance in this perspective. The third perspective is contextual and takes into consideration the conditions of time and place. The factors and situations that are historically linked to the issue at hand are analyzed along with regional issues and conditions that directly relate to the current problem. This could be called a regional or ecological perspective.

The Organizational Perspective

The organizational perspective can be broken into at least three approaches, and each approach can in turn be broken into various orientations or emphases. The three approaches include 1) the separation of powers or the competitive approach, 2) the bureaucratic approach, and 3) the cross-cutting coalitions approach.

The traditional view of the formulation of U.S. foreign policy places the president and his key advisers at the center, the heads of the major departments and agencies such as the National Security Council and the Joint Chiefs of Staff at the next level of influence, and finally Congress, interest groups, and the electorate on the periphery.[2]

The Separation of Powers Approach

The three approaches mentioned above view the foreign policy process a little differently. The separation of powers approach characterizes the president and the Congress in an adversarial-cooperative relationship based on their shared powers within a system of checks and balances. This competitive approach is also used in the study of domestic public policy.

For twenty years after World War II, the president and Congress cooperated on many foreign policy programs. Consensus and bipartisan politics existed in foreign affairs, and there was basic agreement among the principal branches of government. During this same period, however, the powers of the presidency grew tremendously in the areas of foreign and national security policy. In a notable exception to bipartisanship, Congress reacted to this growth in the early 1950s by introducing the Bricker Amendment to

4

circumscribe presidential power to make treaties and executive agreements. This amendment would have given Congress an advice and consent role on most executive agreements similar to that role on treaties. When this amendment failed, Congress became less willing to combat the president.

By 1965, many studies indicated that the president had acquired too much influence in the creation of foreign policy. By the early 1970s, attacks on the Imperial Presidency were commonplace.

Arthur M. Schlesinger, Jr., suggests that by 1977 presidential power had increased so excessively and had been so abused that it actually threatened our constitutional system. Schlesinger argues,

> Congress appeared increasingly impotent in the face of the size and momentum of the postwar institutions of American foreign policy — an institutional array spearheaded by an aggressive Presidency and supported by a military and intelligence establishment virtually beyond congressional reach.[3]

Excess led to a backlash, however, and Congress began exerting some control over the presidency beginning with the now controversial War Powers Act passed over a presidential veto in 1973. This trend raised another question in the scholarly debate over the separation of powers in foreign affairs. A number of experts began to claim that a resurgent Congress had usurped too much influence and was now upsetting and misdirecting U. S. foreign policy.[4]

In addition to passing legislation to constrain the exercise of presidential power, Congress also asserted new powers, through devices such as the recently challenged "legislative veto," to involve itself in executive decisionmaking. Robert Lockwood documents the growth of the legislative veto since 1969, especially in the area of defense policy, and demonstrates significant increases in its use during the past decade.[5]

Cecil Crabb and Pat Holt provide a broader perspective on this competitive approach. Their post-Vietnam War case studies reveal a pattern of continuing struggle and competition between these two branches of government.[6]

Thomas Franck and Edward Weisband take the separation of powers approach one step further, adding a positive normative assessment of congressional reduction of presidential power. They argue that despite the success of some presidential attempts to reduce congressional interference, Congress should not be ignored in the policymaking process.

> . . . But such [Presidential] victories should not obscure the revolutionary new realities of Congressional power that have democratized and legitimized U.S. foreign policy. The Administration would not be acting

prudently, or in the national interest, if it sought to restore the old order of Presidential omnipotence. Neither should it count on an historically determined destiny to swing the pendulum back in its favor.[7]

A different normative assessment is reached by John Spanier and Joseph Nogee in their examination of conflicts between the presidency and Congress over the formulation of foreign policy. To the question, ". . . should Congress or the President have the major voice in formulating foreign policy?" they respond that "the thrust of this essay has been to favor the latter."[8]

Former Congressman Charles W. Whalen, Jr., carries the debate full circle. He argues that the Congress has little right and even less capacity to involve itself in foreign affairs. He argues that every major decision in which Congress has taken an active role has produced a policy that works against the national interest rather than promotes it, and he concludes that Congress has created many more problems than it has solved and that it should leave foreign policy formulation to the executive.[9] From a broad, historical perspective, it would seem that neither normative assessment is conclusive. Arthur Schlesinger, Jr., sums up this debate by stating: "History does not support any general assignment of superior virtue to either branch. . . . Neither branch is infallible, and each needs the other — which is, I guess, the point the Founding Fathers were trying to make."[10]

In an era that now lacks consensus on a foreign policy direction as well as agreement on individual issues, Congress and the president are competitors and opponents in the foreign policy process. Whatever the normative merits of conflict between these two branches of government may be, the practical result is a very inconsistent foreign policy.

The Bureaucratic Approach

Another perspective on conflict in the making of foreign policy is taken by the bureaucratic approach. This focuses on the various agencies of the government as a loosely knit constellation of organizations whose actions and behaviors are often inconsistent and may even conflict. Power is fractionalized and responsibility is divided by specific function: the State Department and diplomacy, the Defense Department and military and strategic policy, and the CIA and intelligence, etc.

According to this view, organizations have parochial priorities and goals. Each works under its own rules and standard operating procedures (SOP's) that prevail during its policy formulation and implementation processes. These internal organizational dynamics yield decisions made on an incremental basis, which involve few major changes in policy except in times of extreme crisis. Problems are solved not by seeking the best

6

solution, but by seeking the first solution that satisfies the needs perceived at that moment. Organizations also seek stability, continuity, and security. These aims reduce flexibility and willingness to break with past behaviors and orientations.

This perspective has the advantage of considering more components in the policymaking process than does the separation of powers approach. It stresses the behavior of a wider variety of organizational actors, but like the first approach it places artificial boundaries around each organizational unit. Conflict and/or cooperation exist as each organization moves toward solutions from the perspective of its own goals, its own standard operating procedures, and its own perceptions of the problem.[11]

The Cross-Cutting Coalition Approach

In contrast to the first two approaches, the cross-cutting coalition approach identifies groups of individuals located in various organizations who coalesce on a particular side of an issue. These could be members of the president's staff, members of the National Security Council, or members of the congressional staff along with various persons in the Departments of Defense and State. Some are likely to line up on one side of the issue; other members of the same organizations might line up on the opposite side. In the analysis of domestic politics, this behavior has been termed subgovernments or iron triangles. According to Grant McConnell:

> . . . the most important political reality is an array of relatively separated political systems, each with a number of elements. These typically include: (1) a federal administrative agency within the agency within the executive branch; (2) a heavily committed group of Congressmen and Senators, usually members of a particular committee or subcommittee; (3) a private (or quasiprivate) association representing the agency clientele; (4) a quite homogeneous constituency usually composed of local elites. Logrolling, rather than a compromise, is the normal pattern of relationship.[12]

An illustration of this type of conflict during the Panama Canal Treaty negotiations will clarify how such coalitions work. In 1975, Representative Gene Snyder (R-Ky), a minority member of the House Subcommittee on the Panama Canal, placed an amendment on State Department appropriations legislation (HR 8121). The amendment would have prohibited the State Department from expending any funds to negotiate a change in U. S. control of the Panama Canal Zone. Members of the State Department, the Defense Department, and the National Security Council who opposed negotiation of a new treaty provided members of the House subcommittee, who were also against the negotiations, with information. At the same time, officials in the State Department, the Defense Department, and on the

7

White House staff who favored negotiations worked with members of the House Merchant Marine and Fisheries Committee and the Senate Committee on Foreign Relations, as well as with the leadership of both houses, to develop a strategy to defeat the Snyder Amendment.[13]

This example illustrates the weakness of organizational boundaries. Officials serving in different organizations may disagree with members of their organization and therefore choose to join with like-thinking individuals in other organizations to advocate a "better solution."

These cross-cutting coalitions, if successful, can thereby alter some of the decision-making dynamics characterized by the other two approaches. Many so-called leaks to the press or to Congress are caused by members of an agency who disagree with a proposed policy and attempt to undercut it by leaking damaging information. A determined coalition can effectively oppose agency-based recommendations and prevent a policy from being approved or implemented. On the other hand, organizational resistance to a policy can be countered if a proponent coalition can obtain strong support within the executive branch, the bureaucracy, and the Congress.

Graham Allison's "Model III, A Governmental Political Model" has elements of both of the previous approaches. The major characteristic that differentiates it from the cross-cutting coalition approach is that Allison keeps the president and his key advisors at the focal point, whereas the cross-cutting model does not necessarily require the participation of officials at the highest level of the executive branch.

Politics is yet another crucial element of both the cross-cutting approach and Allison's model. Allison indicates that in his model the government is composed of several individual political actors and that these actors form groups that constitute the agencies for making decisions.

> Government decisions are made, and government actions are taken, neither as the simple choice of a unified group, nor as a formal summary of leaders' preferences. Rather, the context of shared power but separate judgments about important choices means that politics is the mechanism of choice. Each player pulls and hauls with the power at his discretion for outcomes that will advance his conception of national, organizational, group, and personal interests.[14]

Politics and political considerations are therefore elements that play a more important role than does rationality. Decisions and results of those decisions are based not on a single individual's judgment of what is the best solution, but on the collective bargaining, internal politics, and separate judgments by the various individuals involved in the decision.[15]

The cross-cutting coalition approach, the concept of subgovernments, and the Allison Model III approach all can include groups that are generally

8

on the periphery of the decision-making process. Interest groups, the public, and the media can become actors who join coalitions and make inputs into a decision. Thus, according to these approaches, individuals outside of government can and do play important roles in the making of foreign policy.

The Bargaining Perspective

The term *bargaining* refers to "negotiations among actors concerning the relative distribution of gains, burdens and risks among themselves and/or among other actors."[16] A formal bargaining situation requires at least two parties. Beyond the number of parties, Scott argues that a potential bargaining situation exists when two conditions are present:

a) The relationship between actors must be a mix of common interests and conflicting interests, and b) each actor must perceive that it may have something to gain by negotiations and may have something to lose by not negotiating. That is, each actor must perceive the situation as one of a "variable sum," such that the total gains or total losses will depend upon actions of both of the actors.[17]

The bargaining model takes for granted that conflict exists between two or more parties, but it also implies that more can be gained or at least less lost through negotiations than through confrontation and violence. Each party may or may not know specifically what end result is sought, but each should know what its own interests are. Each may also know what the other party or parties' interests are and have some idea as to a preferred outcome.[18]

On the other hand, a party to a dispute may or may not enter a bargaining situation for the purpose of reaching an agreement. Oftentimes, one or both parties may be seeking another objective, such as stalling for time, looking for an excuse to act when negotiations fail, seeking a third party's support or reaction, or seeking propagandistic, psychological, or prestige benefits.[19]

Nonsolution bargaining may also take place. In this instance, the policymaker may be seeking some of the goals mentioned above or using bargaining to deceive another party as a preliminary step leading to a different strategy at a subsequent time.[20]

If the parties intend to reach an agreement to resolve or reduce the conflict, then the following four conditions must be present, according to Wendzel, for bargaining to succeed:

1. The parties must truly desire such an agreement.
2. The substantive interests involved and the objectives that the parties seek must be reconcilable.

3. Both the process and the outcome of the negotiations must be such that none of the parties' prestige is unduly harmed.
4. The negotiators must have sufficient skill in the use of bargaining tactics to achieve their objectives.[21]

Additional conditions must also prevail in order for a satisfactory agreement to be reached. Timing may be very important. The four conditions specified by Wendzel may exist for only a short period; the "window of time" when these conditions are properly juxtaposed may be quite narrow.

Personality is also important. Some policymakers are movers while others react to events. For any given conflict, movers may be able to respond through negotiations while reactors, perceiving themselves to be caught in a crisis, might consider a violent response preferable to bargaining.

Events in the region or in other parts of the world may also create conditions whereby a bargaining response may or may not be possible. Alterations in the conflict itself or in the nature of the crisis may also complicate the process. The more serious the conflict, the greater the threat to the status quo or to stability, and the shorter the time for decisionmaking, the more difficult it will be for bargaining to occur.[22] Because favorable aspects of all of these conditions must prevail simultaneously, the bargaining window may be very small and temporary.

Treaty negotiations are even more complicated than the bargaining model suggests. Not only do international conditions have to be right, and bilateral circumstances appropriate, but the domestic situation in each country must also be conducive to bargaining. Further, such an atmosphere must be maintained so that each government can approve a treaty once the text is agreed upon by the negotiators.

Bargaining in the domestic arena might therefore take place simultaneously with negotiations or subsequent to them. In either case, the Senate, other political institutions, and the public must be taken into account to a greater degree when treaties are at stake than for other, nonnegotiated foreign policy.

The United States and Panama

In its relations with Panama, the United States chose, for many years, to take a nonagreement or nonsolution bargaining stance on the Canal issue. Neither the four conditions posited by Robert Wendzel nor other facilitating circumstances were present. The United States refused to consider as appropriate for negotiation the two principal issues that were preeminent for Panama: the issue of sovereignty over the Canal Zone and the issue of significantly increasing Panama's economic benefits by having the Canal within its borders.

10

As long as the United States maintained this stance, no lasting solution to the conflict could be obtained. Panama, for its part, demanded to be treated as an equal sovereign state, not as a semi-colony. No real bargaining could take place where one side feared that an unfair solution would be imposed by the more powerful party. In addition, this power imbalance was magnified by Panama's mistrust of the paternalistic attitude demonstrated by the United States since 1903. It was not until the 1970s that a bargaining window appeared. The four conditions emerged when Panama and the United States decided to seek a negotiated solution in the form of a mutually satisfactory agreement. Other necessary conditions that facilitated this change in the U.S. bargaining stance are emphasized by a broader ecological or regional perspective.

Ecological or Regional Perspective

The influence on foreign policy of favorable and unfavorable external conditions is the focus of this analytical perspective. The international environment creates opportunities and restraints for policymakers. Certain features, conditions and circumstances not only influence policymakers' choices but also create situations that affect a policy's operation and success.[23]

In the process of creating new policies, individual decision-makers interact with an environment, which includes geographical patterns, historically established relationships, power resources and capabilities, and prevailing political tensions and ideas.[24] In defining their perspective, the Sprouts explain, "This approach is ecological in the sense that it is constructed around the four integral ideas of environment, environed populations, environmental relationships, and interrelated complexes or communities, that compose in the aggregate an ecosystem coterminous with the earth's surface."[25]

Thus the ecological perspective analyzes dynamic relationships between an individual's actions and the setting and communities in which they are found. Characteristics of the region where activity occurs are also important. The region is a smaller part of the ecosystem described by the Sprouts, having some unique characteristics of its own as well as partaking of aggregate environmental properties.

Another ecological perspective is outlined by John Lovell who stresses several factors specifically related to interstate relations. Lovell identifies four essential elements, primarily political in nature, that yield a more restricted view of the ecosystem:

l) spatial relationships within the environment; 2) the pattern of supply of, and demand upon, natural, material, and human resources; 3) patterns of authority and trends in allegiance to various centers of authority; and 4) the prevailing rules of the game of international politics.[26]

The Geopolitical Ecology of the Canal

Although not all of the following chapters make explicit use of this perspective, it is implied in much of the remainder and explains the context in which policymaking occurred. The geographical ecology of the Panama Canal issue is extremely important to the U.S. and Panamanian policies. These policies and the treaty negotiations cannot be explained without some understanding of historical factors, of the Canal as a resource itself, of the resources that transit the Canal, of Panama's strategic location, and of changing authority and power dynamics in the international and regional arenas.

In the first place, it is important to realize that in the United States, the breakdown of consensus on foreign policy after the 1960s resulted from different perceptions of changes in the structure of the geographical environment. Once some policymakers and opinion leaders perceived the implications of these structural changes for Canal policy, a break with the past was more possible. However, the fact that other policymakers and opinion leaders perceived the environment differently created conflict, between individuals in different agencies and branches and in public opinion, over the merits of a new Canal treaty.[27]

All four of Lovell's factors have affected U. S. policies in the Caribbean region. Of fundamental importance have been the spatial location of the isthmus bridging the oceans and of the need that the United States has for efficient and inexpensive means to convey and acquire resources. Throughout the past century, U. S. policy in the Caribbean Basin has been strongly influenced by the concept of a bridge between the seas and then later by the actual existence of a transisthmian canal. The United States became involved in Colombian, Venezuelan, and Nicaraguan politics during the nineteenth century partially over its, and other countries' hope of eventually bridging the isthmus. Later, in 1898, the Spanish American War (though not fought principally for this purpose) was partly a contest to secure more control over the Caribbean sea lanes and the approaches to the dreamed of canal.

After the site had been chosen and construction begun on the actual Canal, military intervention by the United States and the use of force in the region increased enormously. Eventually, the United States intervened and governed the nations of Nicaragua, Haiti, and the Dominican Republic. Political and military intervention also occurred for short periods of time but on more than a dozen occasions in Cuba and Panama. The U. S. Navy in 1903 occupied and still remains at Guantanamo base in Cuba. The rationale consistently used to justify such intervention and force deployment was defense of the Panama Canal and its sea approaches. Once the Canal was operating, its strategic spatial location and economic importance created large stakes for the United States in the region and in Panama itself. These stakes, combined with the prevailing rules of the international power game that place the weak at the mercy of the strong, prompted the United States to favor force rather than bargaining throughout the Caribbean Basin for over fifty years.

Such activity did not disappear after World War II, although it was on a much smaller scale and was less obtrusive. The CIA intervention in Guatemala in 1954, covert operations against Castro from 1959 to 1962, the invasion of the Dominican Republic in 1965, and the invasion of Grenada in 1983 are all reflections of a similar strategy, relying on the use of force to protect U.S. interests in the region, including a secure environment for continued operation of the Canal.

Two exceptions to this pattern were evident in Franklin D. Roosevelt's Good Neighbor Policy of the 1930s and early 1940s and John F. Kennedy's Alliance for Progress in the early 1960s. Although both attempted to establish more equitable hemispheric relations, Kennedy's policies were characterized by two conflicting goals — cooperative economic relations and militant anticommunism to prevent revolutionary political change.[28] The Bay of Pigs invasion, which used Guatemala and Nicaragua as staging grounds, was typical of the latter goal and the result of the global geopolitical game of Cold War containment.

The Bargaining Window

Spatial location of the Canal was, of course, unchanged, and the volume of resources moved through the Canal actually increased. The rules of containment replaced those of the earlier age, but these also subjected the interests of small states to the security requirements of the strong. That game and the power structure of the region changed during the early 1970s, as a unified Latin American bloc emerged to bargain with the United States on North-South issues. At the same time, an East-West climate of detente and rapprochement eased U.S. strategic concerns in the Caribbean. Then, during the late 1970s, as East-West tensions increased and previously secure regimes in Nicaragua and El Salvador were challenged, U.S. perceptions of its strategic interests in the region changed accordingly, and an interventionist strategy regained its traditional appeal.[29] These developments had a strong and direct impact on the length and scope of the bargaining window available for a mutually acceptable negotiated settlement on the Canal issue. The fate of the 1977 Canal treaties was closely

13

linked to these structural changes in the regional and international environments.

Given the geopolitical features of the issue, it is easy to see why the United States refused for most of the century to bargain seriously with Panama over the main issues of conflict between them. Wendzel's four preconditions for bargaining simply did not exist in the negotiations that occurred throughout most of this period. Also, the power of the two nations was so unequal and the dead hand of the past rested so firmly on the relationship, that the United States usually acted as if no real concessions were necessary. Similarly, nearly all of the elements identified in Lovell's ecological perspective ran contrary to a nonviolent, bargaining resolution of the issues separating these two states. First, the traditional spacial relationships were of such strategic interest to the United States that any major alteration of policy seemed highly unlikely. Second, the pattern of the use of the Canal as a resource, although less strategic by the 1970s than during previous times, was still important to international shipping and to United States naval policy. The Viet Nam War had demonstrated the Canal's usefulness as much of the war material transited the Canal. Third, the patterns of power and allegiance between the United States and Panama remained much as they had in the past. Lovell's fourth element, however, changed during the early 1970s; a new set of rules for international politics emerged and consensus within the United States about the way the Cold War had been waged was breaking down. This allowed for a bargaining window to open during the mid-1970s, a window that was not open earlier and which has since closed.

From this perspective, it appears that the prolonged effort to obtain Senate approval for the 1977 treaties ended with little time to spare. The bargaining window conducive to accepting a new partnership with Panama and relinquishing full U. S. control over the Canal was rapidly closing during 1977 and 1978. Illustrative of this changing environment were constant references during the Senate debate in 1978 to possible threats from Cuba and Castro and a potential for a Communist takeover of the Canal by the Cubans and/or Russians. Another sign of the recent reversal of these ecological elements occurred in June 1979, when the House of Representatives held an extraordinary closed floor session to consider how the Nicaraguan civil war might affect implementing legislation for the Panama Canal Treaties.

If the treaties had not been negotiated and approved before the July 1979 demise of the Somoza regime in Nicaragua, it is doubtful that a nonviolent or nonthreatening bargaining solution could have resulted. After Somoza fell, U.S. perception of the threat of communism in the region increased significantly. The civil war beginning in 1980 in El Salvador and increased violence in Guatemala would also have worked against any negotiated settlement of the Panama Canal issue.

In Panama, the demonstration effect of these events would have played into the hands of the extremists if Panama's grievances against the 1903 Canal Treaty were still unmet. This factor, along with the death of General Omar Torrijos, would surely have made the 1980s a decade of destabilization in Panamanian politics with increased violence and threats to the operation of the Canal.

The bargaining window probably would have been closed by these events, but if not, the events in the South Atlantic during 1982 would surely have sealed it tight. The colonial aspects of the Falklands-Malvinas conflict raised issues well known in Panama, such as demands for territorial integrity and the need for sovereign control over an area claimed and defended by a major power, but perceived as part of the national patrimony. This war in the South Atlantic would have had an extremely deleterious effect on U.S.-Panamanian relations if the treaties had not been in place.

Given all of the influences against a new treaty — the history and the actors involved with the Canal issue, the geographic importance of the area, the events of the past two decades, the tendency for policy once in place to persist, and the reluctance of institutions to alter their standard operating procedures — it is amazing that the Panama Canal Treaties were even negotiated, let alone ratified and implemented.

This act of bargaining, in a region where force and intervention have been so frequent, is a ray of cooperation and conciliation in a storm of confrontation and conflict. It is a real achievement for all parties and persons involved that such a policy could be initiated and carried out in a bilateral atmosphere of relative calm and tranquility.

Understanding U.S. Foreign Policy

An analysis of the 1977 Panama Canal Treaties, from formulation through implementation, provides an unusually rich vantage point for understanding U.S. foreign policy. Encompassing a decade of evolutionary changes in the global and regional environments, from 1972 through 1982, the analysis of this issue explores the effects of moderating and restraining ecological influences on cooperative policy initiatives. As we note in Chapters 3 and 7, these influences were not confined to Canal policy and U.S. relations with Panama. Rather, the Canal treaty initiative was part of a larger shift in U.S.-hemispheric relations. Implementation of the 1977 treaties during the 1980s is being affected by the reversal of moderating trends in the region, and U.S. policies toward other states in the region continue to be shaped by these environmental changes.

The domestic environment also changed, and our analysis of Canal policymaking in this decade provides an equally rich vantage point for exploring the normative and analytical consequences of domestic political developments. Both the presidency and the Congress have undergone dramatic changes since 1972, changes which have obviously given rise to a new orientation and process in the formulation and implementation of foreign policy. An analysis of how the foreign policy process operated for one issue throughout this period allows us to evaluate these changes. Scholars and practitioners frequently question how well the policy process works and whether it can be improved. Our study of Canal policy enables us to address these questions: How does the treaty process work and what are the results? Will treaties that involve controversial and unpopular issues meet with rejection in the U.S. Congress in the foreseeable future? In what ways does the president still dominate the foreign policy process? Has the treaty process become too difficult? Is there too little agreement and too much competition between Congress and the executive? Does the bureaucracy severely limit foreign policy choices and parameters? Has political conflict between the two houses of Congress reached a point where they cannot cooperate in controversial situations? Are single issue political action groups becoming so strong that they can threaten and prevent the approval of treaties? Our in-depth study of the Panama Canal issue provides important insights into the complicated process of treaty making and responses to these normative questions about the state of foreign policy making in the United States today.

The decade of change examined in this study also raises questions about the way foreign policy is analyzed. Models and conceptual approaches must be based on accurate assumptions about political realities. As the nature of politics changes, models and approaches must be evaluated in terms of their continued utility. The complexity of the foreign policy process reflected by the evolution of Canal policy demonstrates the value of using several analytical approaches. In terms of analyzing foreign policy, the contribution of this study lies in constructing an integrated analytical approach and explanation. The three main organizational approaches, supplemented with the two broader ecological perspectives are used, individually, as lenses to view aspects of the foreign policy process. The next step, so frequently neglected in case studies and in the conceptual literature, is an integrated assessment of how the different, dynamic influences combined to affect and delineate policy.

Organizational Format

The organization of this book follows the treaties through the policymaking process. Chapter 2 uses the ecological perspective to structure a short history of U.S.-Panamanian relations and to provide an overview of issues and environmental relationships involving the Canal and the Canal Zone. This chapter also includes background information pertinent to the three organizational perspectives, giving special attention to the roles of Congress and the president in the historical formulation of Panama Canal policy. Chapter 3 examines various problems between Panama and the United States, and suggests why, after fourteen years of negotiations, an agreement was finally reached and accepted by both sides. This chapter places the issue in the broader context of U.S. foreign policy, addresses normative questions about foreign policy formulation in general and focuses specifically on the problems associated with major divisions on foreign policy views. Analytical insights based on the organizational approaches about resistance to new policy initiatives are also discussed in this chapter.

The president's and the bureaucracy's role during the Canal negotiations and the ratification process are the topics of Chapter 4. The nature of the Carter administration's "executive impact" is assessed and compared with the impact of the Nixon and Ford administrations, which presided over the early rounds of the negotiations beginning in 1973. All three organizational approaches are evident in this chapter.

The role of the Congress and particularly the Senate, is discussed in Chapter 5. Questions about the constitutional division of powers, the advantages and disadvantages of a resurgent Congress, and the impact of interest groups, the media, public opinion, and bureaucratic pressures on Congress' treatment of foreign policy are addressed in this chapter. Advice and consent, as well as Congress' continuing responsibility for treaty implementation and oversight are examined in light of the three organizational approaches.

Chapter 6 analyzes the implementation legislation and describes some of its impacts on the operation of the Canal as well as U.S.-Panamanian relations. The role of the House of Representatives in the process is examined. The policies flowing from implementation are analyzed and evaluated in terms of expected and unexpected results and in terms of future prospects.

Chapter 7 reviews the assessments made throughout the preceeding chapters and presents an integrated explanation, in the form of answers to fundamental questions about U.S. Canal policy:

Why did it take so long for the United States to agree to bargain with Panama?

Were new Canal treaties really a necessity?

Did the United States get the best bargain it could?

Is the new partnership between Panama and the United States working and will it last?

What were the principal issues and tactics used by opponents in their attempts to prevent treaty ratification and implementation?

Why was it so difficult to obtain Senate approval for the treaties?

Is the process for making and implementing treaties too complicated and demanding to allow controversial issues to be resolved through negotiations?

Were the new treaties improved by the Senate during ratification and by the actions of the House of Representatives through the implementation legislation?

Which approach or combination of theoretical approaches explains how and why the 1977 Panama Canal Treaties were negotiated and ratified?

What does this analysis suggest about current prospects for cooperative solutions to bilateral and regional problems?

Endnotes

[1] Wilfried L. Kohl identified six major analytical approaches for analyzing foreign policy making; see his "The Nixon-Kissinger Foreign Policy System and U.S. European Relations: Patterns of Policy Making," *World Politics* 27 (October 1975):1-43.

[2] A model of institutional and nongovernmental actors' relative influence in the policymaking process, based on the concept of concentric circles arranged around the president and his closest advisors, is commonly used in the literature. See Roger Hilsman, *To Move a Nation* (New York: Doubleday, 1967), pp. 541-44; John Spanier and Eric M. Uslaner, *How American Foreign Policy Is Made* (New York: Holt, Rinehart, Winston/Praeger, 2d ed., 1978), pp. 49-102; and Charles

W. Kegley and Eugene R. Wittkopf, *American Foreign Policy: Pattern and Process* (New York: St. Martin's, 2d ed., 1982), pp. 316-18.

[3] Arthur M. Schlesinger, Jr., "Congress and the Making of American Foreign Policy" in Thomas E. Cronin and Rexford Tugwell, *The Presidency Reappraised* (New York: Praeger, 2d ed., 1977), p. 218; see also Schlesinger's *The Imperial Presidency* (New York: Houghton, Mifflin, 1973).

[4] See, for example, Thomas Franck, ed. *The Tethered Presidency* (New York: New York University Press, 1981); John G. Tower, "Congress versus the President," *Foreign Affairs* 60 (Winter 1981/82):229-46; and Frans R. Bax, "The Legislative Executive Relationship in Foreign Policy: New Partnership or New Competition?" *Orbis* 20 (Winter 1977):881-904.

[5] Robert Lockwood, "The Legislative Veto and Congressional Control of Defense Policy," paper presented at the annual meeting of the American Political Science Association, New York, September 1981. See also the *Congressional Quarterly* discussion on *Immigration and Naturalization Service v. Chadha*, which possibly strikes down the legislative veto: *Congressional Quarterly*, June 25, 1983, pp. 1263-1268 and 1314-1315 and July 2, 1983, pp. 1327-1334.

[6] Cecil Y. Crabb, Jr., and Pat M. Holt, *Invitation to Struggle: Congress, the President and Foreign Policy* (Washington, D.C.: Congressional Quarterly Press, 1980).

[7] Thomas M. Franck and Edward Weisband, *Foreign Policy by Congress* (New York: Oxford University Press, 1979), p. 9.

[8] John Spanier and Joseph Nogee, eds; *Congress, the Presidency and American Foreign Policy* (New York: Pergamon, 1981), p. 199.

[9] Charles W. Whalen, Jr., "Congressional Influence on National Security Policy Making," paper presented at the annual meeting of the American Political Science Association, New York, September 1981. See also Charles W. Whalen, Jr., *The House and Foreign Policy: The Irony of Congressional Reform* (Chapel Hill: University of North Carolina Press, 1982).

[10] Schlesinger, "Congress and American Foreign Policy," pp. 221-22. See also Schlesinger, *The Imperial Presidency*, pp. 8-9.

[11] The best concise discussion of this approach is found in Graham T. Allison, *Essence of Decision: Explaining the Cuban Missile Crisis* (Boston: Little Brown, 1971), pp. 67-100. For later formulation of the model, see Graham T. Allison and Peter Szanton; *Remaking Foreign Policy: The Organizational Connection* (New York: Basic Books, 1976).

[12] Grant McConnell, *Private Power and American Democracy* (New York: Vintage Books, 1966), p. 244. See also Douglas Cater, *Power in Washington* (New York: Random House, 1964); J. Leiper Freeman, *The Political Process* (New York: Random House, 1965); and Randall B. Ripley and Grace A. Franklin, *Congress, The Bureaucracy, and Public Policy* (Homewood, Ill.; Dorsey, rev. ed., 1980) pp. 6-11.

[13] Stephen S. Rosenfeld, "The Panama Negotiations — A Close-Run Thing," *Foreign Affairs* 54 (October 1975): 8-12.

[14] Allison, *Essence of Decision*, p. 171.

[15] Allison, *Essence of Decision*, pp. 160-80. See also Robert A. Hoover and Lauren H. Holland, *The MX Decision: A New Direction in Weapons Procurement Policy?* (Boulder, Co.: Westview Press, forthcoming, and Robert A. Hoover, *The Presidency, Congress and the Strategic Arms Limitation Talks*, work in progress.

[16] Andrew Scott, *The Functioning of the International Political System* (New York: MacMillan, 1967), p. 172. For a discussion of bargaining theory and conflict, see Thomas C. Schelling, *The Strategy of Conflict* (London: Oxford University Press, 1960). For overviews of the negotiations process, see I. William Zartman, *The Analysis of Negotiations* (New York: Anchor, 1975), and Zartman, ed., *The Negotiations Process* (Beverly Hills, Calif.: Sage, 1978).

[17] Scott, *Functioning of the International Political System*, p. 175.

[18] Albert F. Eldridge, *Images of Conflict* (New York: St Martin's, 1979), pp. 170-83.

[19] Robert L. Wendzel, *International Relations: A Policymaker Focus* (New York: John Wiley & Sons, 2d ed., 1980), pp. 172-75.

[20] *Ibid.*, pp. 175-78.

[21] Ibid., p. 179.

[22] Charles F. Hermann, "International Crisis as a Situational Variable," in James N. Rosenau, *International Politics and Foreign Policy* (New York: Free Press, 1969), pp. 409-21.

[23] Lloyd Jensen, *Explaining Foreign Policy* (Englewood Cliffs, N.J.: Prentice-Hall, 1982), p. 8.

[24] Harold Sprout and Margaret Sprout, *The Ecological Perspective on Human Affairs* (Princeton, N.J.: Princeton University Press, 1965).

[25] Harold Sprout and Margaret Sprout, *Toward a Politics of the Planet Earth* (New York: Van Nostrand, Reinhold, 1971), p. 30.

[26] John P. Lovell, *Foreign Policy in Perspective* (New York: Holt, Rinehart, and Winston, 1970), p. 156.

[27] See, for example, Thomas L. Hughes, "Carter and the Management of Contradictions," *Foreign Policy* 31 (Summer 1978):34-55.

[28] Walker LaFeber, "Inevitable Revolutions," *Atlantic Monthly* (June 1982):74-76. See also Cole Blasier, *The Hovering Giant* (Pittsburgh, Pa.: University of Pittsburgh Press, 1976).

[29] For a discussion of the Carter Administration's responses to these events, see Richard Millett, "Central American Paralysis," *Foreign Policy* 39 (Summer 1980):99-117; for a discussion of the Reagan Administration's policies and responses to events in the region, see Alan Riding, "The Central American Quagmire," *Foreign Affairs: America and the World 1982*, vol. 61, no. 3, 1983, pp. 641-59.

CHAPTER 2
FROM CONCEPTION AND CONSTRUCTION TO
THE NEW TREATIES

From the days of Columbus to that triumphal day in August 1914, when the first ship traveled the Canal from ocean to ocean, explorers and traders have tried to find or create a shorter route from the Atlantic to the Pacific Ocean. The Spanish considered a canal across Panama in the 1500s, but instead had to settle for a narrow road not much wider than a footpath. This route was used for over three hundred years, until some adventurous and enterprising North Americans took up the challenge in 1850 and constructed a railroad close to the trail. The French followed in 1870, but failed in their attempt to build a sea-level canal patterned after the Suez. It was not until 1914 that a route was finally accessible to ships when the water bridge called the Panama Canal was completed.

The tiny Province of Panama, (29,128 sq. miles) just slightly smaller than the state of Maine, was administered as a part of Viceroyalty of New Granada by the Spanish. The area of the Viceroyalty became known as Gran Colombia after winning independence from Spain in 1819 and it included what is now Ecuador, Venezuela, Panama, and Colombia. In 1830, Venezuela and Ecuador established separate states. What is now Colombia and Panama continued to be governed as a single unit under the name of New Granada until 1863 when it was changed to Colombia. Panama continued to be administered as a province of Colombia until it won its independence in 1903.

U.S.-New Granada Negotiations

The government of the United States first showed interest in an isthmian canal somewhere in the Central American-Panamanian region as early as 1826.[1] The U.S. Senate demonstrated continued interest in such a project in 1835 by passing a resolution requesting that the president of the United States consider negotiating such treaties as might be necessary to provide for a future canal.[2] The House of Representatives reaffirmed such a proposal in 1839.[3]

In 1846 the United States and New Granada (Colombia) signed a treaty of peace and friendship (the Bidlack Treaty) that guaranteed the United States freedom of transit in the isthmus "upon any modes of communication that now exist, or that may be, hereafter constructed."[4] In return, the United States guaranteed New Granada "the perfect neutrality of the beforementioned Isthmus."[5] This treaty was ratified by New Granada in 1847 and by the U.S. Senate on June 3, 1848.

It was under the authorization of this initial treaty that the first modern transportation link between the Atlantic and Pacific Oceans was constructed. In that same year — 1848 — three Americans, John L. Stephens, W. H. Aspinwall, and Henry Chouncey, applied to the government of New Granada for permission to build and operate a railway line over the Isthmus.[6]

The concession was granted in 1850, and in May of that year construction began. In January 1855, the road was completed at the cost of approximately $8 million. Between 3,000 and 6,000[7] lives were also lost, mostly to tropical diseases and terrible living conditions.[8] The original contract between the Panama Railroad Company and New Granada was revised five times, the last revision in 1891.[9] For the first twenty years of operation, it was the most successful and profitable railroad of its time.

U.S. and Great Britain

In 1849, the United States attempted to make a treaty with Nicaragua, similar to the 1847 treaty with Granada, for open access to future use of their isthmus, but failed in this attempt to do so. At this same time, Great Britain was seriously considering constructing an isthmian canal and was in the process of acquiring territory in and near Central America. Because the United States feared that Great Britain would construct their own canal, direct negotiations between the United States and Britain were held. These negotiations resulted in the Clayton-Bulwer Treaty of April 19, 1850, which stated that both nations would cooperate in the construction of any isthmian canal and that neither nation would fortify or try to exercise singular control over such a canal. With the aid and support of key senators, who had been consulted during the negotiations, this treaty was speedily ratified by the U.S. Senate. It was, nevertheless, an unpopular treaty as many criticized it for giving up more than was gained. It led Senator Stephan L. Douglas to condemn this agreement as "trucking to Great Britain."[10]

Nicaragua continued to create misunderstandings between the United States and England. The decade from 1850 to 1860 was very conflictual despite the Clayton-Bulwer Treaty. It was so bad in 1854 that the First Lord of the Admiralty declared, "We are fast 'drifting' into a war with the United States . . ."[11]

The problem was further exacerbated by an adventurer from North America, William Walker, who with a small gang of armed men, was able to shoot his way into power in Nicaragua in 1855. He was opposed by other Central Americans; the Cornelius Vanderbilt transit company, which was using the route through Nicaragua to transport people to the California gold fields; and by the British and the French. Walker was finally killed by a Central American firing squad in 1860.[12]

In 1876, Lucien N. B. Wyse was able to obtain a concession from New Granada to construct a canal across the isthmus of Panama. This concession was later transferred to Ferdinand de Lesseps, head of a French company, the Compagnie Universelle du Canal Interoceanique. Work began on the French canal in 1881, and the actual digging of the canal began on January 20, 1882. Work continued until 1889 when the company went bankrupt. Over 78 million cubic yards of earth had been removed and a canal had been constructed along approximately one-third of the route. In accomplishing this task, about $287 million had been spent and over twenty thousand people had lost their lives to dysentery, malaria, yellow fever, and accidents.[13] In 1894, a new French canal company was formed to liquidate the old company's machinery, buildings, and other assets.

Subsequently the United States began to seriously consider the possibility of an isthmian canal in 1897. President McKinley gave the Walker Commission the task of investigating a Nicaraguan route for the canal. The commission submitted its report in 1899. After the 1898 Spanish American War, tremendous pressure began to build for a shorter interoceanic route, especially from the navy. In 1900, Secretary of State John Hay and British Ambassador to the United States Lord Pauncefote concluded a treaty that allowed the United States to construct a transisthmian canal without British help or interference. This agreement had the force of cancelling the Clayton-Bulwer Treaty of 1850.

Under this new treaty, as under the two nineteenth-century treaties, the canal would be a neutral waterway and would be built without U.S. defense fortifications. The U. S. Senate, upon receiving the treaty and reacting to current strong popular sentiment, refused to pass the treaty without amendments. They rejected over fifty years of precedent and passed a reservation to the treaty providing for U.S. fortification of the future canal. Hay had assured Pauncefote that the treaty would be ratified, therefore the British refused to accept this amended version of the original agreement. They would not accept a fortified canal, therefore the whole agreement collapsed in March 1901.[14]

Secretary Hay was so frustrated and angry over this defeat that he bitterly denounced the Senate.

> I long ago made up my mind that no treaty . . . that gave room for a difference of opinion could ever pass the Senate. When I sent in the Canal Convention I felt sure that no one out of a mad house could fail to see that the advantages were on our side. But I underrated the power of ignorance and spite, acting upon cowardice.[15]

Secretary Hay did not give up, however, and in November 1901 after renegotiations, he was able to obtain ratification of a second Hay-Pauncefote Treaty with Great Britain that specifically superseded the Clayton-Bulwer Treaty and gave the United States the authority to build, to control, and to *fortify* any future canal. This time Secretary Hay took a number of senators into his confidence, and with their support the treaty was approved by the Senate, and thus the first step was taken towards the creation of the Panama Canal.[16] By forcing Hay to negotiate a second treaty to include the fortification right, the Senate had demonstrated its power to influence and alter U.S. foreign policy regarding the Canal. This precedent has survived throughout this century.[17]

A New Canal – But Where?

The battle over the site for a canal and the route it might follow was fought within Congress as well as between Congress and the executive branch. This is another good example of the separation of powers approach and the competition between these branches of the government. In December 1901, the House had passed the Hepburn Bill by a vote of 308 to 2, which would have placed a canal in Nicaragua. At this point, President Theodore Roosevelt became more active in the policy formulation, but he had to work with the Congress and especially with the Senate leadership to influence this legislation in the direction he desired. Roosevelt, who had possibly been convinced by a senator, George S. Morison, now had to convince the Senate. Senator Mark Hanna was Roosevelt's kingpin in this process.[18]

The administration was also aided by a New York lawyer, William C. Cromwell, who had legal ties to the French canal company. Cromwell was active in the lobbying efforts in favor of the Panamanian site. After the House passed the Hepburn Act, Philippe Bunau-Varilla, a Frenchman, also helped to convince the Senate to vote for a Panamanian site for the canal by indicating that Nicaragua had a history of active volcanos along the proposed route. He made his point by gluing a postage stamp from Nicaragua with a smoking volcano on it to a sheet of paper and placing it on the desk of each Senator before debate began.

After six months of intensive lobbying, backroom haggling, and some unusual tactics, including the famous stamp episode, the Senate and the House passed the Spooner Amendment to the Hepburn Act. This act allowed a canal to be built not in Nicaragua but in Panama, which was then under the jurisdiction of Colombia, if conditions could be worked out among the United States, Colombia, and the French canal company. This was quite a reversal from what had been expected six months earlier, as most interested Americans had been convinced that the canal would be

24

built in Nicaragua. The fear of active volcanos along the route was probably the single most important reason for rejecting the original Nicaraguan site. After the Panama route was chosen, the major responsibility for what subsequently occurred belonged to the Roosevelt administration, the navy, and the Panamanians. Nevertheless, without the actions of William N. Cromwell and Bunau-Varilla, a representative of the canal company, Congress would probably have approved of the Nicaraguan site instead of the Panamanian one.

Panama was still a province of Colombia, and Colombian officials were not advocating a canal through Panama with any enthusiasm in contrast to the officials of the now defunct French canal company. As a result, it was difficult to resolve the myriad differences between the United States and Colombia. Although Secretary Hay concluded a treaty in January 1903 with Thomas Herran, the Colombian *charge d' affaires* in Washington, the Colombian Congress in August 1903 rejected the treaty. The Colombians objected to a canal zone of ten kilometers (six miles) in width where their sovereignty would be reduced. They also rejected the financial arrangements of a single payment of $10 million and an annual annuity of only $250,000. The $250,000 was equal to what they were already receiving from the railroad concessions. Secretary Hay stated that neither Colombia nor Nicaragua knew how to deal with the United States and that both countries believed they could compel the United States to meet any treaty terms that they might demand.[19] Both Hay and Roosevelt were infuriated by what they regarded as Colombian intransigence.

This rejection by the Colombian government threatened the plans for the canal. Nevertheless, Bunau-Varilla, President Roosevelt, and a number of nationalistic Panamanians were not about to let this happen. If Colombia would not negotiate, then perhaps an independent Panama would. The spirit of independence was very real in Panama, as over fifty rebellions against Colombia had occurred from 1830 to 1903.[20]

Independence for Panama and the Hay-Bunau-Varilla Treaty

Supported by President Theodore Roosevelt and the U.S. Navy, Bunau-Varilla and the Panamanian nationalists succeeded in their bid for Panamanian independence. The United States quickly recognized the new nation, and negotiations between Bunau-Varilla and Secretary of State Hay proceeded immediately. The new treaty was written by Bunau-Varilla, signed by him and Secretary Hay, and shortly thereafter was approved by the U.S. Senate by a vote of 66 to 14.[21] The treaty was so well accepted that one senator stated: "We have never had a concession so extraordinary in its character as this. In fact, it sounds very much as if we wrote it ourselves."[22]

25

The Hay-Bunau-Varilla Treaty gave the United States the right to build a canal and granted in perpetuity the use, occupation, and control of a ten mile, rather than a ten-kilometer, strip of land and all the water it needed for the construction and use of the Canal. (See map 2.1.) The United States agreed to guarantee and help maintain the independence of Panama and to pay Panama $10 million for the Canal and Zone rights as well as a $250,000 annual fee. Article III of the treaty also granted in perpetuity to the United States

> all the rights, power and authority within the Zone . . . which the United States would possess and exercise if it were the sovereign of the territory . . . to the entire exclusion of the exercise by the Republic of Panama of any such sovereign rights, power or authority.[23]

Panama was then told that if it failed to ratify the treaty (negotiated by the Frenchman Bunau-Varilla, and not by Panamanians), that the United States would be forced to withdraw its protection of Panama's newly formed independent government. This action would, of course, have meant a reimposition of Colombian control over the isthmus and death for all of the nationalists. The Panamanian Junta of the provisional government recognized the dilemma and ''for reasons of exterior security'' approved the treaty on December 2, 1903.[24]

The contemporary attitude of the Panamanians toward the United States and their overwhelming desire for a new treaty in the 1960s and the 1970s is largely due to the 1903 Hay-Bunau-Varilla Treaty. This treaty had always been repugnant to the Panamanians and probably violated international law. Bunau-Varilla's authority to negotiate and sign the treaty as well as his unilateral decision to give away Panama's sovereignty in the Zone were all questionable. Bunau-Varilla himself stated that the provisions for the United States to exercise complete sovereignty in the Canal Zone were an ''innovation'' in international law.[25] He believed that this innovation would avoid legal problems and guarantee that the U. S. Senate would approve the treaty.[26]

Besides the basic question of sovereignty, the financial aspects of the treaty deeply offended the Panamanians. While the French canal company (with Bunau-Varilla as one of its principal stockholders) received $40 million, the Panamanians received $10 million and an annual subsidy of $250,000. This latter amount was the same Colombia had been receiving for the operation of the Panama railroad concession.

Although the financial aspects of the treaty remained a continuing problem, the most serious and enduring irritant involved questions of sovereignty. Problems surfaced immediately. Many Panamanians found it difficult to tolerate this loss of sovereignty, but were powerless to prevent it.[27]

MAP 2.1 OLD CANAL ZONE

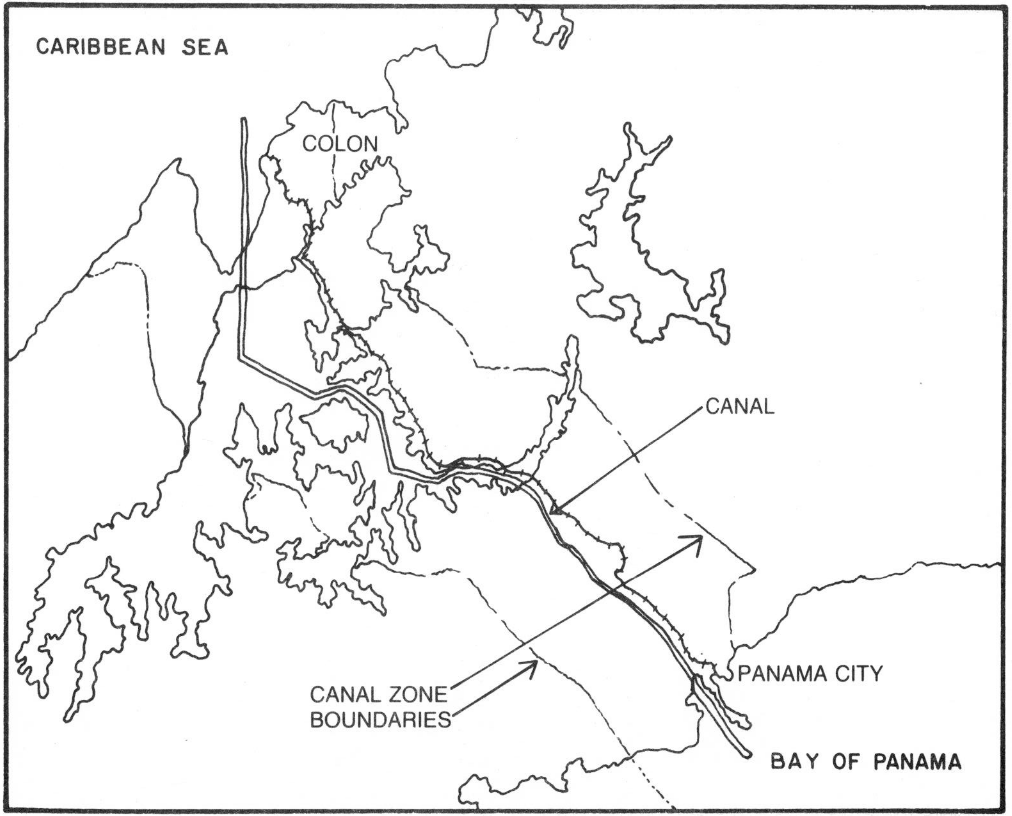

CARIBBEAN SEA

COLON

CANAL

CANAL ZONE
BOUNDARIES

PANAMA CITY

BAY OF PANAMA

Panamanians give three alternative explanations for how this state of affairs came to be: (1) either the men associated with the treaty were weak or were deceived into allowing a foreign nation to act with sovereignty within their territory, or (2) these men were blackmailed and had little alternative choice, or (3) these were very brave and honorable men who did everything they could to gain and maintain independence from Colombia. Nevertheless, the end result was to convert Panama into something just a little less than a colony or a protectorate of the United States.[28]

Questions and opposition were also raised in the United States to such a point that Secretary John Hay was forced to coin the term "titular sovereignty" to describe Panama's rights within the Zone. President Theodore Roosevelt even went so far as to state that "we have not the slightest intention of establishing an independent colony in the middle of the State of Panama . . ."[29] But despite these legal and political questions, work towards construction of the Canal began.

Construction of the Canal

Before serious progress could be made on the actual digging of the Canal, major problems had to be solved. Poor sanitation and the threat of disease, particularly yellow fever and dysentery, had to be reduced. Once this was accomplished, decisions had to be made about the physical aspects of the Canal. The concept of a sea-level canal had to be abandoned and replaced by the concept of a lock canal. The Congress even played a role in this decision. The Chagres River had to be controlled or it would wash away major construction areas. An efficient means had to be developed to move and dispose of the millions of tons of earth that had to be dug. When decisions were made to resolve these problems, the serious construction began in early 1907. The Chagres River was dammed and Lake Gatun was created; nevertheless, land and mud slides continually plagued the construction. The total earth excavated by the U.S. workers amounted to over 230 million cubic yards compared to 78 million dug by the French. In order to understand how much soil that is, consider the following graphic descriptions: enough soil was removed to build a wall as thick and high as the the Great Wall of China and over 2,500 miles long. If the dirt removed from the excavation was placed on a single train, it would have required enough cars to circle the earth four times.[30] As can be seen from these figures, the construction was so immense and so grandiose that it is difficult to imagine.

Until 1914, the Panama Canal project was the most expensive peacetime endeavor undertaken by the U.S. government.

Since 1904, the U.S. has spent $352 million, including the $10 million paid to Panama and the $40 million paid to the French company for the

28

Panama Canal. . . . Yet under the leadership of George W. Goethals, American engineers were able to build the canal for $23 million below what had been estimated in 1907.[31]

It also cost more than all the land purchases the United States had made to that date. Yet when compared to the $287 million spent by the French in their effort, this $352 million seems relatively inexpensive. Beyond this, and despite all of the problems caused by diseases, land slides, and bad weather, the Canal opened six months ahead of schedule. It was also accomplished without any taint of graft or corruption of any kind, unlike the French project.[32]

Technically, the Canal itself was a masterpiece in design and construction. "From the time they were first in use, the locks performed perfectly."[33] The first ship sailed from ocean to ocean in August 1914, but President Woodrow Wilson waited until after World War I was over to officially open the Canal on July 12, 1920.

Not only had the executive and the Congress been very involved with the plans for and the construction of the Panama Canal, but the military establishment of the United States had also been involved from the early beginnings. The navy had been in charge of a number of expeditions exploring and attempting to locate the best route for a canal. The navy was also offshore at the moment of Panama's independence and was involved in countless other ways. The Army Corps of Engineers directed much of the construction, planning, eradication of disease, sanitation, and myriad other tasks. This early and intense involvement in this great project gave the military a very strong sense of creation and ownership that propelled it into an organizational reaction against any alterations suggested by other parties.

U.S. Influence in the Caribbean Basin

During the construction phases of the Canal and its subsequent opening for operation, the United States in general and the military in particular grew concerned over the whole of the Caribbean Basin. The navy wanted a secure and protected sea access and lanes to the Canal. A number of Caribbean states were financially and politically unstable during this period as well. Nicaragua in particular was singled out, probably as it had been the second — and at times the first — choice for the site of the Canal. The United States intervened militarily in Nicaragua in 1912 and remained until 1931, except for a short period from 1926 to 1927. The marines were also landed in and governed over the island of Hispanola in both Haiti and the Dominican Republic for much of this same period. The existence of the Canal was one of the primary reasons for these interventions. The United

States politically and militarily intervened in Panama itself, for very short periods of more than a dozen times in this epoch. Nevertheless, the United States attempted to rebuild its relations with Colombia, which had been very poor since Panama had broken away in 1903.

Subsequent Negotiations and Treaties

In 1914, a treaty was negotiated and signed between Colombia and the United States that settled some of the problems that arose from the establishment of the Republic of Panama in 1903. In the treaty, the United States expressed "sincere regret" for the problems between the United States and Colombia. The treaty further guaranteed certain Colombian goods and warships free use of the Canal and the United States agreed to pay Colombia $25 million to help compensate it for the loss of its province of Panama. This Thomson-Urrutia Treaty was not ratified for six years by the Senate, and then only after the treaty was amended to eliminate the "sincere regret" phrase and to reduce some of Colombia's transit rights. Once again the Senate played a critical role and delayed and altered U.S. foreign policy towards Panama. Although this treaty reduced tensions between the United States and Colombia, it increased those between Panama and the United States.[34] Panama, which now had an operating canal and was a nation split by the Zone, had received only a $10 million one-time payment, whereas the Colombians who had lost out on the first deal, now received $25 million. This action came as a direct insult to Panama for the second time, the first being the $40 million given to the French canal company.

In 1926, the United States and Panama concluded a new treaty modifying some points of the 1903 treaty, but Panama refused to ratify it and requested further negotiations. Ten years later, in 1936, the Hull-Alfaro Treaty was completed and finally ratified in 1939. This treaty reduced the rights of the United States to intervene in the domestic affairs of Panama, terminated the right to expropriate more land for Canal use and increased the annual payment to Panama to $430,000, but it ignored the question of sovereignty. Although Panama ratified the treaty immediately, the U.S. Senate stalled for three full years. The Senate continued to quibble and complain and only with World War II looming on the horizon decided to approve the treaty in 1939.[35] The United States did not want any conflicts with Panama that might disrupt maritime traffic during war.

From 1942 to 1953, the United States concluded various agreements with Panama; most of them were associated with the war effort and its aftermath. The military had established several bases in Panama during the war. It wanted to continue to use those bases after the war was over but the interim accord made during the war now had to be renegotiated. One such case, the 1947 Defense Sites Agreement, was rejected by Panama, however, and the United States withdrew from those bases covered by this agreement.[36] Talks for a new treaty began in 1954 and were completed in 1955. The Panamanians wanted an increase in the annual payment and "justice," which in their minds included the sovereignty issue. The concessions in the treaty, however, were mostly economic. The annual subsidy was increased to $1,930,000, which, in inflated dollars, was actually less than was paid in 1914 when the Canal opened. The Panamanians neither received a percentage of the tolls nor any consideration on the sovereignty issue.[37]

Despite this very one-sided agreement, opposition in the Senate was strong and vociferous. Although the treaty was passed by a vote of 72 to 14, there was great reluctance to alter the status quo. The main issues involved the defense of the Canal, the cost of the new subsidy, the transfer of property, and the alienation of land perceived to belong to the United States.[38] Implementation legislation crept through Congress and was finally completed in late 1957. Again, as in the 1936-1939 period, the Congress obstructed and slowed implementation of an agreement between Panama and the United States. This type of congressional interference in the foreign policy arena is unusual and is unique in the area of U.S.- Latin American affairs. The military establishment also demonstrated its reluctance to change in any way the defense infrastructure or orientations regarding the Canal and the Canal Zone. The Southern Command of the Navy considered the Zone pretty much as its own sovereign territory.

The Caribbean Basin gave the United States a great cause for concern during the 1950s. The "Communist" threat in Guatemala had been met with CIA intervention in 1954 and neutralized. The Cuban situation, however, was different, and Castro's takeover in 1959 and his subsequent confrontations with the United States sent tremors through the "protect the Canal at any cost" syndrome of the military. This is one of the reasons why the Navy tenaciously remained in Guantanamo Base. The Alliance for Progress was begun under John F. Kennedy in 1961 to counteract the threat of communism in Latin America. Panama was not immune to the problems and threats of communism and unrest; therefore, Eisenhower, Kennedy, and Johnson all faced crises over Panama and the Canal.

Flags, Sovereignty, and New Negotiations

From 1959 to 1964, relations between the United States and Panama were marred by the sovereignty issue. Panamanians, long frustrated over the absolute refusal to even allow symbolic changes on this question, demonstrated and rioted over the right of Panama to fly its flag within the Canal Zone. Following such demonstrations in early November 1959, the

31

State Department admitted that "titular sovereignty" over the Canal Zone remained in the government of Panama.[39] President Eisenhower stated in a December 1959 news conference that we should allow Panama to fly its flag in the Zone.[40] The Congress, however, expressed another opinion. Reacting strongly to this attack on tradition, the House, in an advisory vote of 380 to 12, emphatically declared that the Panamanians could not fly their flag within the Zone.[41] Despite this action, in September 1959, President Eisenhower declared that both flags could be flown in the Zone. Congress was outraged and the military was indignant.

From 1960 to 1963, the sovereignty issue in the form of the flag question received considerable diplomatic attention but did not provoke public demonstrations. In contrast, 1964 was the year of confrontation in the streets, of flag riots, and of demands by Panama that the 1903 treaty either be fundamentally changed or replaced. Four days of rioting resulted in the deaths of twenty-four Panamanians and four U.S. soldiers. Eighty-five North Americans and over two-hundred Panamanians were wounded. The Johnson administration made the decision to seriously consider modifying the 1903 treaty. This decision by President Johnson resulted in negotiations on the complete replacement of the Hay-Bunau-Varilla Treaty and also led to the eventual formation of the Atlantic-Pacific Interoceanic Canal Study Commission to examine the feasibility and the possible alternate sites for a new sea-level canal. Before the end of 1965, President Johnson and Panamanian President Marcos Robles announced their agreement on the basic principles for negotiating a series of new treaties.

The 1967 Treaties

On June 26, 1967, Presidents Johnson and Robles announced that an agreement had been reached about three new treaties. One would relinquish U.S. control over the Panama Canal and give up the Zone by the year 2000. The second treaty dealt with defense of the Canal and its neutrality including the concept that U.S. bases would remain in Panama indefinitely. The third treaty would allow the United States to build a sea-level canal in Panama if it chose to do so. The texts of the treaties were never officially released for publication. The *Chicago Tribune*, however, on July 8, 15, and 16, printed what were admitted to be the accurate texts.[42]

The whole issue of what happened to the 1967 treaties is somewhat mysterious. Although agreements were reached between Panama and the United States, the treaties were never formally presented to or acted upon by the legislative branches in either nation. After President Johnson announced the agreement, the House Foreign Affairs Subcommittee on Inter-American Affairs chaired by Armistead I. Seldon (D-Ala) held a series of hearings from July 24 to August 2, 1967. Representative Seldon

32

stated that he realized the House had no responsibilities in the advise and consent procedure, but "it had a duty and a right to express its feelings."[43] Representative Daniel Flood (D-Pa) expressed his reaction and concern in a little stronger language. "If your kidneys are good, I'll tell you what you can do from Cuba to the Canal."[44] On the other hand, Representative Leonor K. Sullivan (D-Mo), chairman of the Merchant Marine and Fisheries Subcommittee on the Panama Canal, warned that if the Panamanians gained control of the Canal they would just allow it "to rot and decay," as they have done with "everything else turned over to them."[45]

Senator Strom Thurmond (R-SC), one of the principal opposition leaders in the Senate to any changes in the status quo on Panama, had the *Chicago Tribune* article and texts of the treaties read into the *Congressional Record* on July 10, 19, and 21, 1967.[46] He strongly criticized the administration for both its secrecy and its lack of trust in the Senate. The administration responded by claiming that the treaties were still in draft form and were not ready to be presented to the Senate.[47]

Opposition to the treaties in the United States revolved around the sovereignty issue, defense issues, Panamanian efficiency in operating and maintaining the Canal, the Communist threat in the area, and Panama's tradition of political instability. Opposition in Panama was also very strong, principally on the sovereignty issue and the continued presence of U.S. military bases there. Financial arrangements on tolls and Panama's share of revenues were also unacceptable to them.[48] Opposition was so strong and vehement in the United States that President Johnson never submitted the actual treaties to the Senate for advise and consent approval. Before the end of 1968, Panama withdrew the treaties from official consideration. Thus, the final drafts of the treaties were never submitted, either to the Panamanian National Assembly or to the U.S. Senate. Congressional opposition, along with other Johnson problems in 1967 and 1968, effectively deferred resolution of this issue for another decade. This delay, however, cost the United States some vital concessions, as the Panamanians toughened their stand on some of the major issues. Again, as in the past, strong congressional input as well as bureaucratic reaction by the military on the Panama Canal issue hampered the president in any attempt to permanently resolve the major disagreements between the two countries.

During this whole process, not only were the Congress and the president at odds over any changes in Canal policy, but the Department of State and the Department of Defense were at opposite poles on the issue as they had different perceptions of the world and different policy agendas. The Department of State had a stake in the negotiations, which they had been advocating and working on for years. This experience had given the negotiators a more political view of the situation, one not shared by the

Department of Defense. The Defense Department continued to consider the Zone and the Canal as their own, and any move towards reducing their power, presence and defense capabilities was rejected without further consideration.

Political Groundwork for the 1977 Treaties

Between 1967 and 1973, the United States was so involved with Viet Nam that other foreign policy issues, especially those in Latin America, were given very low priority. Little was done to ameliorate the Panama Canal problem. In August 1970 the Rio Hato military base, obtained in the 1955 treaty, was returned to Panama. In December 1970, the Interoceanic Canal Study Commission submitted its final report, recommending that if a new sea level canal were built, it should be located within Panama. It also recommended that the United States negotiate new treaties with Panama.

The Turning Point

Panama's Omar Torrijos, who became Panama's strongman leader in a 1968 coup, succeeded in his first major international public relations offensive in March 1973. He was able to get the United Nations Security Council to meet in Panama. During this meeting, a resolution was introduced that would have recognized Panama's full sovereignty over all of its territory including the Canal Zone. The United States was forced to use one of its rare vetoes to prevent the adoption of the resolution. The Third World and even our European allies supported the resolution with only Great Britain abstaining. This became a major turning point in U.S. treatment of the Panama Canal issues. Before 1973 ended, the United States was forced to recognize the importance of this issue and was pressured into taking concrete action towards a new bargaining policy. Ellsworth Bunker was officially confirmed as the new chief Panama Canal negotiator in September 1973, and a new round of negotiations commenced before the year ended. A new era began and the bargaining window opened as serious steps were taken to create a new policy.

As will be discussed in Chapter 4, from 1968 to 1974, the military establishment began to alter its intransigence on Panama. Leaders in the Defense Department began to consider the difficulty of defending the Canal and keeping it operating against a hostile local population or a popular guerrilla movement.[49] The appointment of Ellsworth Bunker as chief negotiator also gave support to those who were now willing to consider negotiations as he was largely trusted by the military.

In 1974, two major changes occurred regarding the status of the Panama Canal. First, in February 1974, Secretary of State Henry Kissinger and Panama's Foreign Minister Juan Antonio Tack signed an eight-point declaration of basic negotiation principles. Then in June, the Panama Canal Company increased its toll fees for the first time in history.

The Kissinger-Tack Agreement included the following principles: the 1903 treaty would be abrogated, the Zone and the Canal would eventually be turned over to Panama, Panama would receive a share of the tolls, the defense of the Canal before Panamanian acquisition would be the joint responsibility of the United States and Panama, and both nations would cooperate on any projects to enlarge Canal capacity or to build a new canal. These points were only moderately stronger than those suggested by the 1965 Johnson-Robles principles and the 1967 treaties, but they were perceived as major concessions to Panama from the United States. Despite these important events and steps towards the treaty negotiations, neither Nixon nor Kissinger discuss these events in their memoirs.

The administration and the treaty negotiators had a tough year in 1975. In March, the talks were deadlocked on three major issues: (1) the United States was demanding a forty to fifty year lease on its military bases due to intense pressure from the Defense Department, (2) neither side could agree on the amount of territory needed within the Zone for defense purposes and Canal use, and (3) disagreement also continued on the duration of the new treaty.[50]

Adding to the problems, Senator Strom Thurmond (R-SC) managed to obtain thirty-eight signatures on a resolution declaring that the United States should not give up its ''sovereign rights'' in Panama.[51] This constituted four more senators than the one-third needed to block any treaty approval as sixty-seven are needed for approval.

This intense senatorial action was also reinforced by action in the House. In June 1975, the House passed the Snyder Amendment by a vote of 246 to 164. L. H. Fountain (D-NC) urged passage of the amendment as a way of ''sending a message'' to the White House and the State Department ''that the time has come to stop giving away the Panama Canal.''[52] It was altered and made less extreme by senatorial action after a second conference committee report was finally accepted by both the Senate and the House in October 1975.

In order to overcome interagency rivalry between the Departments of Defense and State, in late 1975, General Welborn C. Dolvin (Ret.) was appointed as deputy negotiator on the treaties to represent the interests of the Defense Department. At the same time, some of the issues that Defense had been so reluctant to even consider were opened to the negotiations.

1976 Political Campaign and the Canal

Early in 1976, Ronald Reagan in his quest for the Republican presidential nomination against President Ford, sought a dramatic issue. He discovered that the negotiations over the Canal were highly charged politically and seemed to strike a patriotic chord in the U.S. electorate.[53] His statement that "we bought it, we built it, we paid for it and we intend to keep it," was heard across the nation and was accepted as fact by many U.S. citizens. The Panama Canal issue lasted through the primary elections and became a continuing issue in the general campaign between Jimmy Carter and President Ford. It climaxed in the October debates during which Carter stated, "I would never give up complete control or practical control of the Panama Canal Zone."[54] This political campaign placed the Canal negotiations in such a contentious political position that little was accomplished, and negotiations came to a standstill in May 1976.

At the time that these political arguments were occurring, economic issues were causing problems at the Canal. From March 15 to 20, 1976, over seven-hundred U.S. employees initiated a "sickout-strike," which resulted in a slowdown of Canal traffic and an eventual traffic jam of over 175 ships awaiting transit through the Canal. The issue was not the treaty negotiations, but a freeze in wages. This created the most serious work stoppage in the Canal's sixty-year history.[55]

As the political campaign intensified in the United States, the Panamanians became more and more frustrated with the lack of progress on the negotiations. They also became angry about the accusations made against them and by some statements made by the Reagan campaign. For example, in April, Panama's newly installed foreign minister, Aquilino Boyd, responded to Reagan's campaign statements and labeled them irresponsible and inflammatory. He went on to say that Reagan "talks like a jolly cowboy who doesn't appear to have gone to school nor to have much knowledge about present foreign affairs."[56]

In October 1976, General Omar Torrijos responded to the presidential campaign debates between Carter and Ford by stating that "the superficial manner in which the most explosive topic in U.S. relations with Latin America was broached constitutes a great irresponsibility toward the American people."[57]

Commitment to a Resolution of the Negotiations

Even before taking office, President-elect Jimmy Carter became committed to continued negotiations over the Panama Canal (despite his earlier statements). He hoped to carry out serious negotiations that could result in a new treaty by June 1977.[58] Ambassador Ellsworth Bunker was asked to continue the negotiations, and former OAS Ambassador Sol Linowitz was assigned to join him. Ambassador Linowitz, however, was given only a temporary six-month assignment that did not require the approval of the

36

Senate. This action angered opposition senators who later used it in arguments against the administration and the treaties.

During and after the major negotiation round of February 23 to March 1, 1977, negotiation teams and their staffs were hard at work on specific details of the treaties. Briefings with the Senate and House leadership and with the various committees and their staffs concerned with the treaties began to take place with more frequency, and interactions increased significantly, as the negotiators continued consulting with congressional leaders through the end of May.[59]

Secretary of State Cyrus Vance stated that consultations were sometimes as often as once or twice a week with key Senators. According to him: "This almost unprecedented consultation . . . was vital in building Senate confidence in the treaty. This would serve us well once the bitter ratification debate began." [60]

The Treaties are Completed

Negotiations continued from May through August 1977. Progress was made, and finally on August 10, 1977, the negotiators announced agreement "in principle" on two new treaties. The treaties then went through a formal drafting stage and were ready for signing in September. On September 7, 1977, in a ceremony not to be forgotten in Washington, President Carter and Panamanian Chief of Government Omar Torrijos signed the two new treaties in the presence of leadership from most of the Latin American nations. On October 23, the Panamanians, through a popular, open plebescite, approved the treaties by a 2 to 1 margin. Now it was up to the U.S. Senate to act. For the next seven months, the Senate played out its part on the treaties. Finally, on March 16, 1978, the Neutrality Treaty was approved, and on April 18, 1978, the Senate gave its approval to the new Panama Canal Treaty.

Implementation Legislation

The Carter administration finally submitted its proposed implementation legislation to the Congress in January 1979. After months of conflict and numerous defeats of White House positions, two pieces of legislation passed the House and the Senate. The conference committee had the difficult task of putting the two bills together into an acceptable compromise, one that would be acceptable to Panama, the White House, the Senate, and the House. It was nearly an impossible task and their efforts were thwarted and rejected. Finally, the implementation legislation was approved by both houses on September 26, 1979 and signed into law by the president the next day. On October 1, 1979, the treaties and the implementation legislation went into effect.

37

Major Treaty Provisions

The Canal Treaty

The treaties that finally went to the Senate broke completely with the traditions of past U.S.-Panamanian agreements. Panama was clearly given sovereignty over all of the former Canal Zone and the Canal itself. The United States was granted the right to manage, operate, maintain, improve, and defend the Canal until December 31, 1999. Article I of the new treaty simply states that the "Republic of Panama, as territorial sovereign, grants to the United States of America . . . certain rights, necessary to keep the Canal in operation."

All previous treaties, including the 1903 treaty are specifically abrogated by this treaty. Panama is given increasing responsibility in the operation of the Canal while the U.S. is specifically restricted from any intervention in the internal affairs of Panama. The United States can only fly its flag in a few designated places in the former Zone.

A new Panama Canal Commission established by the treaty and by the implementation legislation will operate the Canal until January 1, 2000. This commission is to be composed of five citizens of the United States and four Panamanians. A U.S. native or citizen will be the administrator of this commission until January 1, 1990 when a Panamanian will then become the chief administrator and a U.S. citizen will be the deputy administrator.

Approximately sixty percent of the Canal Zone was turned over to Panama when the implementation legislation became effective on October 1, 1979, and the Zone as a separate territory ceased to exist. Other segments of the Zone will be transferred to Panama during the twenty-two-year life of the treaty. In the year 2000, all remaining territory and property, including the Canal itself, will be turned over to Panama.

During a thirty-month transition period, legal activities and police services shifted from U.S. law to Panamanian law. Since April 1982, Panamanian law applies to all areas of Panama. Starting in October 1979, Panama received a $10 million annuity in addition to thirty cents per net ton in tolls amounting to about $50 million per year. Panama also receives an annual payment of $10 million for the provision of public services such as water, sewer, garbage collection, public lighting and street maintenance; as well as an additional $10 million contingency payment to be taken from profits when Canal revenues exceed expenditures. These benefits are much smaller than those demanded by Panama during negotiations, when Panama requested a one-time payment of about $1 billion and an annual subsidy from tolls of from $150 to $200 million.

The question of a sea-level canal and/or a third lane of locks was part of the original agreement, but the U.S. Senate altered this section on the sea-level canal and it is left completely open and outside the treaty.

The treaty discusses at length employment practices and guarantees. For example, it states that North Americans can still hold secure jobs, but that Panamanians must be trained to eventually replace most of them. Early retirement and other benefits are granted to those U.S. citizens currently employed. This section created a lot of technical problems, difficulty with specific job-related questions, and makes up the bulk of the implementation legislation.

The Neutrality Treaty

The Neutrality Treaty — officially the Treaty Concerning the Permanent Neutrality and Operation of the Panama Canal — took effect simultaneously with the Panama Canal Treaty. It declares that the Canal shall be permanently neutral, secure, and that it will remain open to peaceful transit by vessels of all nations equally in times of peace and war. To this end, the United States and Panama agree to maintain and defend this neutrality. After the year 2000, only Panama is to operate the Canal and maintain defense forces and defense installations within its national territory. Hence, administrative as well as protective responsibilities, will eventually rest on the government of Panama whereas the United States will continue to defend the Canal from external threats. The treaty further states that vessels of war and auxiliary vessels of the United States and Panama shall be entitled to "expeditious" passage.

Summary

This chapter has provided the reader a brief overview of the Panama Canal as a U.S. foreign policy issue, with special emphasis on the policy formulation. A number of aspects of this process should now be evident. First, although in some of the cases, the executive had initiated or formulated policy towards Panama, such policymaking needed to be tailored to suspected congressional reaction. In the 1800s, however, it was Congress that initiated policy and made the final choice of the current site of the Canal. Policies surrounding the construction and operation of the Canal were more jointly formulated, deliberated, and resolved by the executive and the Congress working together. The Canal and the Canal Zone were perceived by those policymakers to be so much a part of the United States that Canal policy and issues always received special consideration and attention. Canal policy remained atypical to most other U.S.-Latin American foreign policies, which were largely products of decisions of the president and a small body of key advisors.

In the second place, Congress historically took an active but negative role in the implementation of any alterations of the 1903 treaty. This was particularly true with regard to Colombia from 1914 to 1922. It was equally true from 1936 to 1939 and again from 1955 to 1957. During these years, Congress was always reluctant to approve and implement changes in treaties even though they may have already been ratified. Hence, given this history of intensive involvement by Congress and its negative reaction to change, it is not surprising that it played similar roles from 1977 to 1979.

Third, the bureaucratic model helps to explain the actions of the Departments of State and Defense regarding the Canal and the Canal Zone. The State Department generally supported negotiations and accommodations with Panama, while the Defense Department resisted any changes to the 1903 treaty. Very little changed through the 1950s and most of the 1960s. However, the cross-cutting coalition approach helps to better explain much of the activity of various groups in these agencies as they interacted with each other, with the Congress, and with the White House in the late 1960s and early 1970s. Proponents, as well as opponents to change openly operated to influence policy in all of these institutions. Divisions on the issue were more important than institutional boundaries.

The regional or ecological perspective is also helpful in understanding the historical background. Many aspects of U.S. foreign policy in the Caribbean Basin from 1903 to the present are better understood when the Panama Canal is held in ecological perspective. In many activities, the subtle driving force behind decisions is the concern that U.S. policymakers have had for the Canal and its importance to the military and to trade.

Despite the many attempts to fundamentally alter the 1903 treaty in the 1920s, 1930s, 1950s, and 1960s, no significant changes were made that were acceptable to both the United States and to Panama. It was not until 1973 that the bargaining window really opened and allowed for serious bilateral negotiations. The next two chapters describe in detail how and why bargaining took place and the results of those negotiations.

Endnotes

[1] U.S. Congress, Senate, Committee on Foreign Relations, *Background Documents Relating to the Panama Canal*, 95th Congress, 1st Session, by Congressional Research Service, Library of Congress, committee print (Washington D.C., Government Printing Office, November 1977). Hereafter cited as *Background Documents*.

[2] Ibid., p. 4.

[3] Ibid., p. 5.

[4] Ibid., p. 8.

[5] Ibid, p. 9.

[6] Forbes Lindsay, *Panama and the Canal Today*, (Boston: Boston and Co., rev. ed., 1912) p. 41.

[7] Because no accurate records were kept, an actual body count does not exist.

[8] Joseph Bucklin Bishop, *The Panama Gateway* (New York: Charles Scribner's Sons, 1913), pp. 48-50.

[9] Ibid., p. 53.

[10] Thomas A. Bailey, *A Diplomatic History of the American People*, (New York: Appleton-Century Crafts, 7th ed., 1964), pp. 275-276.

[11] Ibid., p. 277.

[12] Ibid., p. 277-78.

[13] David McCullough, *The Path Between the Seas*, (New York: Simon and Schuster, 1977), pp. 131, 235.

[14] Bailey, *A Diplomatic History*, pp. 275-276, 486-488.

[15] Quoted in Bailey, *A Diplomatic History*, p. 487.

[16] Alfred L.D. Dennis, *Adventures in American Diplomacy* (New York: E.P. Dutton and Co., 1928), p. 162.

[17] Consistently the Congress was centrally involved in U.S. relations with Panama contrary to the model constructed by Franck and Weisband in *Foreign Policy by Congress*. Congress in periods of resurgence as well as during periods of a strong presidency influenced and altered U.S. policy with Panama.

[18] McCullough, *Path Between the Seas*, pp. 305-328.

[19] Dennis, *Adventures in American Diplomacy*, p. 312.

[20] Ibid., p. 313.

[21] McCullough describes this fascinating story of intrigue and political strategy in exciting detail.

[22] Dough, *Path Between the Seas*, p. 397.

[23] U.S., *Statutes at Large*, v. 33, p. 2235; also Treaty Series 431 and in *Treaties and Other International Agreements of the United States of America 1776-1949*, compiled by Charles Bevans, Washington D.C., Department of States, Aug. 1972, v. 10, p. 664.

[24] *Background Documents*, p. 51.

[25] Philippe Bunau-Varilla, *From Panama to Verdun: My Flight for France* (Philadelphia, PA: Dorrance and Co., 1940), p. 158.

[26] Ibid., pp. 158-159.

[27] Domingo H. Turner, *Tratato Fatal !* (Panama: Ferguson & Ferguson), 1974, pp. 47-56.

[28] Moises Chang M., *Historia de Panama* (Bogota, Columbia: Editorial Ltda., 2nd ed., 1973), pp. 199-200. (High School history textbook used in Panama.)

[29] Walter LaFeber, *The Panama Canal*, (New York: Oxford University Press, 1979), pp. 42-46.

[30] Willis J. Abbott, *Panama and the Canal in Picture and Prose*, (New York: Syndicate Publishing Co., 1913), pp. 134-35.

[31] *Background Documents*, p. 55.

[32] McCullough, *Path Between the Seas*, p. 611.

[33] Ibid.

[34] Wendzel, *International Relations*, pp. 215-18. The author discusses this condition as one of "differential effects." He defines this as, first, all decisions have both costs and benefits, and second, that each decision has an impact on more than one actor, and that it affects difference actors differently.

[35] LaFeber, *Panama Canal*, pp. 86-88.

[36] U.S. Senate Committee on Foreign Relations, *A Chronology of Events Relative to Panama Canal*, 1977, 95th Congress, 1st Session, Washington, p. 6. Hereafter cited as *Chronology*.

[37] LaFeber, *Panama Canal*, pp. 116-20.

[38] U.S. Congress, *The Congressional Record*, 1955, 84th Congress, 1st Session, Vol. 101, Part 9, Washington, pp. 11999-12019.

[39] *Chronology*, p. 7.

[40] Ibid.

[41] LaFeber, *Panama Canal*, p. 128.

[42] *Congressional Quarterly Weekly Report*, Vol. 25, July-Sept., 1967, p. 1627.

[43] Ibid, p. 1351.

[44] Ibid.

[45] Ibid.

[46] U.S. Congress, *The Congressional Record*, 95th Congress, 1st Session, Vol. 123, Parts 15 and 16, June 7-22, 1977, pp. 18114-18119, 18940-18948, 19739-19746.

[47] *Congressional Quarterly Weekly Report*, Vol. 25, July-Sept. 1967, p. 1633.

[48] *New York Times*, November 7, 1967.

[49] U.S. Senate Committee on Foreign Relations, *Panama Canal Treaties: Hearings*, Exec. N., 95th Congress, 1st Session, Washington D.C., 1977, part III, pp. 97, 99, 101 and interviews in 1979 and 1980 with military personnel involved in the negotiations.

[50] LaFeber, *Panama Canal*, p. 185.

[51] Ibid.

[52] *Congressional Quarterly Almanac*, Vol. 31, 1975, p. 805.

[53] *New York Times*, February 29, 1976.

[54] *New York Times*, October 7, 1976.

[55] *Background Docments*, pp. 15-16.

[56] Ibid., p. 1.

[57] *Congressional Quarterly Almanac*, Vol. 32, 1976, p. 22.

[58] *Washington Post*, Jan. 13, 1977, pp. 4, 12.

[59] *Washington Post*, May 29, 1977, and Cyrus Vance, *Hard Choices: Critical Years in America's Foreign Policy* (New York: Simon & Schuster, 1983), pp. 144-146.

[60] Vance, *Hard Choices*, pp. 144-45.

CHAPTER 3
WHY CHANGE PANAMA CANAL POLICY?

This chapter examines the basic questions that faced each president from Eisenhower to Carter: What Canal policy would best serve U.S. interests? Should Canal policy be changed? A simple answer was given by Eisenhower, Kennedy, Johnson, and initially by Nixon: make no change that would diminish effective U.S. control over the Canal. Only during the watershed year 1973 were the merits of cooperation and true partnership with Panama seriously considered. Then, in negotiations that spanned the rest of the Nixon presidency and the administrations of President Ford and Carter, the details of a partnership were slowly constructed. To explain why a fundamentally different relationship was not advocated until the 1974-77 negotiations, this chapter analyzes the types of control the United States sought to exercise over a canal in Panama from 1903 to 1972. The chapter then assesses the merits and risks of the new partnership envisioned in the 1977 treaties from the viewpoints of supporters and opponents.

The chapter analyzes the evolution of U.S. Canal policy objectives. This discussion builds upon the historical background presented in Chapter 2 and demonstrates the alternative treaty arrangements that the United States considered to prolong its control.

Evolution of U.S. Canal Policy Objectives, 1903-1972

At the turn of the century, the United States was not only determined to build an interoceanic canal in Central America but also to exercise unilateral control over that facility. While the Panama Canal would serve as a commercial asset for all nations, it would be operated, administered, and defended by one, the United States. More was at stake than the simple premise that the country making the investment for construction should run the Canal. As an interoceanic passage, the Panama Canal would be more than a commercial asset; its military value, in times of war and preparation for war, was equally significant. An interoceanic canal would alter the geostrategic horizons of the United States as an Atlantic and a Pacific power. Consequently, to use the waterway to its best advantage and to prevent the Canal from becoming a military asset for any potential enemy, the United States felt compelled to exercise unilateral control. National security required that no other nation be allowed to interfere in Canal operations, administration, and defense. These rights, which amounted to a grant of sovereign authority over a canal and a canal zone, were contained in the 1903 Hay-Bunau-Varilla Treaty; maintaining these rights became the primary objective of U.S. Canal policy during the next six decades.[1]

Although the Frenchman Bunau-Varilla added a perpetuity clause to the 1903 treaty, U.S. presidents from Theodore Roosevelt to Dwight Eisenhower maintained a permanent, nonterminating relationship with Panama and refused to change the basic rights the United States had acquired. Despite periods of U.S. isolationism and cooperative hemispheric initiatives such as the Good Neighbor Policy, the United States strongly identified its national interests with unilateral control, in perpetuity, over the Panama Canal. Neither the 1936 Hull-Alfaro Treaty nor the 1955 Remon-Eisenhower Treaty diminished or affected the U.S. ability to exercise unilateral control over Canal operations, administration, and defense rights equivalent to sovereignty over the Zone. The most the United States could concede, in response to Panamanian charges that it was exceeding the rights granted in the 1903 treaty, was to relinquish control *outside* the Canal Zone and to modify some Canal Zone government procurement policies. Neither treaty addressed Panama's basic demands: recognition of its sovereignty and elimination of the perpetuity clause.

Anti-American riots in Panama in 1959 caused the Eisenhower administration to reexamine Panama's demands and U.S. objectives concerning the Canal. Additional economic and symbolic concessions beyond those granted in the 1955 treaty were considered. Later that year, after a prolonged and acrimonious interdepartmental debate between the Departments of Defense and State, the United States adopted a new "flags policy." This decision was particularly significant. For years, Panama had demanded that its flag be flown in the Canal Zone. Opponents to such a policy postulated that such a decision would also be a decision about sovereignty. Nevertheless, the Eisenhower administration finally accepted Panama's demand, which it had adamantly rejected during the 1955 treaty negotiations, and agreed to fly the Panamanian flag at one site, Shaler Triangle, in the Zone.[2]

Critics viewed this decision as the beginning of the erosion of U.S. sovereignty and control, a process that could culminate with the loss of the Canal. From this perspective, Panama would be emboldened by its success on flags policy to demand further concessions from the United States. Canal Zone Governor Potter, for example, argued:

> I am sure that the flying of the flag is not an ultimate step; it is merely the next step . . . First, economic concessions from the United States and the right to fly the flag over the canal. Second, move for a 50-50 split for Panama's revenues. Third, when that is realized, demand for the canal itself.[3]

One of the administration's advocates for a change in flags policy, Assistant Secretary of State Rubottom, agreed that Panama "would press for other things as well.'"[4] He disagreed, however, that a new flags policy would jeopardize U.S. rights.

> I certainly acknowledge that flying the flag has political overtones and is subject to varying interpretations . . . There are a number of variations on the idea that could be done, and none of them, in my opinion, encroach to one degree on our rights and jurisdiction and our right to act as if we were sovereign in the Canal Zone.[5]

But, as Secretary Rubottom's statement makes clear, the Eisenhower administration did not intend the new flags policy to signal fundamental change. It was a symbolic gesture, a minimal response designed to ease tensions and reduce the likelihood of violence directed at U.S. citizens and property in Panama and the Canal Zone. For this and subsequent administrations, unilateral control over Canal operations, administration, and defense was not affected by flags or economic concessions. The authority and ability to exercise these more critical rights depended upon a U.S. presence: people in operations, management, and defense positions who were ready and willing to exercise their responsibilities.

Indirect Control

When Panama requested renegotiation of the 1903 treaty during the Kennedy administration, a new definition of control emerged from internal policy debate. The idea of building a new canal in Panama, constructed at sea level by nuclear excavation technology, was first discussed during the Eisenhower administration. This idea formed the basis for the Kennedy administration's plan for a new type of control. A different type of canal, a sea-level trench without locks and dams to operate and defend, entailed the possibility of sharing administration and internal defense with Panama, while maintaining unilateral external defense based at sea. Advisers in the White House considered growing Panamanian nationalism a threat to permanent, unilateral control based on a U.S. presence.[6] When they learned of the possibility of building a sea-level canal, they suggested that U.S. interests could be maintained and protected through indirect control. A multilateral management agency, with voting power weighted in favor of the United States and an inter-American defense force composed largely of U.S. troops under a U.S. commander, could replace the Panama Canal Company, the Canal Zone government, and U.S. bases in Panama. These multilateral agencies would effectively protect U.S. interests, defined as an open and efficient canal, because a sea-level canal would be much easier to administer and defend. A sea-level canal would have no network of locks and dams that could be depleted or sabotaged; therefore it would not require a large administrative area or a U.S. labor force, and it would be defended

46

from its approaches rather than its banks. These characteristics would allow the United States to eliminate a persistent source of Panamanian grievances and demands: a highly visible U.S. presence in the middle of their country where U.S. employees enjoyed a standard of living far higher than most Panamanians could attain. In addition, the perpetuity question would be moot because a sea-level canal would not become obsolete or vulnerable. No nonterminating rights for defense or management would be needed because this type of canal would be like a large river; it would always be open and could always be defended by naval forces at sea. Building a sea-level canal would thus allow the United States to relinquish the right "to act as if sovereign." A new treaty relationship based on indirect control through multilateral agencies could thus replace direct control.

The only drawback to these proposals was uncertainty over the feasibility of constructing a sea-level canal, an excavation project that would require using nuclear cratering devices. Nonetheless, in 1962, President Kennedy authorized additional feasibility studies of the peaceful uses of atomic energy similar to the studies which had already begun during the Eisenhower administration. Kennedy also authorized bilateral discussions short of negotiations to resolve Panama's grievances arising from existing treaties. The administration planned, once feasibility was demonstrated, to negotiate a new treaty for a new canal.[7]

Token Sharing of Control

Two years later, after the 1964 Flag Riots, the concept of indirect control over a sea-level canal was reformulated. President Johnson authorized two simultaneous actions consisting of a major program of sea-level canal feasibility studies and negotiations to establish new, bilateral agencies to manage and defend the Panama Canal and a new canal. The Flag Riots caused Johnson to actually begin treaty negotiations in 1965, long before the feasibility studies were completed.

The Johnson administration preferred bilateral to multilateral control, and the 1967 treaties contained provisions for joint administration and defense that severely circumscribed Panama's participation; the partnership envisioned in these treaties clearly relegated Panama to junior rather than equal status.[8] Effective control over Canal administration and defense would continue to be exercised by the United States with some "token" sharing of control with Panama. Although the Johnson administration, like its predecessor, rejected perpetuity as the basis for a relationship with Panama, it attempted to prolong the U.S. presence well into the next century. Instead of nonterminating rights, the 1967 treaties contained a

47

complex, extendable duration formula that would allow a dominant role for the United States for another 97 to 100 years if a new canal were constructed.

These changes in U.S. objectives — from unilateral control in perpetuity, to indirect control through multilateral agencies, to a token sharing of control through bilateral management and defense — reflect an evolution toward partnership made possible by the option of building a new and different canal facility. When that option was foreclosed, a conclusion reached in the 1970 report of the canal study commission authorized by President Johnson, the accomodative trend in U.S. Canal policy objectives was temporarily reversed.

At negotiations held from 1971 to 1972, the U.S. negotiating team advocated stronger unilateral defense and management rights for the United States and diminished participation by Panamanians as compared to the 1967 treaty package. A U.S. draft treaty offer presented in December 1971 contained a duration formula that would allow termination in fifty, eighty-five, or ninety years, depending upon whether the United States made no Canal improvements, constructed an additional lane of locks for the Panama Canal, or built a sea-level canal. Since the latter two options were unlikely, this draft treaty contained strong provisions for U.S. control through U.S. government agencies until the year 2022. Although minimal Panamanian participation would be allowed in a joint administration and some defense activities, this draft treaty was much more favorable to the United States than the 1967 treaties had been.[9]

Panama firmly rejected this offer in late 1972. After eight years of unsuccessful negotiations and in the context of progressively less favorable treaty proposals by the United States, Panama decided to enhance its bargaining position. The strategy it chose was a diplomatic initiative designed to embarrass the United States and to demonstrate widespread international support for its demands. Panama's strategy — to internationalize the Canal issue by inviting the United Nations Security Council to meet in Panama — was formulated during 1972, while bilateral negotiations were suspended. This successful initiative was a major determinant of fundamental changes in U.S. Canal policy objectives and the successful ratification, five years later, of two new Canal treaties.

From Control to Partnership, 1973-1974

Why did the same administration that made the 1971 draft treaty offer also accept the eight principles of the Kissinger-Tack Agreement? How could the administration that favored prolonging U.S. control well into the twenty-first century agree, two years later, to establish a partnership based

48

on Panamanian consent? How could the Panamanian government, after demanding full sovereignty and an immediate end to the U.S. presence in Panama, accept shared control until the year 2000?

Panama's internationalization strategy created a context that brought several previously inoperative factors to bear on Canal policy. Each was conducive to a fundamentally different treaty relationship. First, Panama's strategy focused the attention of a broader group and higher level of policymakers on the Canal issue. This altered the personnel involved with Canal policy from a small, insulated group of experts on the Panama Canal and its defense, which had handled the 1971-72 negotiations, to a larger group including National Security Adviser Kissinger and State Department officials with expertise in Latin America, hemispheric affairs, and Panama. Second, the success of Panama's strategy forced high-level officials to reexamine existing objectives, Panama's bargaining position, and U.S. interests. Third, sustained pressure from Panama and Latin American states kept the attention of high-level officials focused on Canal policy and the costs of failing to resolve the issue. Fourth, accommodative initiatives on other issues, ranging from SALT and rapprochement with China to the Vietnam peace negotiations, were influencing the overall framework of U.S. foreign policy. The Department of Defense, in particular, was rethinking counterguerrilla warfare tactics as these would apply to internal threats to Canal security. Within this broader context of changes, accommodation with Panama was considered a legitimate option.

Panama's internationalization strategy succeeded in convincing the Nixon White House and the Department of State that the Canal issue could no longer rest at the bottom of the foreign policy agenda. Columnist Stephen S. Rosenfeld described the effect of this strategy: "The propaganda and political beating administered in the United Nations helped transform the issue within the U.S. government from a modest regional matter, which could safely be left in a state of stagnation, into a major priority."[10] The situation in Panama was perceived as highly volatile. Officials in the Department of State believed that anti-U.S. demonstrations were likely to occur if positive steps were not taken. Demonstrations could lead to a military confrontation, threaten the security of the Canal, disrupt Canal operations, damage U.S. property, and threaten U.S. citizens living in Panama as well as those living in the Canal Zone. The conclusion drawn from these projections was that the situation must be stabilized by an effective approach that demonstrated a willingness to accommodate Panama. These conclusions were later summarized by Secretary Kissinger during the signing ceremony for the Kissinger-Tack Agreement on Principles.

A stable world cannot be imposed by force; it must derive from consensus. Mankind can only achieve community on the basis of shared aspirations . . . In the past our negotiation would have been determined by relative strength. Today we have come together in an act of conciliation. We recognize that no agreement can endure unless the parties want to maintain it. Participation in partnership is far preferable to reluctant acquiescence.[11]

Ambassador Bunker, who later headed the U.S. negotiating team, also stressed the administration's new emphasis on the importance of Panamanian consent.

For many years the level of Panama's consent has persistently declined. And by Panama, I mean the Panamanian people of all strata, not simply their government. Governments in Panama may change. But I am persuaded that governmental change will never again divert the Panamanian people from the course of legitimate nationalism they are now pursuing.[12]

Before the Security Council meeting had been held, the officials involved in the 1971-72 negotiations had believed that the Panamanian government was only attempting to draw international attention to the Canal issue in order to divert its citizens' attention from severe domestic problems. The outcome of the Security Council meeting — having to veto a resolution endorsing Panama's demands — caused these officials to reexamine this belief and to adopt two new assumptions. The first of these was, as the statements by Secretary Kissinger and Ambassador Bunker reflected, that Panama would reject any offer that perpetuated U.S. control over the Canal and Canal Zone. The second was that the Panamanian government and people would reject anything less than a substantial increase in their economic return from Canal operations and removal of the U.S. civilian and military presence in the Canal Zone.[13]

These assumptions formed the basis for reassessing Panama's intentions and bargaining strength. Apparently the Panamanian government was willing to risk additional confrontations with the United States in order to improve and maintain its bargaining position. During 1973, the Torrijos regime continued to demonstrate this resolve, broadening its bilateral relations to include ties with Communist states, particularly Cuba, as well as nonaligned nations. Moreover, Panama was not the only nation applying pressure on the United States. The Security Council meeting had demonstrated wide support for Panama's demands, both throughout Latin America and the Third World. Following the meeting, pressure from Latin American states continued to take the form of statements supporting Panama's legitimate aspirations and urging the United States to be for-

50

thcoming at the negotiating table.[14] Consequently, the Nixon administration revised its strategy. The White House decided it was inadvisable to ignore Panamanian preferences; it would be wiser to consider Panama as a more equal partner.

Although the Nixon Administration's negotiating team with its new advisers concluded that a different approach to the negotiations must be taken, they did not begin formulating a new strategy immediately. Rather, during a predicted "cooling-off period" following the Security Council meeting, a high-level, interdepartmental review of Canal policy was initiated to guide the next negotiations.[15]

Thus, the outcome of the Security Council meeting also produced changes in the personnel involved with U.S. Canal policy. The high-level review, which began soon after the U.S. delegation returned from Panama, provided an opportunity for the president's National Security adviser to intervene for a short but critical time in Canal policymaking.

The significance of Kissinger's involvement was twofold: it brought new participants with different interests and experiences into the process and broadened the range of ideas and options considered. During 1971 and 1972, the negotiating team and its Canal- and defense-oriented advisers had operated in relative isolation from experts on canal policy, Panama, and Latin America in the Departments of Defense and State. Dr. Kissinger's involvement in Canal policymaking added representatives from these departments plus experts on the National Security Council staff. The use of high-level interdepartmental review groups to construct consensus positions was another development that facilitated the negotiations and the ratification process.

These personnel and procedural changes provided an opportunity for high-level officials to relate Canal policy to the broader objectives of a cooperative hemispheric policy outlined by President Nixon in an address on Action for Progress in October 1969. Kissinger's direct involvement in Canal policy was only temporary, but it occurred while his attention was focused on developing a constructive dialogue on hemispheric and North-South issues. Consequently, review processes for hemispheric initiatives and a new round of Canal negotiations coincided with mutually reinforcing consequences.

These developments enhanced the likelihood that a conciliatory approach toward Panama would be adopted. A positive response to Panama's demands was seen as contributing to better inter-American relations. Similarly, an emphasis on improving U.S. relations throughout the hemisphere was seen as enhancing U.S.-Panamanian relations.[16]

Kissinger reacted positively to these ideas. Rosenfeld reports that "as Kissinger started dipping into Latin affairs, he found that there was more actual community of interest and more personal responsiveness than he had been led to believe."[17] Agreeing to negotiate a new treaty could enhance this "community of interest." Such a step would eliminate a highly symbolic rallying point for Latin American and Third World grievances against the United States. And while a new Canal treaty would not resolve other problems on the hemispheric agenda, it was likely to improve the environment in which those problems would be addressed.

Although the Kissinger-Tack Agreement was the most positive development in U.S.-Panamanian relations in many years, the idea of negotiating a new Canal treaty to establish a partnership based on Panamanian consent was strongly criticized at home. It was soon obvious that the views expressed by Secretary Kissinger and Ambassador Bunker did not reflect beliefs widely shared by members of Congress, the attentive public, veterans' and national security interest groups, and public opinion. Rather, they represented one bloc or segment of opinion in what opinion analysts have labeled the post-Vietnam consensus.[18] Unlike the relatively unified Cold War consensus of the 1950s and early 1960s, the post-Vietnam consensus is fragmented into several blocs. These include a small isolationist bloc; a larger conservative or cold war internationalist bloc; an equally large liberal or nonisolationist, but noninterventionist group of internationalists; and a small group concerned with global problems and nonmilitary solutions.[19] With such an array of foreign policy beliefs, less than a majority of elite opinion was predisposed to agree with the Nixon administration's new approach on Canal policy. Many observers rejected the views represented in the Kissinger-Tack Agreement and argued that the United States would regret giving up unilateral control granted in the 1903 treaty.

Merits and Risks of Changing Canal Policy

The foregoing analysis of the different types of control systems that the United States was willing to accept has demonstrated the large degree of change the 1977 Canal treaties represent. The Canal, formerly considered a vital defense asset, was downgraded to the status of a military convenience. A long-standing commitment to unilateral U.S. control over Canal operations, administration, and defense, once seen as an essential requirement for guaranteed use of the Canal, was replaced with a willingness to accept a permanent regime of neutrality, temporarily shared control, recognition of Panamanian sovereignty, and finally, full Panamanian control over Canal administration and operations in the year 2000. The new treaties were designed to ensure continued U.S. access to the Canal through incentives rewarding Panamanian cooperation rather than a permanent U.S. presence in the Canal Zone.

When compared to the forms of control the United States considered acceptable between 1903 and 1972, shared control reflects different axioms or premises for the conduct of U.S. foreign policy: how it deals with small nations, protects its security interests, and structures long-term, mutually advantageous relationships.[20] The 1974-77 negotiations and the treaty texts submitted to the U.S. Senate generally reflected respect for Panama despite its size and small military stature; a preventive, rather than a reactive diplomatic strategy; a cooperative view of security relations with Panama as an ally; and a belief that long-term relationships should be built on positive incentives rather than coercive sanctions. Consequently, the Canal treaty ratification debate concerned the merits of these premises as well as the content of the new treaties.

A Clash of World Views: Liberal versus Conservative Internationalists

Support for the new treaties and the premises they reflect is consistent with what William Schneider calls "liberal internationalism," one element in the currently fragmented foreign policy consensus.[21] A liberal internationalist supports cooperative international solutions to global problems and coexistence with non-Western countries, especially the Soviet Union and the People's Republic of China.[22] Schneider also finds that liberal internationalists are willing to take "a broader world view, to understand more complex and remote causes, to give more support to policies that involve no immediate, palpable benefit."[23] Clearly, the changes embodied in the 1977 treaties are compatible with this outlook or world view.

Opposition to the 1977 treaties is associated with entirely different views. Instead of perceiving the treaties as a cooperative, mutually beneficial solution, opponents viewed them as blackmail by a greedy, ungrateful, fourth-rate nation. Opponents believed that the only way the United States could guarantee access to the Canal was through a permanent military presence in Panama and the use of force. Moreover, they saw the treaties as another U.S. retreat from superpower status, as a sign of weakness, and as appeasement of Soviet and Cuban threats.[24]

These opposition views are compatible with the other dominant element in the currently divided foreign policy consensus, "conservative internationalism."[25] Conservative internationalists favor a strong and active U.S. role as leader of the Free World. They also support making and maintaining military commitments and the use of force to counter Communist aggression. Conservative internationalists distrust non-Western nations; instead, they support closer relations with states which are socially, economically, and politically similar to the United States. Although liberal internationalists support efforts that redirect U.S. foreign policy in cooperative and conciliatory directions, conservative internationalists support a return to the Cold War.[26]

Views of treaty supporters and opponents can be found in the text of the Senate debate and in two articles frequently cited by members of Congress during the treaty ratification debate.[27] Several representative statements from these sources are presented below to illustrate the different foreign policy premises and views held by treaty supporters and opponents. Chapter 5, which provides a detailed discussion of the role of the Congress, also reviews statements and views of treaty supporters and opponents. Given these fundamentally opposing views, neither side could persuade the other of the merits of its case. The fate of the 1977 treaties rested on the number of proponents and opponents in the Senate and, more importantly, on the last minute decisions of a few truly undecided senators.

The basic disagreement between supporters and opponents was over the merits of cooperation versus confrontation. This theme also differentiates liberal from conservative internationalists. Paralleling the theme of cooperation versus confrontation was the basic choice facing the Senate during the ratification debate: to accept the new cooperative partnership or to reject the 1977 treaties and face a period of heightened bilateral tension and confrontation. Senator Sam Nunn (D-Ga) succinctly summarized the choice: "'Save the Canal,' is a common theme of those who oppose the treaties; however, it is also an appropriate theme for those who will vote for the treaties. The question is how do we save it for our own use — by ratifying or by rejecting the treaties?'"[28]

Two analysts, Abraham Lowenthal and Milton Charlton assessed the implications of this choice for treaty proponents.

> The Congress will then have to choose between two different approaches for protecting U.S. economic, military, and political interests. One way is to cling — in the face of rising opposition from Panama, on the international scene, and even from within the United States — to the terms of the Hay-Bunau-Varilla Treaty of 1903 . . . The other is to forge a modern partnership between the United States and Panama so that the two countries can protect an efficient, secure and neutral canal. One path assures an era of bitter and continuing confrontation . . . the other way promises closer cooperation.[29]

For Senator Harry F. Byrd, Jr. (I-Va), however, such an argument was misguided and inappropriate. U.S. security was too directly related to the Canal to give it up for any reason, especially under duress from Panama. Instead, he argued that broader national security concerns should take precedence.

This is not the first time a President has proposed surrendering our sovereignty over the Panama Canal and the Canal Zone. In 1967, President Johnson put a head of steam behind Panama's resolve to wrest the canal away from undisputed American control . . . I see no fundamental difference between the Johnson proposal and the Carter proposal. Each would surrender U.S. control. The Congress was told in 1967 that there would be a series of anti-American riots in Panama if the U.S. Government did not give the Panamanians what they want. We are being told the same thing today. It is vitally important that the United States maintain a position of strength in Latin America and the pivotal point in our defense arrangements is the Panama Canal and the Canal Zone.[30]

Similarly, Senator John Stennis (D-Miss) reacted negatively to the idea that the spectre of violence in Panama should result in surrender of the Canal. "We cannot afford to gamble with our national security to appease Panama — that is irrational — or to appease others with whom we are friendly."[31]

Opposition to appeasement was a major theme articulated by treaty opponents, who frequently referred to the Carter administration's negotiations as concessions made "at the point of a gun." This view of the negotiations and the 1977 treaties was particularly strong among opponents who perceived the Canal issue as another example of U.S. retreat from superpower status during the 1960s and 1970s. Hanson Baldwin articulated this position quite forcefully.

. . . The distinct possibility of a physical confrontation — perhaps an armed one — must be faced. This does not mean that we must cut and run. The avoidance of bloodshed is devoutly to be desired, but for some things we must be prepared to fight. If we establish as our goal peace at any price — if, faced with the threat of force, we continuously concede and compromise — we shall lose the world. Since the Bay of Pigs the United States has been in retreat . . . Somewhere the line must be drawn — this far and no farther. Sometimes the resolution and will of the American people must be made manifest. Panama is the place and now is the time.[32]

This statement shows the continuing appeal of antiappeasement as a reason for opposing changes in Canal policy. Officials in the Eisenhower administration who had opposed the new flags policy had argued that concessions should not be made to appease Panamanian threats. During the 1960s and 1970s, the appeal of this reasoning was enhanced when treaty opponents perceived threats to U.S. interests that made appeasement seem even more foolhardy. Perceived threats were, in fact, the basis for Baldwin's conclusion that "the line must be drawn." His view of recent international events contained a clear and strong perception of that threat:

Throughout the world, Soviet communism has tried to secure control, or influence over, the global maritime choke points. For a considerable period the Soviet Union was dominant in Egypt and the Suez Canal, and a pro-Soviet Communist underground, smashed just in time, came close to making that dominance permanent. Now, rebuffed in Egypt, Soviet communism is highly influential on the Horn of Africa, which gives access to the Red Sea and the southern approaches of the Suez Canal, and it is jockeying for position to threaten the Strait of Bal-el-Mandeb, through which most of the world's oil traffic from the Persian Gulf flows . . . It is, therefore, no accident that the Panama Canal has been the object of so much Soviet and Cuban attention. A Communist Panama, in control of the canal and dominated or greatly influenced and supported by Havana and Moscow, would indeed represent another major defeat for the United States and a strategic victory for communism, this time in an area vital to the United States.[33]

Senator John Stennis also perceived this threat and argued that "this is no time to be weakening in any substantial way sea passages that are to our advantage, particularly one that we now control."[34] While Baldwin emphasized direct and indirect threats, Communist domination or influence, Stennis emphasized the critical nature of the Canal in an uncertain and threatening world.

In time of national emergency, the availability of the Panama Canal could be decisive if we are to be able to counter the growing Soviet threat. That threat is certainly increased by the presence of a Communist Cuba astride the Atlantic approach to the Canal. Cuba, a Soviet satellite, now has over 30,000 military troops in faraway Africa, and is growing in military sophistication each day. Who would have dreamed of a situation like that coming true? Who would have dreamed of it just a few years ago? Certainly it tells us today, "Do no go too fast, and do not go too far in assuming that if you pull out of the canal some other powers are not going to immediately try to find a way to come in." Those with the power and enough cooperation will find a way to come in.[35]

In addition to perceiving events as part of a global Soviet strategy to dominate the sea lines of communication, Baldwin also perceived a domino effect operating in the international environment.[36] Belief in a domino theory is consistent with conservative internationalism, and Baldwin's views about this foreign policy premise were quite clear.

The much maligned domino theory was valid for Southeast Asia; along with Vietnam, Cambodia and Laos fell to Communist governments; Thailand expelled our forces; the Philippines immediately announced a shift away from the United States and demanded a revision of our base agreements; and all over the world, U.S. resolution and will were questioned. The domino theory is equally valid for the Caribbean: if Panama goes, all our positions there may eventually follow.[37]

Treaty supporters, as typified by Lowenthal and Charlton, perceived events differently. Although treaty opponents viewed the Canal as an important target in a long-term Soviet expansionist strategy, treaty supporters attached much less strategic significance to the Canal and a U.S. military presence in Panama. Lowenthal and Charlton argued that while the Canal might once have been " 'vital' to this country . . . it is not today, and it will be even further from reality in coming years.' '[38]

Instead of perceiving Communist expansionist threats in the region or directed against the Canal, treaty supporters perceived a new relationship with Panama as an opportunity.

> What is at issue in Panama, more than anything else, is our own country's conception of our international role. Some Americans would pick Panama as the right place to "draw the line", to show the world that the United States cannot be pushed around, that it will not withdraw in retreat from its outposts around the world . . .
>
> We would argue, however, that Panama is not the place to vent national insensitivities but rather that the United States knows well how to best protect its real interests in a rapidly changing world. Building the Panama Canal early in the twentieth century was a great American accomplishment, requiring ingenuity and audacity above all. Keeping it open and secure in the latter part of this century and into the next will be another impressive feat, requiring intelligence and tact.[39]

Thus, while Baldwin reflects a belief that the world has not greatly changed since the beginning of the Cold War, Lowenthal and Charlton emphasize changes in the external environment that require changes in U.S. foreign policy. Senator Frank Church (D-Idaho) summarized this point: "The world has changed. It used to be that gunboat diplomacy would serve to enforce our will in the Caribbean and in Central America. But now it takes some respect for the rights of others . . ."[40]

These conflicting beliefs were also expressed during the Senate debate. Senator Pat Moynihan (D-NY) saw the 1977 Treaty as an opportunity for the United States to reverse world opinion.

> This treaty, far from being a retreat in American policy, has the potential to become an extraordinary forward movement in our relations with the rest of the world. In a space of ten year's time, we may well reverse completely the understanding in the United Nations, for example, of what the United States stands for and what Cuba stands for.
>
> A decade ago Cuba said it stood for resistance to imperialism, for resistance to militarism, for all those wonderful things. We were said to stand for armies, for occupation of other people's lands. But pass this

treaty and we will be the people of the future, while the Cubans, murdering and killing and burning their way through Africa, will be discredited militant imperialists, which in fact they are, and they will be completely rejected in Latin America. The turning point will be this treaty.[41]

Senator Church argued in favor of the treaties because they represented positive and worthy values rather than weaknesses.

No one perceived our country as weak when we granted independence to the Philippines or when we returned Okinawa and Iwo Jima to Japan. Quite the contrary — these were seen as the acts of a self-confident nation, as acts of justice, as adherence to our principles — acts which benefitted our relations significantly in the Pacific. These treaties with Panama also will represent an act of self-confidence and of justice and of principle.[42]

For senators who opposed the treaties, promises of future benefits and investments to earn good will were insignificant in comparison to the concrete advantages the Panama Canal, under U.S. control, could provide. Senator Harry Byrd strongly valued the status quo.

With sovereign rights, existing rights which we have held for many years, the United States has been able to garrison troops in the Canal Zone and control access to the U.S.-owned areas immediately adjacent to the canal. In this way the United States has kept the canal secure, even during two world wars and the Korean and Vietnam conflicts.[43]

Senator James Allen also emphasized the tangible advantages of the status quo.

No amount of words in no amount of amendments, no matter how carefully drafted, could ever provide the same needed guarantees as are provided by actual possession . . . if we give up physical control the country will still, sooner or later, find itself at the mercy of some petty dictator who decides, probably with the backing of the Soviet Union, to cause difficulties for the United States in using this vital strategic waterway.[44]

Instead of resorting to physical pressure and force to protect perceived U.S. interests, Lowenthal and Charlton, like many treaty supporters, advocated another alternative.

Confrontation with Panama — the almost inevitable consequence of clinging to the 1903 treaty — can be avoided by negotiating a new and more modern treaty relationship. The United States can protect its essential interest in an open, efficient, secure, and neutral canal while satisfying Panama's desire to regain jurisdiction over all of its national territory.

58

.

In so doing, the two countries would eliminate the greatest real threat to the canal's security: Panamanian bitterness.[45]

Thus, while treaty opponents emphasized the Canal's role in the global strategic context and threats arising from Communist expansion and patterns of falling dominoes, treaty supporters emphasized threats arising from the situation in Panama and the 1903 treaty.

Consequently, opponents and supporters held very different images of Panama and its leaders, particularly General Torrijos. Predictably, treaty opponents emphasized General Torrijos's and Panama's relationships with members of the Communist bloc. Baldwin argued:

> Far more important from the point of view of U.S. security is the character of the Torrijos regime and its relationships to Communist powers. A kind of neo-Marxist establishment rules the country, even though there is no proof that Torrijos himself is a Communist (of either Soviet, Cuban or Chinese coloration). Known and open Communists occupy high positions in the Torrijos regime.
>
> The ties between Torrijos, Castro's Cuba, and the Soviet Union have been cordial and close, though some of their most important manifestations have been hidden . . . .[46]

Treaty supporters, in contrast, emphasized long-standing grievances of the Panamanians, rather than the ideological cast of the current regime. Their views emphasized nationalism instead of leftism, and perceived Panamanian demands for sovereignty over the Canal as arising internally and as likely to persist long after General Torrijos's tenure ended. Supporters' views of Panama's motivation in seeking a new treaty and control over the Canal emphasized the historical context in which Canal policy evolved.

> Americans are brought up to think of the building of the Panama Canal as one of the most glorious chapters in our nation's history . . . The first step toward understanding the Panama problem is to realize that Panamanians learn a very different history. They are taught that the United States seized the opportunity to build the canal through the heart of Panama's territory by combining brute force with political chicanery. For Panamanians, the Canal Zone created by, the 1903 treaty is a daily affront . . . For Panama, and for most of the rest of the world, the Canal Zone is a colony, a vestige of the era when great powers could at will set up non-self-governing territories abroad. For Panama, the Canal Zone is a source not of national pride but of humiliation. The central question for the United States in Panama is whether U.S. interests require Panama's continuing humiliation.[47]

This sampling of statements by treaty supporters and opponents demonstrates the ideological differences that separated them. These differences are consistent with premises and views associated with liberal and conservative internationalism. Because these broader world views entailed irreconcilable foreign policy premises, opposing sides in the ratification debate failed to convince each other with their arguments. The 1977 Canal treaties were almost defeated in the Senate, and later, when the Carter administration's implementing legislation was debated, the same question — why change Canal policy — was raised again.

Endnotes

[1] For a discussion of U.S. motivation and interests in an interoceanic canal and the 1903 treaty, see Samuel Flagg Bemis, *The Latin American Policy of the United States* (New York: Harcourt, Brace, 1943); William D. McCain, *The United States and the Republic of Panama* (New York: Russell & Russell, 1965); McCullough, *Path Between the Seas*; and LaFeber, *Panama Canal*.

[2] The "United States Agreement 'To Have the Panamanian Flag Flown in the Canal Zone': Note from Ambassador Farland to Panamanian Acting Foreign Minister Miro Grimaldo, September 17, 1960,'' is reprinted in *Background Documents*, p. 1058.

[3] U.S. Congress, House of Representatives, Committee on Foreign Affairs, *United States Relations with Panama*, subcommittee hearings, 86th Cong., 2d Sess. (Washington: Government Printing Office, 1960), pp. 42-43.

[4] Ibid., p. 74.

[5] Ibid.

[6] These plans were developed by a special Task Force on Latin America established by President Kennedy soon after his inauguration. The Task Force review of Canal policy was completed in July 1961 and its recommendation for negotiating a new Canal treaty that would allow the United States to build a sea-level canal was contained in a memorandum described in confidential interviews; confirmation of the content of the memorandum and its rationale can be found in Ambassador Farland's testimony in U.S. Congress, House of Representatives, Committee on Merchant marine and Fisheries, *Panama Canal Problems*, subcommittee Hearings, 88th Cong., 1st Sess. (Washington: Government Printing Office, 1963), pp. 26-28.

[7] These events are discussed in Atlantic-Pacific Interoceanic Canal Study Commission, *Interoceanic Canal Studies 1970* (Washington: Government Printing Office, 1971).

[8] The texts of the 1967 Canal treaties have been declassified and can be found in *Background Documents*, pp. 1149-1370.

[9] For a discussion of the 1971-72 negotiations, see U.S., Congress, House of Representatives, Committee on Foreign Affairs and Committee on Merchant Marine and Fisheries, *United Nations Security Council Meeting in Panama*, 93rd Congress, 2d session, joint subcommittee hearings (Washington: Government Printing Office, 1973).

[10] Rosenfeld, "The Panama Negotiations," p. 4.

[11] "U.S. and Panama Agree on Principles for Negotiation of a New Panama Canal Treaty," address by Secretary of State Kissinger, February 7, 1974, *Department of State Bulletin* 70 (February 25, 1974):181.

[12] "Panama and the United States: A Design for Partnership," address by Ellsworth Bunker at Center for Inter-American Relations on March 19, 1974, Department of State *Bulletin* 70 (April 29, 1974):455.

[13] Both authors conducted several indepth interviews with people involved in the treaty process. Senators, Congressmen and their staffs; Congressional Committee staffs; members of the U.S. negotiating team; White House staff; and personnel of the departments of State and Defense were among those interviewed. Professor Scranton did most of her interviewing in Washington in 1977 and 1978. Professor Furlong did most of his interviewing in Washington in 1978 and 1979. Follow up interviews with a few selected key people were done in 1980, 1981 and 1983. Many of those who were interviewed preferred to remain anonymous. The authors have abided with this request. Thus, throughout the text, many footnotes will refer simply to "interviews" rather than being more specific. In a few cases, the dates and names of people interviewed are included with their permission.

[14] For examples of Latin American initiatives to support Panama's position, see *Background Documents* pp. 165, 168, and 176.

[15] Interviews.

[16] State Department officials close to the negotiations reported in confidential interviews that Kissinger was anxious to take positive action on the Canal issue prior to attending the Latin American Foreign Minister's Meeting scheduled for February, 1974. Secretary Kissinger and others in the State Department were determined to avoid a "replay" of the 1973 Security Council Meeting in Panama.

[17] Rosenfeld, "The Panama Negotiations," p. 4.

[18] The term consensus is used in the literature on public opinion to refer to the distribution of views reflected in public opinion surveys that use a Likert-type scale. That distribution can take one of several shapes: a normal distribution with few strongly agreeing or disagreeing and a majority falling in the middle categories of agree, neutral, or disagree; a skewed distribution, with a majority falling in either the strongly disagree/disagree categories or strongly agree/agree categories; or, the distribution may be bimodal, with opinion closely divided into strongly disagree and strongly agree categories and few respondents taking more neutral positions. During the 1950s and early 1960s, public opinion reflected in foreign policy belief surveys was usually characterized by a normal, bell-shaped distribution. Hence, the term *Cold War Consensus* was used to describe these shared views. Once the Cold War consensus began to erode a bimodal distribution of foreign policy views emerged in opinion surveys. While it may seem odd to use the term consensus to describe the two competing sets of views reflected in such a distribution, the literature on foreign policy beliefs and opinion continues to use the term consensus to refer to the distribution of views whether it be normal or bimodal. For an early work on the subject, see James N. Rosenau, *Public Opinion*

and Foreign Policy (New York: Random House, 1961); for more recent studies, see William Watts and Lloyd A. Free, "Nationalism, Not Isolationism,"*Foreign Policy* 24 (Fall 1976):3-26; Ole R. Holsti and James N. Rosenau, "Vietnam, Consensus, and the Belief Systems of American Leaders," *World Politics* 32 (October 1979):1-56; Holsti and Rosenau, "America's Foreign Policy Agenda: The Post-Vietnam Beliefs of American Leaders," in Charles W. Kegley, Jr., and Patrick J. McGowan, eds., *Challenges to America: United States Foreign Policy in the 1980s* (Beverly Hills, Calif.: Sage, 1979), pp. 231-68; and Michael Mandelbaum and William Schneider, "The New Internationalisms: Public Opinion and American Foreign Policy," in Kenneth A. Oye, Donald Rothchild, and Robert J. Lieber, eds., *Eagle Entangled: U.S. Foreign Policy in a Complex World* (New York: Longman, 1979), pp. 34-88.

[19] These are William Schneider's terms; see Mandelbaum and Schneider in *Eagle Entangled* and also see William Schneider "Internationalism and Ideology: Foreign Policy Attitudes of the American Public, 1975," paper presented at the 19th Annual Conference of the International Studies Association, Washington, D.C., February 1978. Holsti and Rosenau use the terms *Cold War* and *post-Cold War internationalists* to refer to these two dominant opinion blocs; the terms *cooperative internationalism* and *militant internationalism* are used by Michael A. Maggiotto and Eugene R. Wittkopf in "American Public Attitudes Toward Foreign Policy," *International Studies Quarterly* 25 (December 1981):601-31. All of these analysts reach similar conclusions: a bimodal or bifurcated distribution of opinion began to characterize U.S. public and elite opinion during the early to mid-1970s.

[20] Holsti and Rosenau use the term axiom to refer to fundamental foreign policy beliefs about "the contemporary international system, a proper role for the United States in it, the nature of adversaries, and the aspirations, strategies and tactics that should constitute the core of this nation's external relations" in "Cold War Axioms in the Post-Vietnam Era," paper prepared but not presented at the Annual Conference of the International Studies Association, Washington, D.C., February 1978, p. 2.

[21] The terms *post-Cold War internationalist* or *cooperative internationalist* can be substituted for Schneider's liberal internationalist.

[22] Schneider, "Internationalism and Ideology," pp. 37-38.

[23] William Schneider, "Behind the Passions of the Canal Treaty Debate: A Matter of Pride and Property," *Washington Post*, February 12, 1978.

[24] For another discussion of treaty opponents' and supporters' views, see Chapter 5, "Congress and the Treaties."

[25] Schneider, "Internationalism and Ideology," pp. 38-39.

[26] Mandelbaum and Schneider, "The New Internationalisms," pp. 63-64; these views are the reason some analysts have used the terms *Cold War internationalists* and *militant internationalism* to characterize this set of beliefs.

[27] These articles were published in the *AEI Defense Review*, Number Four, "A New Treaty for Panama?" August 1977; see Abraham F. Lowenthal and Milton

Charlton, "Pro: The United States and Panama: Confrontation or Cooperation," and Hanson W. Baldwin, "Con: The Panama Canal: Sovereignty and Security."

[28] *Congressional Record*, Vol. 124, pt. 6, Senate, March 14, 1978, p. 6748.

[29] Lowenthal and Charlton, "Pro: The United States and Panama," p. 2.

[30] *Congressional Record*, Vol. 124, pt. 5, Senate, March 8, 1978, p. 5990.

[31] Ibid.

[32] Baldwin, "Con: The Panama Canal," p. 30.

[33] Ibid.

[34] *Congressional Record*, Vol. 124, pt. 5, Senate, March 8, 1978, p. 5990.

[35] Ibid.

[36] Baldwin, "Con: The Panama Canal," p. 15.

[37] Ibid.

[38] Lowenthal and Charlton, "Pro: The United States and Panama," p. 4.

[39] Ibid., p. 11.

[40] *Congressional Record*, Vol. 124, pt. 3, Senate, February 10, 1978, p. 3215.

[41] *Congressional Record*, Vol. 124, pt. 4, Senate, February 23, 1978, p. 4281.

[42] *Congressional Record*, Vol. 124, pt. 3, Senate, February 10, 1978, p. 3214.

[43] *Congressional Record*, Vol. 124, pt. 5, Senate, March 6, 1978, p. 5587.

[44] *Congressional Record*, Vol. 124, pt. 6, Senate, March 16, 1978, p. 7165.

[45] Lowenthal and Charlton, "Pro: The United States and Panama," p. 8.

[46] Baldwin, "Con: The Panama Canal," p. 27.

[47] Lowenthal and Charlton, "Pro: The United States and Panama," p. 4.

CHAPTER 4

ASSESSING EXECUTIVE IMPACT: PRESIDENTS, THEIR ADMINISTRATIONS, AND THE TREATIES

This chapter examines the impact of three presidents — Nixon, Ford, and Carter — and their administrations on the Panama Canal Treaty negotiations. Throughout the negotiations, positions taken by the United States were most strongly affected by the negotiating team and its advisers. Nonetheless, other parts of the administration also played significant roles. The negotiators acted within guidelines approved by the National Security Council and under the direction of the president. And although the language of treaty articles can be attributed to bargains struck among bureaucratic coalitions and between negotiating teams, presidential decisions set the basic direction of Canal policy.

The first section of this chapter focuses on several executive activities that typically occur during the formulation phase: setting priorities, setting basic policy guidelines, selecting negotiators, timing initiatives, and resolving interdepartmental conflicts. The second part focuses on executive activity during the advice and consent phase, particularly consensus and coalition building, and examines the Carter administration's campaign to successfully ratify the 1977 Canal treaties.

What do we expect presidents and their administration to do in the field of foreign policy? Ideally, we expect them to exercise leadership: to set priorities among issues, to provide direction for experts in the administration, to select personnel for key positions who will advocate presidential interests, to make strategic choices about the timing of initiatives, and to decide questions that cannot be successfully resolved at lower levels of the executive branch. For treaty negotiations, we expect the experts involved — negotiators and their staff — to be primarily responsible for formulating proposals. But we expect the president and his advisers to set general guidelines for U.S. positions and to coordinate policymaking through the National Security Council. Direction setting and coordination are especially important when several executive departments are involved in negotiations. Performed well, these activities can prevent mixed signals to other governments. Performed poorly, just the reverse can occur. Finally, we expect presidents to select chief negotiators. In addition to representing the United States externally, chief negotiators also advocate the president's views vis-a-vis executive departments and agencies; in this capacity, negotiators may help resolve interdepartmental conflicts.

These expectations about presidential leadership structure our analysis of Canal policymaking during the Nixon, Ford, and Carter administrations. The first part of this chapter contains discussions of the events and policy activities that occurred during formulation and the advice and consent phase. The last part contains a comparative analysis of executive impact and our conclusions about the three administrations' contributions to Canal policy.

Early Formulation Phase

Three administrations presided over the negotiations that produced the 1977 Canal treaties. The Nixon administration was responsible for the most fundamental decision: to seek an entirely new Canal treaty that would terminate U.S. control over the Canal and Canal Zone and establish a new partnership for managing the Canal. This change in policy objectives was formally outlined in the 1974 Kissinger-Tack Agreement on Principles (see Appendix A).

This agreement was broad in scope and contained vague language. Consequently, when negotiations were conducted under the Ford adminis-. tration, important decisions had to be made about specific positions and draft treaty texts. Most of the provisions of the 1977 treaties were approved during this administration.

When the Carter administration took office in January 1977, only a few issues remained on the agenda. President Carter made a strong public commitment to bring the negotiations to a speedy but mutually acceptable conclusion, and this administration was responsible for the final and most controversial stages of the negotiation process.

The Nixon Administration: New Directions for Canal Policy

The process of formulating new Canal policy objectives began in the spring of 1973, after Panama invited the United Nations Security Council to hold a special meeting in Panama City. The outcome of this meeting was a diplomatic setback for the United States. Panama's demands for sovereignty over the Canal and the Canal Zone were supported almost unanimously, and the United States vetoed a resolution on the Canal question. After this embarrassing event, a high-level review was undertaken, and the conclusions reached set an entirely new direction for Canal policy.[1]

Previously, as we saw in Chapter 3, the primary U.S. objective had been to prolong its control over Canal administration and defense, hoping to maintain U.S. control well into the twenty-first century. Positions taken by the United States, during negotiations in 1965 to 1967 and 1971, reflected an assumption that Panama would accept token U.S. concessions in return for a new treaty that would overwhelmingly favor the United States. After the Security Council meeting, these views changed: U.S. objectives were redefined and Panama's bargaining position was reassessed. Members of the U.S. negotiating team argued that Panama's successful diplomatic initiative should be interpreted as a sign of determination; apparently, Panama would not accept a new treaty that perpetuated the old relationship. Therefore, the United States would have to set a new objective, and attempt to negotiate a new treaty that would create a more equal partnership. Several months later, Ambassador Ellsworth Bunker, the U.S. chief Canal treaty negotiator, publicly summarized this conclusion, "We can serve those [U.S.] interests in continued operation and defense of the canal adequately only if we move to change — to modernize the nature of the presence of the United States in the Canal Zone."[2]

The high-level review was completed in June 1973. Beyond affirming the decision to seek a new treaty, the review group identified past mistakes that should not be repeated. First, the administration would not enter negotiations by proposing a revised version of the 1971 draft treaty that had been rejected by Panama. A formal agenda would not be set until negotiations were actually underway. Second, the National Security Council (NSC) would not issue new guidance on Canal policy before negotiations formally opened and preliminary discussions with the Panamanian negotiating team were held. In essence, the review group recommended waiting to hear Panama's demands before making substantive decisions. Thus the Nixon administration's new direction for Canal policy was to take a bargaining approach. That is, instead of beginning negotiations, as the United States had in the past, by proposing a plan created solely by its own negotiators, a joint plan for a new treaty would evolve during discussions between Panamanian and U.S. officials.[3]

The administration then faced the problem of repairing U. S. relations with Panama. Panama had taken the initiative with the UN Security Council meeting, and the United States needed to make a countermove signaling its willingness to bargain.

A New Chief Negotiator

One obvious signal was to appoint a new chief negotiator. National Security Adviser Kissinger decided that Ellsworth Bunker would be the administration's best choice. Bunker was experienced; he had participated in many seemingly intractable negotiations. In addition, Bunker had firsthand experience in Panama, having served as a mediator after the 1964 Flag Riots. Another positive signal, one typical of Kissinger's style, was personal diplomacy. Kissinger decided that he and Ambassador Bunker

66

would conduct the preliminary discussions with Panama's representatives. Kissinger's participation would confer status on Panama and demonstrate the priority the administration set for the Canal issue. And, the personal involvement of Bunker and Kissinger would set a positive tone during the sensitive prelude to formal negotiations.

These plans received an unexpected boost from Panama during the summer of 1973. In June, Panama's Foreign Minister Juan Antonio Tack wrote to Ambassador Bunker and suggested that the two negotiating teams formulate a statement of principles reflecting both governments' objectives. This suggestion pleased Ambassador Bunker; it signified Panama's willingness to begin serious discussions, and a joint statement would provide an excellent vehicle for the administration's new bargaining approach.

A second step was taken in July, when Foreign Minister Tack invited the United States to hold negotiations in Panama. A draft statement of principles accompanied the invitation. Ambassador Bunker interpreted this development as another positive signal from Panama. Tack's draft statement was very similar to ideas that had been circulating within the administration. Secretary Kissinger[4] and Ambassador Bunker conveyed a positive response to Foreign Minister Tack, and the negotiating team estimated that a final text could be reached after one or two meetings with the Panamanian team.

The Kissinger-Tack Agreement

An indication of the high priority of the Canal issue was that each government's top officials participated in the first bilateral discussion. Secretary Kissinger, Ambassador Bunker, and Foreign Minister Tack met at UN headquarters in New York during October 1973. Both countries considered the meeting a success, and they agreed to schedule several working sessions in Panama to draft an official text.[5]

Substantial progress was made at the first working session, held from November 26 to December 3, 1973. During the next three weeks, the deputy negotiators, S. Morey Bell and Nicolas Gonzales Revilla, held informal sessions to refine the working text. Although the Panamanian government and the Department of State accepted this draft text, it failed to satisfy the Department of Defense. Difficulties in obtaining Defense Department concurrence delayed a meeting between Ambassador Bunker and Foreign Minister Tack until January 6-8, 1974. Then, after a final round of executive branch consultations, both governments accepted the text of the Kissinger-Tack Agreement, and a signing ceremony was scheduled for February 7, 1974.

67

Having reached an agreement with Panama, the administration had to begin building a consensus at home supporting its new Canal policy objectives. In an attempt to build bipartisan support for the Kissinger-Tack Agreement, a congressional delegation — including Senate Majority and Minority Leaders Mike Mansfield (D-Mont) and Hugh Scott (R-Pa) and five members of the House of Representatives — was invited to the signing ceremony. With a dramatic style seldom witnessed by Panamanians, Secretary Kissinger, Ambassador Bunker, and the congressional delegation arrived in Panama aboard the presidential jet, Air Force Two. At the ceremony, Secretary Kissinger informed Panamanian officials and observers that the occasion marked "the advent of a new era in the history of our hemisphere."[6]

Clearly, both parties' hopes were raised by this event. One administration official stated that a new Canal treaty might be negotiated by the end of the year.[7] Although this prediction proved to be premature, the Kissinger-Tack Agreement marked a significant turning point and established the outlines of the 1977 treaties.

The First Negotiating Round, 1973-1975

After meeting with Foreign Minister Tack in December 1973, Ambassador Bunker decided that Panama was still uncertain about the strength of the U.S. commitment to negotiate a mutually satisfactory treaty. He felt that additional positive signals and concrete demonstrations of conciliatory intentions were necessary. Bunker envisioned a "dual track strategy": combining formal negotiations with a series of "visible actions" that would reduce the most objectionable aspects of the U.S. presence in the Canal Zone.[8]

Bunker expected this strategy to produce several benefits. First, the visible actions would provide immediate and continuing evidence of the U.S. good faith and willingness to change the treaty relationship. Second, these actions would also reduce tensions between Panama and the Canal Zone by demonstrating that the United States was already beginning to respond to Panama's grievances. Third, an orderly reduction of U.S. activities in the Zone would serve as a prelude to transition. Incremental transfers of responsibility to Panama, made while U.S. authorities still controlled the Zone, should diminish Zone residents' apprehensions and bolster their confidence that Panamanians could provide needed goods and services. These visible actions would also prove to domestic treaty opponents, Zone residents, and skeptical administration officials that a partnership could work. Finally, in terms of U.S. bargaining resources, a program of visible actions would constitute a continuing source of incentives for

Panamanian cooperation. Throughout the negotiations, Panamanian accommodation could be rewarded with additional actions, while intransigence could be countered by delaying implementation of further changes.

Thus Ambassador Bunker's strategy was designed to produce more than successful negotiations; he was also hoping to improve prospects for ratification and to pave the way for implementing a new treaty. But these long-term political considerations were not equally shared by other policy makers. Despite the forceful arguments made by Ambassador Bunker, administration officials and members of Congress responded negatively. Of the twenty-odd action proposals jointly drafted by the two negotiating teams, only two or three were eventually "squeezed out of the administration."[9] Congress refused to authorize implementation of most of the action proposals, and Ambassador Bunker was forced to abandon this part of his strategy.

Another step taken by Ambassador Bunker to improve the chances of obtaining a new treaty involved a change in negotiating style. He decided to shift from the formal atmosphere of previous negotiations held in Washington to a private and informal setting in Panama. A change in negotiating style was easy to implement because neither Congress nor intransigent vested interests in the executive branch could veto this decision. The Canal treaty negotiations were therefore held at a resort area on Contadora Island, where Ambassador Bunker met with Minister Tack at six-week intervals beginning in June 1974.[10] In the interim, the U.S. deputy negotiator remained in Panama conducting working-level discussions with Minister Tack's deputy.

When the negotiating teams first met, they set two ground rules that also contributed to the success of the negotiations. First, easier issues on the agenda would be resolved before more divisive issues were discussed. Second, basic or conceptual agreements on each major issue would be drafted prior to specific provisions. Once all major issues were resolved at a conceptual level, the package of conceptual agreements would be progressively enlarged with specific details. This would allow the negotiators to bargain over specific provisions within a larger, mutually acceptable basic framework.

Shared Participation

The easiest issue on the agenda, Panamanian participation in Canal administration and operations, was discussed at the first negotiating session. The concept of "growing Panamanian participation" emerged at this meeting as a foundation for the first agreement. The Conceptual Agreement on the Increased Panamanian Participation in the Administration of the Canal states:

The primary objective of Panamanian participation is to guarantee that Panama is prepared to assume complete responsibility for the efficient operation of the interoceanic waterway once the new treaty expires.

This objective shall be reached by guaranteeing a sufficient number of Panamanian personnel, qualified and available to operate the interoceanic waterway when the treaty expires.[11]

The negotiators agreed that the second paragraph meant that training programs and affirmative personnel policies would be established, and that Panamanians would be placed in jobs with responsibilities over Canal operations during the treaty period. In return, Panama agreed that the United States would retain "primary responsibility for Canal operations and the transit of ships" throughout this period.[12] This was an important right for the United States to obtain; the negotiators insisted that U.S. control be maintained while Panamanian participation increased.

During the period of growing Panamanian participation, economic benefits for Panama would also increase. Services provided for Zone residents by U.S. agencies would be progressively reduced and replaced by Panamanian businesses. By simultaneously enlarging Panama's service and operational responsibilities, the negotiators sought to build reinforcing incentives into the new partnership that would enhance its effectiveness. Each progressive step taken to meet Panama's demands would also increase Panama's stake in maintaining the new relationship.

Shared Defense

The concept of growing Panamanian participation was also the center-piece of a conceptual agreement on defense. And, like the first agreement, the second also specified a primary role for the United States and new responsibilities for Panama during the treaty period. To enable Panama to assume responsibilities for Canal defense when the new treaty expired, Panamanian forces would begin participating in joint military training exercises and in a joint defense planning board.

The portion of this agreement that was especially significant to the United States was a guarantee for the "permanent and effective neutrality" of the Canal and its nondiscriminatory operation.[13] If the Canal were threatened during the treaty period, the United States and Panama would each retain the right to act unilaterally to meet "the common danger."[14] In addition to these unilateral rights, the Conceptual Agreement on the Protection and the Defense of the Canal specified a division of defense responsibilities: "Panama, as territorial sovereign, has the responsibility for defending its territory. The United States shall have the main responsibility of protecting and defending the maritime waterway until the expiration of the treaty."[15] Although Panama would be primarily responsible for

70

defending the Canal after the treaty expired, U.S. defense rights would not necessarily terminate at that time. These rights could be extended if both parties agreed to negotiate another agreement five years before the new treaty expired.

The Canal Zone

The third and most important issue on the agenda during this round of negotiations involved transferring jurisdiction over the Canal Zone to Panama. Bilateral bargaining on this issue centered on the length of the transition period and the scope of Panamanian jurisdiction.

Panama wanted to obtain immediate jurisdiction over Canal Zone territory and Zone government functions. This was the most important and politically sensitive demand it made during this negotiating round. For the United States, ensuring an incremental and orderly transition was of paramount importance. Its negotiators believed that retaining sufficient U.S. control over Canal administration and operations, as well as substantial territory, would be necessary to keep the Canal running smoothly during the transition period. They also wanted to retain U.S. jurisdiction over certain Zone government functions; this would encourage U.S. employees to keep working after the new treaty entered into force.

Both sides perceived significant issues to be at stake. The choice between immediate or incremental transition would determine the extent of ''growth'' in Panamanian participation in Canal administration and defense. Acceptance of the first two conceptual agreements was therefore contingent upon the third. In this context, the jurisdiction and transition issue posed the first major test of each side's commitment to the negotiations and of each side's willingness to compromise in order to obtain a mutually acceptable treaty.

The U.S. team initially proposed a fifteen-year transition period, but this was flatly rejected by the Panamanian team. Ambassador Bunker then requested and received authorization to reduce the offer to a five-year period. This, too, was rejected. Then, in a dramatic move designed to break the negotiation's first stalemate, Ambassador Bunker exceeded his instructions and offered a three-year transition period. In return, the Panamanian team dropped its demand for immediate jurisdiction, and negotiation of the third conceptual agreement proceeded smoothly. The Conceptual Agreement on Jurisdiction and Right of Use outlined the structure of a ''new relationship of association'' between the United States and Panama.[16] Full sovereignty over the Canal Zone would be transferred to Panama within three years. Panamanian laws and police powers would apply throughout the Zone as soon as the treaty entered into force, with only a few exceptions for U.S. employees and standard diplomatic im-

71

munities. During the transition period, responsibilities for criminal and civil jurisdictions would be divided between the United States and Panama.

In return for gaining jurisdiction over the Zone, Panama would grant the United States rights to use necessary lands and facilities for "operating, maintaining, protecting, and defending the canal," rights similar to those contained in the Hay-Bunau-Varilla Treaty of 1903.[17] The United States would also retain control over Canal employee relations, toll rates, and rules of Canal transit. U.S. responsibilities would be exercised under a new administrative agency directed by a board composed of Panamanian and U.S. representatives.

U.S. Military Forces

Having successfully established the outlines of a new management agency that would replace the Panama Canal Company, the negotiators then addressed a relatively easy issue: negotiating a Status of Forces Agreement (SOFA) for U.S. troops and bases in the new Canal area. Since SOFAs had been drafted during previous negotiations, and since these were similar to agreements with many other nations, few disagreements arose during these discussions.

Conclusion of the SOFA marked the final issue that both teams were prepared to discuss during this round of negotiations. Both teams planned to draft general position papers during April for conceptual agreements on outstanding issues. Negotiations were scheduled to resume in May, but a disagreement within the executive branch caused a six-month delay. Throughout the spring and summer of 1975, two bureaucratic coalitions waged "interdepartmental guerrilla warfare." One coalition, composed of State Department officials and the negotiating team, supported accommodative positions on all outstanding issues; the other, composed of Defense Department advisers and officials, supported minimal changes in order to maximize U.S. control.[18]

The Guidance Fight

An opportunity to resume a general debate over Canal policy arose at this time because detailed National Security Council (NSC) guidance was required to formulate negotiating positions for remaining issues. Existing guidance on Canal policy was contained in National Security Decision Memorandum (NSDM) 302; issued by the NSC in early 1974, it only reiterated the eight principles in the Kissinger-Tack Agreement and therefore contained ambiguous language on duration and neutrality. At that time, the Department of Defense had accepted this language because the principles referred to "a fixed termination date" and to agreeing "bilaterally on provisions for new projects which shall enlarge canal capacity."

72

When proposals specifying how these principles would be fulfilled were debated in the spring of 1975, unresolved conflicts between State and Defense, over the implications and operational definitions of these principals, resurfaced.[19]

The neutrality issue was also subject to renewed debate because the new conceptual agreement on defense also contained vague language. Neither the negotiating team nor its Defense Department advisers knew what "permanent neutrality" meant, and they disagreed on how best to ensure the neutrality of the Canal.

According to one participant, several members of the negotiating team viewed this debate as an opportunity to obtain "forthcoming positions" from the Department of Defense; that is, authorization to make accommodative offers on all outstanding issues. They hoped to secure a comprehensive decision by President Ford that would "overwhelm the Pentagon" by setting the year 2000 as the date for terminating shared control over Canal administration and defense. By making such a generous offer on duration, the negotiating team planned to gain Panamanian concessions on rights the United States wanted to exercise during the treaty period. Thus, this strategy was designed to bring the negotiations to a rapid and advantageous conclusion. Panama's strong interest in shortening the treaty period could be used for the advantage of the United States. In fact, however, this strategy underestimated the Department of Defense's interest in prolonging U.S. control, and the resulting conflict over new guidance prevented completion of the negotiations during the Ford administration.

The Department of Defense advocated a hard-line position: a forty to fifty-year duration for the new treaty plus an option to defer termination for another thirty years if the United States decided to build a sea-level canal in Panama.[20] This proposal linked the Kissinger-Tack principles on termination and Canal expansion; by combining the two, a new treaty would last for ninety-nine years. If the United States built a new canal, it could maintain a military presence and shared control well into the next century. This linkage was not new; as we noted in Chapter 3, an option for building a new canal had been used during negotiations in 1965-67 and 1971-72 to extend the duration of proposed treaties. Both of those offers had been rejected by Panama, however, and more importantly, the final report of the Atlantic Pacific Interoceanic Canal Study Commission, which had been established by President Lyndon B. Johnson, had advised against building a sea-level canal in Panama.[21] Why was this defunct option revived?

The Department of Defense justified its proposal in terms of global security interests in the post-Vietnam period. Under the 1903 treaty, the United States had permanent access to military bases in the Canal Zone. Earlier, during debate over the Kissinger-Tack Agreement, Defense had objected to the idea of negotiating a new treaty because fewer overseas bases would be available during the next two decades. In 1975, officials in the Department of Defense reacted even more negatively to the idea of voluntarily relinquishing base rights in Panama because base agreements with Turkey, the Philippines, Japan and Portugal were due to be re-negotiated. Why, many asked, when the global network of overseas bases was diminishing, should the United States agree to withdraw from the strategic Caribbean?[22]

Given these concerns, many Defense Department officials, including Secretary of the Army William Clements advocated maintaining perma-nent base rights in Panama and exempting U.S. rights to defend the Canal from any duration proposal. Secretary Clements viewed the sea-level canal option as the best means for securing permanent rights for the United States. Moreover, Secretary Clements felt that this option could be used to influence Panama's position on other issues. "Certainly, if we are looking for any leverage with respect to Panama — either with regard to the security or the economic package, or the future rate structure or the operation of the canal — our leverage is in our ability to build another canal."[23]

The negotiating team strongly objected, characterizing Defense's prop-osal as a new perpetuity clause that would doom the negotiations. A mutually acceptable treaty could only be obtained, they asserted, if United States positions on duration and neutrality were much closer to the Panamanian position, namely termination in the year 2000.

The Defense and State Departments also differed on the issue of "lands and waters": identifying which areas of the Zone were necessary for the operation, maintenance, administration, and defense of the Canal, and which "unused" areas could be transferred to Panama. The Department of Defense favored retaining control over at least eighty-five percent of the Canal Zone, much "more than the State Department" believed could "be negotiated."[24] For its part, the Panamanian team demanded transfer of more than ninety percent of the Zone; the U.S. negotiating team advocated a compromise between these two extremes.

While the administration debated these issues, treaty opponents in the House of Representatives and the Senate attempted to influence the negoti-ations, using the tactic of politicizing the Canal issue. This unanticipated development further prolonged the fight over new guidance. It also pro-vided an opportunity for each bureaucratic coalition to gain congressional supporters. As the number and interests of participants expanded, a wider set of arguments about the merits of a new Canal treaty surfaced. These arguments are discussed below in some detail as well as in Chapter 5 because they exemplify consensus and coalition building during the Ford administration as well as the difficulties the Carter administration faced during debate over ratification of the treaties.

Congress Debates the Canal Issue

The Canal issue was raised in Congress when a State Department appropriations bill, HR 8121, was debated in the House. On June 26, 1975, Congressman M.G. (Gene) Snyder (R-Ky) offered an amendment that would prevent using these funds for "negotiating the surrender or relinquishing of any U.S. rights in the Panama Canal Zone."[25] Although Representative Snyder did not expect a loss of funds to halt the negotiations, he did hope to demonstrate substantial opposition to any major changes in the status quo. "We can negotiate with them, we just cannot negotiate to surrender or relinquish our rights."[26] His attempt succeeded: the Snyder Amendment passed the House by an overwhelming vote of 246 to 164.

Several members of the House supported the Snyder Amendment in order to "send a message" to the Department of State expressing public opposition to "giving away" the Panama Canal. Congressman Symms' (R-Idaho) remarks represented these views.

> I think it would behoove Members of this House to vote for this amendment and give a strong message to the State Department that the American people want no part of it and their Representatives are telling them what to do. This way we can get a little direction in at the beginning rather than just wait until they have taken action, then try to close the door.[27]

Like Congressman Symms, several other members also wanted to register opposition to major changes in Canal policy while negotiations were still underway. Congressman Glenn M. Anderson (D-California) made a forceful statement on this point.

> I think it is high time that we in the House of Representatives indicate what our position is. It has been said by some, "Let us wait until a treaty gets to the Senate and then we can go over there and express our views." I say that is too late. Now is the time to express ourselves.
>
> I think this is a good time to bring it up. I think we should vote for this amendment and let the world know we want to keep the Panama Canal, that we want to keep control of it, and that we do not want anybody else to move in and take our place.[28]

Security concerns were another theme stressed during the debate. Congressman L.H. Fountain (D-NC) viewed the Canal as a vital asset that should remain under U.S. control "But, our vital commercial and strategic interests are at stake in this matter and I just do not see how we can insure that our interests will be protected if we surrender sovereignty over what we built and paid for.''[29] Congresswoman Marilyn Lloyd (D-Tenn) viewed the strategic value of the Canal in historical terms.

We saw during World Wars I and II the strategic value of the Panama Canal to the national security of the United States. If we give up our rights in the Canal Zone, any change of Panamanian leadership could lead to the United States being denial [sic] full access to the Canal and possibly preferential treatment of our ships.[30]

The amount of support the Snyder Amendment obtained can be partially credited to Pentagon lobbying. Defense Department officials were aware of Congressman Snyder's long-standing opposition to a new treaty, and they used the appropriations debate to generate support for their duration proposal.

Prior to this vote — and doubtless contributing to it — there had been contacts between the Pentagon and the Congress that suggested major Pentagon reservations. The military volcano had started to rumble, and legislators found Pentagon officials easing off their posture of noncommittal neutrality. . .and sliding into outright opposition. The Navy took 20 Congressmen for a boat ride while a full admiral delivered a Canal message.[31]

In an attempt to prevent a similar outcome when the appropriations bill reached the Senate floor, the Department of State mobilized its own lobbying campaign. This campaign was directed against a companion measure to the Snyder amendment that was introduced by Senator Harry F. Byrd, Jr., (I-Va). First, the Office of the Legal Adviser prepared an analysis of the unconstitutionality of these amendments, which infringed on the executive's power to negotiate, and circulated it to members of the Senate.[32] A second appeal, also based on the need for leadership by the executive branch in the treaty-making process, was made by Secretary of State Kissinger in personal letters to Senate leaders. Secretary Kissinger urged senators ''not to interfere with the Administration's attempt to negotiate a new treaty'' and pledged ''the closest possible consultation with the entire Congress'' on the negotiations.[33]

To counter their opponents' arguments, State Department officials used a violence argument.

Put bluntly, high-ranking American officials are predicting that Panama will explode into rioting or open battle unless the U.S. presence and authority are changed in accord with both Panamanian and American long-term interests. Not only would such a contingency endanger the vital waterway but all of Latin America would back Panama in any confrontation with the United States, Administration officials fears.

76

Apprehensive policymakers envision a far bloodier collision than the mini-war that U.S. troops fought with Panamanian rioters in 1964 in which 20 Panamanians and three Americans died.

It is not going too far to say that the U.S. government feels it might have to send combat troops to Panama in the event that the negotiations break down and fighting begins. The administration wants to avoid this contingency at all costs.[34]

To substantiate this argument, the findings of a secret Central Intelligence Agency report were circulated on Capitol Hill by treaty supporters and leaked to the press. This report stated that a new treaty was "essential on the ground that perpetuation of the current arrangement could lead a sabotage in the Canal Zone and the possibility that operations would be shut down."[35] Secretary of State Kissinger then issued a dire warning. "Panama could become a focal point for the kind of nationalistic guerrilla type of operation we have not yet seen in the Western hemisphere, directed against the United States."[36]

Another argument used by treaty supporters might be called an anticolonialism argument. A new treaty was necessary to remove the U.S. colonial presence from the Canal Zone. One columnist wrote, "Colonialism is on the way out all over the world, and this applies to the United States."[37] Carl T. Rowan reiterated this theme.

Faced with . . . lessons of imperialistic folly (France in Algeria, Portugal in Angola and Mozambique), it seems utterly beyond belief that members of Congress are luring the United States toward the same kind of tragedy regarding the Panama Canal.

But the frightening truth is that a band of people steeped in racism and the Colonel Blimp mentality which long had lain at the heart of Western imperialism are now riding high in Congress.[38]

Neither of these arguments — that the United States should negotiate a new treaty to end colonialism in the Canal Zone and that only a new treaty would prevent guerrilla war in Panama — convinced treaty opponents. Instead, opponents dismissed charges of U.S. imperialism and colonialism as misplaced guilt and asserted that the U.S. presence had actually benefited Panama. The violence argument proved particularly counterproductive, prompting treaty opponents to charge that the administration was being blackmailed and negotiating "at the point of a gun."[39]

Treaty opponents asserted that the Canal Zone was U.S. territory and that the Canal and other facilities in the Zone were U.S. property. Even more persuasive to opponents was a national security argument that the Panama Canal was still a vital strategic asset. The "American Canal in

77

Panama,'' as veterans groups called it, was essential to national and hemispheric security.

To counter charges that a new treaty would injure U.S. interests, administration officials attempted to redefine the meaning of security in a changing world. Assistant Secretary of State for Latin American Affairs William D. Rogers argued that U.S. foreign policy should be updated to correspond to changing conditions, and that these changes should be seen as constructive opportunities instead of threats. In an interview in the *Denver Post*, Rogers said:

> Latin America, like many areas of the world, is undergoing great change. There are also changes in the U.S. role in the world which dictate change in U.S. policy toward Latin America. We no longer dominate the world as we once did. A new pattern of relations and power structure is emerging. Military and economic strength are only part of them. Our future well-being will be determined, to a much greater degree than in the past, by our ability to adapt to changing world circumstances.[40]

Assistant Secretary Rogers' remarks constituted one of the Ford administration's few attempts to articulate a positive rationale for a new Canal treaty. More typically, administration officials used defensive and reactive arguments designed to counter treaty opponents' charges. Meanwhile, Senator Harry Byrd's Snyder-like amendment continued to be considered in the Senate.

needed to go against congress

Reaching an Executive Branch Consensus

In the absence of agreement within the administration on new guidance and the Senate's concern over the Byrd Amendment, the date for resuming negotiations had to be postponed. Ambassador Bunker said that he would not negotiate under a ''cloud of domestic opposition,'' so the second negotiating round, which was to begin in May 1975, was rescheduled for early July.[41] This date also passed before the guidance fight was resolved, and negotiations did not resume until September.

When interdepartmental conflict could not be resolved through routine clearance and concurrence procedures, the two departments presented their positions to the National Security Council (NSC). At a NSC meeting in late July, arguments on a range of issues were presented, including Panama's ability to defend the Canal, threats of domestic violence in Panama, in the absence of an agreement, the decline of the vital nature of the Canal, the possibility of building a sea-level canal, the problem of the Defense Department's intransigence; the U.S. public reaction to a new treaty, and the diplomatic catastrophe for President Ford if no treaty was forthcoming.[42] Neither side was persuaded by the other's claims, and this meeting ended inconclusively. A second NSC meeting was held on August 9, and when it also failed to produce a consensus, President Ford demanded that the departments produce a unified recommendation within a few weeks.

According to Secretary of State Kissinger's account of the guidance fight: "Defense was not leaned on. Before that they just didn't have a position."[43] In fact, and in contrast to what an organizational approach would expect, several different positions had been advocated by different Defense Department officials, ranging from a hard-line to a more moderate stance. Cross-cutting coalitions had formed, but the scope of agreement on any one position was not wide because the Canal negotiations were low priority and received little high-level attention. When President Ford's directive forced Defense to reexamine these positions, a new consensus on duration and neutrality slowly evolved. After conferring with their advisers, the Joint Chiefs of Staff "all generally" agreed that "there could be no treaties if there were to be a U.S. presence beyond a certain specified date."[44]

The State-Defense deadlock was finally broken when Ambassador Bunker proposed a compromise. Bunker suggested a "dual — duration" formula: transferring control over Canal operations to Panama by the year 2000 and maintaining U.S. defense rights for a longer period, perhaps forty to fifty years.[45] Realizing that this formula was the only reasonable means for prolonging U.S. defense rights, the Department of Defense accepted Ambassador Bunker's proposal.

Since the guidance fight had been so bitter, the negotiating team suggested that General Brown and Secretary Clements visit the Canal Zone to "improve the Pentagon's perspective" on the negotiations and to publicly demonstrate their support for the new, united U.S. negotiating position.[46] President Ford agreed that the trip would be useful; it would signal Defense's position to the Senate and strengthen the negotiating team's leverage with Panama. Secretary Clements later reported:

> This was a fruitful trip in the spirit that we impressed upon Mr. Torrijos that the single-most thing in any treaty negotiation had to be the security of the canal and as it affected our national security on a world wide basis.
>
> General Torrijos understood this; he agreed that the security aspects of this had to be clear, and that the rest of the treaty could be accommodated to this basic building block.[47]

Personnel and organizational changes were made following this visit. The most important change added a representative of the Defense Department to the negotiating team. Lt. General Welborn C. Dolvin (Ret.) was appointed deputy negotiator for the Department of Defense. General Dolvin was also appointed cochairman of the department's Panama Canal Negotiations Working Group, the internal task force that developed and reviewed Canal policy. These changes were designed to improve communications within the Defense Department, and by providing direct participation in the negotiations, to improve communications between Defense and the Department of State. This Working Group was also reorganized to improve its capacity to formulate treaty positions and provisions; this change also strengthened the organizational resources and skills of the Department of Defense.

Once an interdepartmental consensus was established, the appropriations controversy was relatively easy to resolve. Senator Byrd was persuaded to withdraw his Snyder-like amendment, and a House-Senate conference report containing compromise language on the negotiations was passed in October 1975. This temporarily ended debate on the Canal issue in the Congress and the press.

The Second Negotiating Round, 1975-1976

The second round of negotiations began inauspiciously. The first two sessions were unproductive, and no conceptual agreements were achieved during this round. Simply put, the meetings accomplished little because the issues discussed — duration and neutrality — were so difficult to resolve. These substantive difficulties were compounded by two disruptive events. The first and least damaging of these occurred in September 1975 during the first negotiating session. While this session was underway, Secretary of State Kissinger addressed a meeting of the Conference of Southern Governors. Following Kissinger's speech, Governor George Wallace asked whether the United States could afford to give up the Canal. Kissinger's reply contained a mistatement. "The United States must maintain the right, unilaterally, to defend the Panama Canal for an indefinite future, or for a long future. On the other hand, the United States can ease some of the other conditions in the Canal Zone."[48] According to Henry Bradsher's report in the *Washington Star*, Secretary Kissinger also said, "nobody is in favor of turning over the defense of the Canal and nobody is in favor of turning over essential operating requirements."[49]

In Panama, the U.S. negotiators had just presented the new dual-duration formula. Secretary Kissinger's comments seemed to contradict this proposal, and the Panamanian team angrily demanded clarification. A series of conciliatory statements were issued by the Department of State, but the negotiations recessed the next day and the U.S. team returned to Washington. Several days later the Panamanian government indicated its

80

displeasure by releasing the positions both teams had just presented. Negotiations did not resume until November.

This negotiating session also failed. The problem that developed during the November session was much more serious than the diplomatic flap that interrupted the first. Between August and November, the executive branch consensus supporting Bunker's dual-duration formula dissolved. Defense Department officials reverted to a hard-line position and advocated defining permanent neutrality as "non-terminating defense rights." This development was a direct result of organizational changes within the Department of Defense and of the assessment, developed by General Brown and Secretary Clements during their visit with General Torrijos, that a bargaining chip strategy based on a tough position would be more successful than one based on the accommodative strategy preferred by the negotiating team. The negotiating team agreed to present this position at the November session, in order to avoid another guidance fight. The consequences were predictable because this proposal was much less favorable to Panama than the forty to fifty years specified in the dual-duration formula presented in September. The Panamanian team flatly rejected the idea of nonterminating defense rights and both teams described the session as "unsuccessful."[50]

Because no progress was made at these sessions, the Ford administration had to revise its estimate of when a new treaty would be concluded. Instead of late 1975 or early 1976, it now appeared that a treaty could not be drafted until mid-1976, at the height of the presidential election campaign. Since President Ford was being challenged for the Republican nomination by Ronald Reagan, who held more conservative views on foreign policy, White House advisers concluded that the Canal issue could become a "potential embarrassment" during the campaign.[51]

Formal negotiations were then suspended for the rest of 1975 and 1976, but both negotiating teams viewed this decision as a necessary political constraint that would only delay the U.S. ratification process. They agreed to continue informal negotiations at the working level so that rapid progress could be made when formal negotiations resumed.

Recessing the negotiations did not, however, prevent the negotiations from becoming a salient issue in the presidential primaries and the election campaigns. When the negotiations were first mentioned, on February 26, 1976, Governor Reagan attacked the Department of State rather than President Ford.

> State Department actions for several years now have suggested that they are intimidated by the propaganda of Panama's military dictator, Fidel Castro's good friend, General Omar Torrijos. Our State Department apparently believes the hints regularly dispensed by the leftist Torrijos regime that the Canal will be sabotaged if we don't hand it over.

Our Government has maintained a mouse-like silence as hard criticisms of the give-away have increased.

I don't understand how the State Department can suggest we pay blackmail to this dictator, for blackmail is what it is.[52]

Then Governor Reagan made a statement that became a familiar slogan for treaty opponents and a hallmark of his campaign: "When it comes to the Canal, we bought it, we paid for it, it's ours, and we should tell Torrijos and company that we're going to keep it."[53]

President Ford later expressed his reaction to Governor Reagan's use of the canal issue and the choices he and his advisers faced as they decided how to respond to Reagan's success:

> Reagan's statements were inflammatory and irresponsible. But my advisers were split on how I should respond. Kissinger wanted me to tackle him head-on and say that his reckless rhetoric was endangering our position in the world. Morton and Cheney disagreed. Mention of his charges, they said, would give them a dignity they didn't deserve. I felt the voters were smart enough to realize that his verbal swipes were the final lunges of a desperate man. I should be affirmative, ignore my challengers and just stress my own record of accomplishments. And they made another valid point. If I criticized Reagan personally, I would infuriate conservatives whose support I would need in November. That made sense. In the interests of party unity, I would stick to the high road and hope for the best.[54]

Thus, President Ford initially countered Governor Reagan's charges by trying to minimize differences between their positions on the Canal issue, but as Reagan's popularity increased, President Ford took as tough a line as his challenger. By April, President Ford's comments had so hardened that they contradicted the Kissinger-Tack Agreement. When asked about a new Canal treaty at a press conference in Texas, President Ford replied, "I can simply say, and say it emphatically, that the United States will never give up its defense rights to the Panama Canal and will never give up its operational rights as far as Panama is concerned."[55]

As debate on the Canal issue intensified, a climate of growing uncertainty clouded the working-level discussions in Panama. President Ford's opponent, Governor Jimmy Carter, did little to ease either negotiating teams' doubts about the future of U.S. Canal policy. Carter took an ambivalent position, designed to placate treaty opponents and supporters. "I would never give up complete control or practical control of the Panama Canal Zone, but I would continue to negotiate with the Panamanians."[56] Thus, for most of 1976, little progress was formally made on negotiations. It was not until after the election that progress could be renewed.

Although little was accomplished in negotiations between the United States and Panama in 1976, one major breakthrough did occur within the U.S. bureaucracy. General Dolvin ordered a realistic assessment of the extent of Zone lands and waters needed to operate and defend the Canal during the treaty duration phase. Based on this assessment, the Department of Defense reduced its earlier stand from 90 to approximately 40 percent. This major breakthrough proved invaluable when serious negotiations began again after the election.[57]

During the transition period between November 1976 and January 1977, President-elect Carter began sending signals that his administration would vigorously pursue treaty negotiations consistent with the Kissinger-Tack Agreement.

The Third Negotiating Round, 1977

During the transition period, President-elect Carter, his staff, and visiting advisers set an agenda of foreign policy priorities for the coming year. Members of the transition team agreed that the Carter administration should restructure U.S. foreign policy commitments through a series of bold initiatives. This, they realized, would require an early victory on a salient issue that would set the stage for future successes. After surveying the status of issues already on the agenda, the transition team concluded that the Panama Canal treaty negotiations were the best choice for a "keynote" success.[58] Several factors contributed to selecting the Canal issue for this role including Carter's interest in Latin America, the issue's moral appeal, and an effective lobbying campaign by a vigorous treaty advocate, Sol Linowitz. Linowitz had consulted with Carter during the campaign and had chaired a commission on U.S.-Latin American Relations. The commission's report, issued in December 1976, strongly endorsed the Kissinger-Tack Agreement and urged a speedy conclusion of the Canal treaty negotiations.[59] The moral appeal of a new Canal treaty, to the new president and his advisers, should not be underestimated. According to National Security Adviser Brzezinski:

> When Jimmy Carter assumed office, U.S. foreign policy appeared to him and his team to be stalemated on the level of power and excessively cynical on the level of principle. The new administration therefore decided to move on a broad front and to tackle several key issues at once while the President's prestige was at its highest. We were determined to demonstrate also the primacy of the moral dimension in foreign policy.[60]

Brzezinski later recalled that he and Secretary of State Vance "both felt that we had to bite the bullet on the politically sensitive Panama Canal Treaties."[61] Vance's commitment on the Canal issue was particularly strong. Following the 1964 Flag Riots, Vance was sent to Panama as President Johnson's special representative and was involved in sensitive and difficult negotiations to resolve that crisis. Those events led him "to the conclusion that almost all Panamanians regarded exclusive U.S. authority over the canal and zone as an affront to their national dignity and sovereignty.'"[62] Thus, when the transition team surveyed the Canal issue, it found that substantial progress had been made in directions that closely corresponded to those the administration planned to pursue.

The Treaties in Context

Although the Canal treaty negotiations were given a high priority, other, more significant issues were also given priority status on the new administration's agenda. In fact, the transition team planned to initiate a general reorientation of U.S. foreign policy in which a new Canal treaty was only a first step. According to their plans, victory on the sensitive Canal issue would expose conservative foreign policy critics as flag-waving chauvinists clinging to an imperial past. These opponents would be further weakened by normalization of relations with Cuba and Vietnam. Debate on establishing diplomatic relations with these two minor powers would set the stage for normalization of relations with the People's Republic of China. This victory would be the first major achievement of the administration's foreign policy. Its second and most important achievement, a new Strategic Arms Limitation Treaty (SALT II), would then follow, capping a series of positive and constructive initiatives that would mark an end to the "post-Vietnam syndrome" in U.S. foreign policy. Secretary of State Vance later recalled the positive mood that permeated the president's foreign policy team:

> In those early days, I was optimistic that we were on the threshold of an important period in American diplomacy. We had the confidence and support of the American people. The president, the vice-president, Brown, Brzezinski, and I agreed on the shape and direction of our foreign policy. Our priorities were clear to us: a stable military balance; a stronger, more confident NATO; a new SALT agreement; progress toward peace in the Middle East; a Panama Canal Treaty; a settlement of the racial and political crises in Southern Africa; an improving and positive relationship with the People's Republic of China; a strong and involved East Asian policy; a sensible energy policy; and a principled yet pragmatic defense of basic human rights.[63]

Carter's transition team thus viewed the Panama Canal Treaty negotiations as part of a larger foreign policy program. Later, as the ratification campaign progressed during 1977 and 1978, the Canal treaties assumed unwarranted and unexpected proportions, both in relation to other, more

84

important initiatives, and in the amount of attention and resources they consumed. Carter acknowledged in his diary entry for January 28, 1977 that too many initiatives might be underway. "Everybody has warned me not to take on too many projects so early in the administration, but it's almost impossible for me to delay something that I see needs to be done.' '[64] Brzezinski, in reflecting on the crowded foreign policy agenda, later stated that "the competing goals came into conflict and, indeed, one additional major objective-normalizing relations with China - was temporarily put on hold.' '[65]

In his memoirs, Carter explained his decision to tackle the Canal issue despite the risks entailed. "Despite the opposition of Congress and the public, I decided to plow ahead, believing that if the facts could be presented clearly, my advisers and I could complete action while my political popularity was still high and before we had to face the additional complication of the congressional election campaigns of 1978.' '[66] Instead of a relatively quick success, however, victory on the Canal issue became a lengthy test of President Carter's leadership, his ability to conduct U.S. foreign policy, and his credibility to conclude other agreements.

But during the transition period, before the Canal issue assumed such proportions, Carter's top political advisers viewed ratification of a new Canal treaty as another type of test. Public debate on the Canal issue was seen as a prelude to major foreign policy debates on China policy and SALT II. These advisers freely admitted that the Canal treaty ratification campaign would serve as a "dry run" for ratification of SALT II.[67] According to plans developed by the transition team, each initiative would make subsequent victories easier to achieve. They were aware that public opinion was sharply divided into contrasting world views and foreign policy beliefs, but they hoped that each policy debate would weaken their opponents, particularly those identified with the New Right, who favored a return to the Cold War, U.S. hegemony, and interventionism. After a series of administration victories, those few opponents remaining would be perceived by the public, if this strategy succeeded, as a small minority advocating an obsolete and dangerous course for U.S. foreign policy.

Carter administration officials perceived the Canal treaty negotiations as part of a larger shift in U.S. foreign policy. Linking a new Canal treaty to wider hemispheric policy changes and, more broadly, to a general reorientation of U.S. foreign policy, strengthened the conceptual and organizational basis for Canal policy actions taken by the Carter administration. Secretary of State Vance recalled in his memoirs:

> One of my special concerns was that we should forge a sounder, more equal relationship with Latin America. I recommended that we drop the notion of a "special relationship," which smacked of paternalism, and

85

deal with each Latin American and Caribbean nation as a sovereign
power with different problems, except when it came to multilateral
issues. The first step toward a mature Latin American policy, I believed,
was the successful completion of the stalled Panama Canal Treaty negotiations.[68]

These linkages between hemispheric and Canal policies guaranteed that
high-level officials would pay close attention during negotiations and
invest considerable resources during the ratification campaign.[69]

Executive Guidance

The president, Secretary Vance, and National Security Advisor
Brzezinski accepted the Kissinger-Tack Agreement as a foundation for a
new Canal treaty, and to provide continuity in the negotiations process,
they agreed that Ambassador Bunker should continue to serve as the U.S.
chief negotiator. But they also wanted "to put the Carter stamp" on a new
treaty, so they decided to appoint a well-known treaty advocate, Sol M.
Linowitz, as conegotiator.

Although Ambassador Linowitz was eminently qualified, his appointment angered treaty opponents in the Senate. First, he was appointed to a
six-month interim position that did not require Senate approval. Second, he
was widely known to strongly favor new treaty negotiations with Panama.
Lastly, he did have some important connections with multinational corpo-
rations doing business in Panama which suggested that he might have some
problems with conflicts of interest.

On the other hand, he was qualified, spoke Spanish, had been very active
in Inter-American Affairs, and was well known and trusted in Panama. He
was also recognized as a hard bargainer and a person who could work out
details in complicated negotiations.

The six-month appointment in order to circumvent Senate approval was
probably made in order to avoid as premature debate on the treaty negotiations and an early vote which the administration might have lost. The short
appointment also set a time limit for the negotiations and helped push the
negotiations to completion within the six month time frame.

One of the Carter administration's first tasks was a high-level review of
Canal policy. At their first "informal NSC meeting," held on January 5,
1977, the decision was made "to move rapidly with the conclusion of the
Panama Canal Treaties" and to rapidly develop the first Presidential
Review Memorandum (PRM 1) so that we could meet in order to make
more substantive decisions during the week of January 24.'"[70] The result,
PRM 1, confirmed existing National Security Council guidance on Canal
policy. Secretary Vance later recalled that "we wanted to give our
negotiators as much latitude as possible to explore various formulations

86

without being constrained by detailed instructions.''[71] Although the new administration made no major changes in guidance, its decision to give a high priority to the negotiations produced changes in Canal policy actions. The third negotiating round was treated much more seriously than the first and second had been. Carter later described his appointment of Linowitz as ''a clear signal that we meant business.''[72] And, for the first time since 1974, both negotiating teams were confident that domestic political constraints would not prevent the United States from beginning the ratification process.

Negotiations Begin

The third negotiating round began with a preliminary meeting, held in Washington on January 31, 1977, to identify outstanding issues. Secretary Vance told Foreign Minister Aquilino Boyd that the United States remained committed to the Kissinger-Tack Agreement and that ''reaching an agreement on a treaty termination date depended on his government giving the United States the right to defend the canal after the treaty expired. I stressed that while the new administration wanted to be fair, we would not jeopardize our national security interests in the canal.''[73] In addition to duration and neutrality, final agreements were needed on proposals discussed at working-level meetings during 1976: lands and waters, the new administrative agency, employee rights and guarantees, and economic benefits.

The first formal negotiating session was held in Panama from February 13 to 23, 1977.[74] There, all of these issues were discussed in depth, but no substantive or conceptual agreements were reached. Alternative proposals for a neutrality formula constituted the main area of disagreement. Secretary Vance felt that ''the Panamanians were testing us. We were determined not only to stand firm, but to make it clear to the Congress that we were doing so.''[75] The U.S. team advocated Ambassador Bunker's dual-duration formula, while the Panamanian team set forth a new proposal: having the United Nations guarantee the neutrality of the Canal during the post-treaty period.[76]

President Carter later recalled that the February session showed ''the Panamanians to be as tough as we were at the bargaining table'' and that for a while thereafter:

> ''it seemed that we would be spared the trouble of a Senate ratification fight and be faced instead with another confrontation with Panama and the other Latin American countries. Although the Panamanians considered our conditions an infringement on their sovereignty, there was no way I could yield on two or three important points. We had to have assured

87

Thinking of bad thing what he get to things congress.

priority of access to the Canal, and we had to have the right to defend it against external threats at *all* times in the future.''[77]

During March and April, specialized working groups prepared working papers on each of the outstanding issues. At one of the U.S. working sessions, a two-treaty formula on duration, defense, and neutrality emerged as a possible solution for these thorny issues.[78] Ambassadors Bunker and Linowitz agreed that to be acceptable to the president and the Congress a new treaty must contain unilateral defense rights even after U.S. military forces were withdrawn from Panama. They proposed drafting two separate treaties: a treaty containing U.S. defense rights and neutrality guarantees during the post-treaty period, and a basic Canal treaty, terminating by the year 2000, that would establish an orderly transition from partnership to full Panamanian control over the Canal and Canal Zone.

Two-Treaty Formula

The U.S. negotiators were enthusiastic about this new formula because it would "allow clearly for an American security role while giving the least offense to Panama's sensitivity about intervention."[79] Secretary Vance described the two-treaty formula as "a brilliant stroke." He continued by stating that "Carter and I saw the political importance of this suggestion, and immediately authorized Linowitz and Bunker to pursue this course."[80] The new formula would improve prospects for Senate approval by strengthening U.S. defense rights and establishing nonterminating guarantees for the neutrality of the Canal. The formula also had the advantage of meeting Panama's major objectives, gaining control over the Canal, and obtaining a withdrawal of U.S. military forces and bases by the year 2000. Once all of the necessary executive branch concurrences were obtained, the two-treaty formula was presented to the Panamanian team at an "unannounced working session" held at the Department of State from March 11 to 13, 1977. At first, the Panamanian team flatly rejected the two-treaty formula, and restated their proposal for United Nations neutrality guarantees. By late April, the negotiators learned that Panama was interested in the formula if certain defense provisions could be clarified.

Panama accepted the two-treaty formula at the next negotiating session, held in early May, when the U.S. team presented a modified version of the proposed neutrality treaty. This version, unlike previous offers, distinguished between external and internal defense of the Canal's neutrality. In response to Panama's concerns, the Department of Defense developed the idea of making this distinction. "Secretary of Defense Harold Brown and Chairman of the Joint Chiefs of Staff George Brown both approved this language in the developing agreement (some called it the Brown-Brown language).''[81] Under this proposal the United States would be responsible for defending the Canal from external threats, such as attacks by third parties, while Panama would be primarily responsible for defending the Canal from internal threats, such as sabotage.

The U.S. negotiators also obtained clarification of U.S. rights to guarantee the neutrality of the Canal. Given Panama's reluctance to endorse specific language in the treaty text, this clarification was confined to the written record of the negotiating session. According to Secretary Vance:

> In an effort to allow a ''decent ambiguity'' in the Neutrality Treaty rather than insisting on formal language in the text, we stated to the Panamanians as part of the negotiating record that we would interpret our right to guarantee permanent neutrality to mean that the United States could take any steps necessary to defend the canal after we transferred it to Panama. The Panamanians accepted our interpretation.[82]

At this session the United States also suggested drafting a protocol to the Neutrality Treaty that could be endorsed by Latin American nations and deposited at the Organization of American States. This suggestion resolved Panama's remaining doubts about accepting the two-treaty formula. From the U.S. perspective, a protocol would add a welcome multilateral component to the new agreement without disturbing the bilateral partnership.

Once Panama accepted the neutrality portion of the two-treaty formula, on May 18, the negotiations became even more ''serious'' and ''intensive.''[83] One participant reported that both teams realized that a final, major breakthrough had occurred and that the two treaties could be concluded within a few months. When the negotiations recessed on June 1, 1977, conceptual agreements on all of the major issues except economic benefits had been reached. Since ''substantial portions'' of both treaties were completed during this session, participants predicted that the new treaties would be initialled by the end of June.[84] President Carter recalled that ''by the last week in May, we were so encouraged that we began detailed briefings for the members of Congress, concentrating our efforts in the Senate . . . We also began gearing up for the ratification campaign.''[85]

Delays

These optimistic expectations were soon shattered. Two unforeseen disturbances delayed conclusion of the negotiations until August. The first, a new Panamanian proposal on economic benefits, resulted in a separate agreement on economic development assistance. The second, and less serious of the two, occurred in July when President Carter raised the previously settled issue of Canal expansion rights.

While attending a town meeting in July at Yazoo City, Mississippi, President Carter surprised the U.S. negotiating team by announcing that the United States "might well need a new canal at sea level. I would say we will need a new Panama Canal to solve problems of transporting Alaskan crude oil needed on the U.S. East Coast."[86] The next day, July 22, President Carter stated that "he would 'guess' that before the year 2000 a 'larger, wider, deeper' Panama Canal without the multiple locks of the present one 'might be in the interest of our national security militarily as well as economically'."[87]

These statements about a sea-level canal, an issue successfully resolved at working sessions in 1976, took the negotiating team by complete surprise. How did the president's interest in this defunct option arise?

President Carter learned about the possibility of a sea-level canal when Senator Mike Gravel (D-Ala) urged him to consider building a new canal rather than continental pipelines for transporting Alaskan oil to the East Coast. Senator Gravel also attempted to interest other administration officials in a sea-level canal project. These efforts were unsuccessful, but the president was so intrigued with the idea that he requested briefings by canal construction experts. These briefings provided the basis for Carter's statements.[88]

The Panamanian government was reluctant to consider granting these additional rights to the United States; but at President Carter's insistence, additional language was added to the Canal expansion provision of the Panama Canal Treaty.

Revision of this draft article resolved the disturbance caused by the president's intervention. In contrast, Panama's demands for greater economic benefits were "an almost fatal blow" to the negotiations that caused a short-lived but heated controversy in the executive branch, Congress, and the press.[89]

When the negotiations resumed on June 8, the Panamanian team presented a financial proposal characterized by one participant as "totally unacceptable" and by President Carter as a "ridiculous request". Panama wanted a $1 million lump sum down payment as soon as the treaty goes in effect" and "an annual payment of nearly $200 million."[90] According to Secretary Vance, "We were told that these exorbitant demands reflected the conviction of a large number of Panamanians that the United States had exploited Panama's main economic asset for sixty years and that we owed them adequate compensation."[91] Why, when the negotiations were so close to a successful conclusion, did the Panamanian team submit a proposal which they knew the United States would reject?

Members of the U.S. negotiating team viewed these "last minute financial demands" as resulting from severe pressures on General Torrijos, including Panama's deteriorating economy and "greedy financial interests." In addition, the Torrijos government was apparently being advised to extract major concessions to increase elite and public support for the treaties. Secretary Vance cited another reason, "their desire for a major U.S. concession to draw attention away from the permanent rights accorded to us under the Neutrality Treaty."[92]

Ambassador Bunker and Ambassador Linowitz refused to consider Panamanian demands for "reparations" within the context of the principle in the Kissinger-Tack Agreement that referred to an "equitable share" of benefits derived from canal operations. Instead, they adopted a two-part strategy for dealing with these financial demands: First, they insisted that any payments to Panama under the treaty be derived solely from Canal-operating revenues; second, they considered any other financial demands as requests for economic development assistance. The U.S. negotiating team presented a counterproposal similar to financial provisions contained in the 1967 and 1971 draft treaties, agreeing to pay Panama a progressively increasing proportion of Canal revenues and a substantial annuity payment. Panama would be paid $10 million a year for municipal services and an increasing portion of Canal tolls, beginning at thirty cents/canal ton, for the duration of the Canal treaty. "Discussions" were initiated between a delegation of Panamanian economic experts and administration officials and agreements on economic assistance were drafted; these were entirely separate from the negotiations and the new Canal treaties.[93] At first, Panama refused to accept the U.S. proposal. Personal and direct intervention by President Carter was required to overcome the "stalemate":

> On July 29, I met with the American and Panamanian negotiators, and was told that only a direct communication from me to General Torrijos could resolve the argument.
> I personally wrote a letter to Torrijos for the Panamanian negotiators to deliver, stating in effect that we were making our last offer, and that it was "generous, fair, and appropriate." After consulting with other Latin American leaders, Torrijos announced on August 5 that Panama would accept our economic proposals.[94]

Despite a barrage of press reports that focused treaty opponents' attention on Panama's financial demands, this strategy for resolving the economic benefits issue succeeded. When the negotiations resumed on August 8, 1977, only one issue remained unresolved: final agreement on "lands and waters." This issue was finally resolved, based on the Dolvin Assessment, and completed in 1976. Technical working groups discussed Panama's latest proposals for property transfers while the negotiators reviewed the entire treaty package. Press reports indicated that new Canal treaties would be completed at any moment, and on August 10, after two days of "review and tidying up exercises," the negotiators announced that an agreement had been concluded.[95] Ambassadors Bunker and Linowitz also announced that they would present the draft treaty package to President Carter the next day, while legal specialists would remain in Panama drafting the final texts of the new treaties.

The August 10 announcement and the formal initialling of treaty texts on September 6, marked the successful conclusion of the formulation phase. After four years of negotiations, the United States and Panama had finally concluded draft treaties that met the objectives set forth in the 1974 Kissinger-Tack Agreement.

Groundwork to Build Support

The groundwork for the Carter administration's plans for ratification of the Panama Canal Treaties was laid during the transition period in late 1976. Ratification of a new Canal treaty was to be a keynote success in a larger program of initiatives, and debate on the treaty was to be the first in a series of foreign policy debates that would forge a new, post-Vietnam consensus. The architects of this strategy, however, underestimated two critical factors: the ease with which a new Canal treaty could be negotiated and ratified, and negative public reactions to the administration's foreign policy initiatives.

The administration initially expected a draft Canal treaty to be completed by June and approved before Congress recessed in October. Even when treaties were not completed until August the administration still hoped to complete the ratification process by the end of the year. Senate leaders asserted however, that the advise and consent process could not be rushed. At a meeting with the president in mid-August, the Senate Majority Leader Robert Byrd (D-WVa) counseled that neither a majority of the Senate nor public opinion was ready to approve the treaties.[96] As a result, the administration's ratification campaign was repeatedly delayed and its public education effort was not fully mobilized until January 1978.

In contrast to the administration, treaty opponents began their campaign before the negotiations ended. While the administration considered its foreign policy initiatives to be positive and constructive, opponents disagreed. These initiatives, plus the administration's announcement that it would withdraw U.S. troops from South Korea, were perceived and decried by opponents as a pattern of weakness and withdrawal from great power status. The Carter administration had boldly announced each of these moves and was proceeding to simultaneously alter long-standing

U.S. commitments in several strategic areas. As a result, each initiative, which might not have seemed so drastic to some opponents, was linked by the New Right into a larger, more threatening pattern. New Right spokesmen, including Ronald Reagan, Congressman Philip Crane (R-Ill), and Senator Paul Laxalt (R-Nev), launched a campaign denouncing the Canal treaties as a "giveaway" and a symbol of defeat and retreat from U.S. commitments abroad.[97] This campaign is described in detail in Chapter 5.

Developments in the international arena also complicated the administration's task and strengthened opponents' claims. The involvement of Cuban troops in conflicts in Africa fueled opponents' claims that conciliatory moves only encouraged adversaries to 'push American around.' New Right spokesmen asserted that policies of appeasement in Panama would only encourage Soviet and Cuban intervention in other regions. Congressman Philip Crane (R-Ill), for example, argued in his book *Surrender in Panama*:

> Quite aside from the security which the current American military presence in the zone provides for the Canal, yielding it would also mean the loss of a vital American presence in the Caribbean, an area already menaced by Cuba's Castro, a Marxist government in Guyana, and the recent rise to power of a pro-Marxist Jamaica.
>
> Constitutionality aside, there is a deep moral issue at stake in Panama. In the past decade, the United States went through something very close to a collective national breakdown. Assassinations, rioting, war, campus violence, Watergate, and the tragic humiliating collapse of Indochina have all contributed to a global climate in which most of the world — but especially those nations and those ideologies who wish us ill — are watching the United States through wolfish eyes, searching for any trace of irresolution or weakness of purpose. In Korea, in Taiwan, throughout Africa, Asia, Europe, the Middle East, and Latin America, wherever freedom is on the line and men must choose, America's image strong or weak, will help to determine their fate. . . .[98]

Crane further asserted:

> This is no time for America to abandon a just claim to a symbol of our national resolve and a vital safeguard of economic and military security for the entire world. . . . There must be no surrender on Panama.'"[99]

Public reaction to the "Singlaub affair," where a General on active duty openly criticized the administration's decision to withdraw troops from South Korea, indicated the strength of an increasingly popular perception that U.S. foreign policy was headed in the wrong direction.[100] Secretary of State Vance later recalled that he and President Carter "were keenly aware of the deep emotions that were aroused by the idea that the United States would voluntarily relinquish the Canal and Zone. To many, they symbolized America's will to maintain its global predominance."[101] The Canal issue, according to Vance:

> Brought together, into a single explosive issue, contending ideological cross currents.
>
> The debate over the Canal treaties would reflect the political and philosophical differences brought about by the searing events of the last decade: Vietnam, Watergate, inflation, the energy crisis, accelerating social change, intractable international problems, loss of economic and military supremacy. Those developments shook American self-confidence and fed fears of national decline.[102]

Just as Ronald Reagan's charges had put President Ford on the defensive during 1976, the Carter administration responded to treaty opponents in a defensive and counterproductive manner. Instead of using the ratification debate to build consensus supporting its view of a new U.S. role in world affairs, the administration stressed essentially negative themes. A familiar theme, used without success by the Ford administration, was resurrected. It was the violence argument that raised the specter of riots and sabotage of the Canal by irate Panamanian nationalists if the treaties were not ratified. As we noted in Chapter 3, this theme played directly to the opponents' strongest suit, namely, that the Carter administration was yielding to threats, being blackmailed into giving away the Canal, and negotiating at the "point of a gun." The administration did not deliberately fall into this unfortunate position. President Carter asserts in his memoirs,

> . . .both we and the Panamanians had to be careful not to present this crucial argument ["that the Canal was in serious danger from direct attack and sabotage unless a new and fair treaty arrangement could be forged"] in the form of a threat, because there would, understandably, be a negative reaction from Congress and the American public.[103]

Nevertheless, in a televised "fireside chat," for example, President Carter devoted most of his time to debunking opponents' criticisms of the treaties. He stated, "We're not giving away the Canal, we're not giving up our defense rights, and we're not paying Panama to take the Canal." On several occasions, President Carter and other treaty advocates made constructive arguments for the Canal treaties. More often, however, their rationale of contributing to "a more humane and stable world," dealing with other nations on the basis of "good will and fairness," and building a "new partnership," was overshadowed by defensive and negative reactions to opponents' charges.[104] And, when administration officials made positive claims for the treaties, they tended to oversell and exaggerate their potential benefits.[105]

94

Brzezinski provides a revealing insight about the process of persuading others to support the treaties and the advantages of forceful rhetoric over a constructive but less effective conceptual justification:

> I conducted numerous briefings for community leaders from all over the country and met with many senators to lobby for their support. After several ineffective initial briefings, in which I attempted to present a broad conceptual perspective on the agreement and its history, in keeping with my general approach to Latin America, I realized that if the treaty was to pass, the presentation would have to be much rougher and more to the point. This political reality was made clear to me by the reception given my new approach. I gave a briefing in early September to a group of political leaders in the East Room. I noted in my journal that at the end of the meeting which was attended by Senator [Robert] Byrd, I was asked the question "But what if after the year 2000, the Panamanian government simply and suddenly announced that it is closing down the canal for repairs?" Without a moment's hesitation I replied, "In that case, according to the provisions of the Neutrality Treaty, we will move in and close down the Panamanian government for repairs." This brought the house down and I think assured a great deal of additional support for our efforts on behalf of the Panama Canal Treaty.[106]

Brzezinski's account reveals an important explanation for the nature of the arguments the administration ended up using in its ratification campaign. He found that matching a tactic used by opponents — relying on emotion-laden slogans — proved to be more effective than presenting a complex conceptual rationale. Administration officials were, indeed, capable of the latter, but the former tactic had a higher probability of success.

Formulating a Ratification Strategy

Advisors in the White House and the Department of State began planning a ratification campaign in April 1977, when a it seemed that a draft treaty would be completed during the next few negotiating sessions. Hamilton Jordan, top political aide to President Carter and the architect of his successful primary and election campaigns, was the principal strategist for the administration's public education drive. In a twelve-page memorandum to the president, Jordan outlined likely obstacles, opponents' strategies and strengths, potential sources of support for the new treaty, and a detailed campaign plan for obtaining a two-thirds majority vote in the Senate.[107]

Jordan predicted, correctly, that the Canal issue would generate a divisive debate similar to the one between President Ford and Ronald Reagan during the 1976 primary elections. However, Jordan did not see the Canal treaty as a no-win proposition. Instead, he estimated that only a few hard-core conservatives, much less than one-third of the Senate, would be irrevocably opposed to a new treaty. Similarly, only a few liberal senators were likely to automatically support the new treaty. Consequently, the major task facing the administration was to persuade the remaining sizeable, but disinterested majority to vote for the treaty. Many of these senators might be willing to support the president, but they were likely to remain uncommitted for quite some time to avoid adverse political reactions in their states. President Carter later confirmed this aspect of the ratification plan. "The task force set up for this purpose developed a somewhat limited objective: not to build up an absolute majority of support among all citizens, but to convince an acceptable number of key political leaders in each important state to give their senators some running room."[108] Jordan's strategy was dictated by the view that the administration must reduce the pressure on potential supporters by creating a climate of closely divided, if not approving, public opinion nationally and in selected states.

To succeed, the administration had to influence several targets: first, undecided senators; second, national public opinion; and most importantly, public opinion in fifteen states where one or both senators were uncommitted. Many events were planned to reverse antitreaty opinion in these states: 1) White House briefings for state opinion makers — including civic, business, and political leaders — conducted by high-ranking officials and the president; 2) speeches, public appearances, and media interviews with members of the negotiating team, high-ranking officials, especially from the Department of Defense, and by Foreign Service Officers; 3) town meetings in particularly crucial states, with telephone connections to the White House for question-and-answer sessions with the president; and 4) campaigns to mobilize grass roots opinion coordinated through a bipartisan Committee of Americans for the Canal Treaties (COACT).[109] The COACT would also counter the activities of the antitreaty truth squad organized by the New Right. President Carter later reported how these plans were implemented.

> We worked closely with the individual senators on lists of state leaders, and we brought hundreds of editors, college presidents, political party leaders, elected officials, campaign contributors, and other influential people into the White House for personal briefings by me. Depending upon the makeup of each group, I would invite State Department or Pentagon officials to join me, including highly effective members of the Joint Chiefs of Staff. At times, the military uniforms were of great help. We also briefed our top administrators at the State Department about the terms of the treaties and how best to present the facts. Altogether, they

made more than 1500 appearances throughout the nation to explain the treaties directly to the public.[110]

White House strategists were confident that their public education campaign would be effective despite antitreaty views that dominated early opinion polls. They found several reasons for dismissing these surveys. The questions were biased, the public lacked information about the value of the Canal and the worth of the new treaty, and the public was being swayed by misleading rhetoric. They assumed that hard-core treaty opponents were a minority, and that "the bulk of public opinion" was "really unformed and susceptible to persuasion. . ."[111]

This assumption dictated the timing of the administration's ratification campaign. Because the most important element in this strategy was the "facts" — the treaty text specifying U.S. defense rights and neutrality guarantees — a full-scale public education campaign could not begin during the negotiations. Consequently, the administration planned to open the campaign with an impressive treaty signing ceremony in either Washington or Panama City. This media event would focus public attention on the treaty and its strong support throughout the hemisphere and among current and former U.S. officials. Then, with the text in hand, the administration would take its case directly to the people.

In order for this strategy to succeed, however, a network of protreaty opinion leaders in target states had to be mobilized before the treaty was signed. Bipartisan support for the treaty would be sought as soon as a treaty text was available, particularly from former officials, such as President Ford, his Secretary of State Henry Kissinger, and President Johnson's Secretary of State Dean Rusk. Endorsements from these officials would symbolize one of the administration's major themes: that the treaty culminated "fourteen years of negotiations." Even Ronald Reagan was considered, although as a long shot, as a potential member of this group. In addition, a series of endorsements from prominent U.S. citizens and their participation in the bipartisan Committee of Americans for the Canal Treaty (COACT) would be solicited.

This bipartisan committee would also be used to mobilize potentially supportive interest groups which, it was hoped, would then activate their grass roots networks and generate protreaty communications to senators and local media. These group activities would serve as a counterweight to the New Right's direct mail operations. The administration realized that neither COACT nor other protreaty groups could outspend or outmail the New Right; they could, however, generate some tangible evidence of support for the treaty, support which could be useful to senators testing the opinion climate at home. These expectations were largely fulfilled.

Labor unions, business leaders, the Jaycees, garden clubs, religious groups, senior citizens, schoolteachers, Common Cause, and other organizations joined us in our effort. Counter-acting the Ronald Reagan opposition, such distinguished conservative leaders as John Wayne and William Buckley spoke out for ratification. By the end of the year, about half of the nation's newspapers were in favor.[112]

The administration hoped that protreaty letters to editors, postcards, telegrams, and letters to senators would encourage the undecided senators to feel more confident about voting for the treaty. The COACT could mobilize a number of former officials and nongovernmental experts to handle overflow requests for treaty briefings and speakers. The cumulative result hoped for was that these efforts would shift public opinion in undecided senators' states.

While the administration's strategy for affecting public opinion in target states relied on personal contacts and face-to-face interactions, it planned a media campaign to influence national opinion polls. A series of media events were planned, involving members of the negotiating team, ranking administration officials, and prominent supporters. At least one "fireside chat" by the president was also included in Jordan's plan for the media campaign. Later, television broadcast of the Senate Foreign Relations Committee hearings and radio broadcast of the entire Senate debate provided an unanticipated windfall for the administration's media strategy.

Hamilton Jordan's strategy for persuading undecided senators to vote for the treaty had pre- and post-signing stages. While the negotiations were still in progress, members of the negotiating team would arrange numerous briefings for members of Congress and their staff, and participate in private consultation with key members of the Senate and its leaders. As soon as the treaty was signed, the administration would provide background information, personal consultation with ranking officials in the Departments of Defense and State, briefings for constituents, and other services to help undecided senators make up their minds and present their position to constituents.[113]

Treaty Opponents' Aims and Strategies

Canal treaty opponents in the Senate may be divided into two ideologically compatible but differently motivated groups: standard or "old right" conservatives led by Senators Allen, Thurmond, and Goldwater; and the New Right, led by Senators Laxalt, Helms, Garn, and Hatch. Old right opposition was primarily based on foreign policy beliefs and world views. These senators believed that permanent, unilateral control over the Canal was essential to U.S. national security. The New Right, although using similar rhetoric, viewed the Canal issue as an opportunity for enlarging its political base and discrediting moderate Republicans. For these senators, and the broader alliance of neoconservative strategists, such as Richard Vignerie, and organizations such as the America Conservative Union and Conservative Caucus, the security value of the Canal was secondary to the political value of the Canal issue. Senator's and Representative's views of the new treaty are discussed more fully in Chapter 5.

The opponents' public education campaign was largely planned, coordinated, and financed by the New Right. It duplicated previous, successful drives by the New Right to build support for conservative positions on domestic issues, relying on direct mail operations for funding and generating grass roots communications to senators. The strategy used by opponents was similar to the administration's; both identified undecided senators and public opinion as their targets. Opponents attempted to influence votes by creating a public opinion climate that would raise the costs of voting for the treaties to unacceptable levels. In contrast to treaty supporters' emphasis on costs to the president's prestige if the treaties failed, the New Right emphasized the political costs of a protreaty vote to senators' chances for re-election.

Turning Points in the Ratification Campaign

Three turning points can be identified during the ratification campaign, where strategic choices allowed the Carter administration to avoid defeat of the treaties. Each of these turning points involved three-way negotiations involving the administration, the Panamanian government, and key figures in the U.S. Senate. Each was necessitated by the fact that the ratification process required President Carter and General Torrijos to sell "the same product to two different audiences."[114] Naturally, each executive emphasized the concessions it had gained and minimized those that had been made. In an era of instant transnational communication, and with opponents in each country eager to find reasons to challenge the treaties, the rationales each government provided for domestic consumption were perceived by opponents abroad as official foreign policy. In overcoming each of these turning points, both governments maintained their commitment to bargaining throughout the ratification process.

Statement of Understanding

The first turning point arose in October 1977 when President Carter invited General Torrijos to visit Washington to clarify discrepancies in the two governments' interpretations of the Neutrality Treaty. As President Carter later related:

All was not going well, however. Some Panamanian leaders, in their eagerness to prove that they had negotiated a good deal, were publicly interpreting parts of the treaty texts differently from my explanation of the same items to Congress. I knew I was right, but it was necessary to eliminate the confusion about the points of controversy — military intervention, the definition of neutrality, and priority for American ships' use of the Canal in an emergency.[115]

At this point the administration made a crucial decision: to make a concession to demands by moderate senators in order to obtain their votes. Previously, the administration had refused to admit that the treaty texts might be "perfected" by the Senate. It soon appeared, however, that the understanding of U.S. defense rights reached by the negotiating teams, which had been noted in the record of the negotiations but not explicitly spelled out in the text of the Neutrality Treaty, would have to be made public. Panamanian officials were claiming that the treaties did not give the United States a right of intervention; translations of speeches made by one of Panama's negotiators, Romulo Escobar, and by Ambassador Carlos Lopez-Guevarra, were challenged by the Senate Foreign Relations Committee and treaty opponents in the Senate. Earlier, Ambassador Linowitz and Secretary Vance had testified at Senate hearings that the United States had, in fact, obtained Panama's understanding and acceptance that the United States could intervene and that U.S. warships had a right of expeditions passage through the Canal in an emergency. Then, on October 4, 1977, "Senator Robert Dole, a leading treaty opponent, released a classified cable from our embassy in Panama that reported continuing Panamanian differences of view over our defense rights under the Neutrality Treaty."[116]

The administration initially tried to convince the Senate Foreign Relations Committee that despite the ratification rhetoric in Panama, the government of Panama had accepted the U.S. interpretation of the treaty. According to Secretary Vance:

> On October 5 we sent a letter to Senator John Sparkman, Chairman of the Foreign Relations Committee, emphasizing that the administration stood firmly behind the interpretation we had given to the Panamanians during the negotiations, but stating that "The treaty does not give the United States the right to intervene in the internal affairs of Panama, nor has it been our intention to seek out or to exercise such a right." Nowithstanding, Senator Byrd told the President that unless these differences were settled in a formal way, the Senate would not approve the treaties.[117]

This and other signals sent the Carter administration an unmistakably clear message: the treaty texts would have to be modified in some way, both to accommodate senators' concerns about U.S. defense rights and to allow the Senate to claim credit for improving the treaties. Secretary Vance later disclosed:

> Carter then met with key senators on October 11 to explain the purpose of the Torrijos visit, which was kept secret. The president said he understood the importance of clarifying the U.S. right to take military action to preserve the Canal's neutrality, and that later that week he and General Torrijos would discuss a joint statement. Carter then disclosed the contents of a draft to see if it met the senators' concerns, warning that Torrijos might insist on some changes. He told them we needed to issue the joint statement prior to the October 23 plebiscite [in Panama].[118]

By inviting General Torrijos to join in a clarification, President Carter hoped to prevent defections by moderate treaty supporters and to avoid having to accept amendments or reservations. This meeting provided the first post-neogotiations test of President Carter's and General Torrijos's commitment to resolve the Canal issue through bargaining. Both governments had already made all of the concessions they believed could be sustained politically at home. In Panama, General Torrijos faced growing opposition to the treaties, opposition partly aroused by the nature of some sentators' demands and statements about him, his regime, and the Panamanian people. Panama's ratification process, a national plebecite, was scheduled for October 23, less than two weeks away. President Carter also faced mounting opposition to the treaties, caused in part by Romulo Escobar's statements about the treaties and comments about the United States. Carter estimated that he could count on only fifty-five of the sixty-seven votes needed in the Senate and that twenty-five senators remained undecided.[119] Both leaders realized that a mutually satisfactory compromise must be reached if the treaties were to be saved from defeat by either or both national ratification processes.

Tactically, Carter and Torrijos appeared to have three alternatives: an oral declaration, a memorandum or statement of understanding, or an exchange of letters. President Carter, given the pressure from the Senate, preferred a written clarification; Torrijos preferred an unwritten affirmation of U.S. defense rights. Secretary Vance provided an account of how a fourth option that accommodated both governments' preferences, an unsigned statement of understanding, was developed.

> Linowitz, who was listening to the two leaders, did not want to let Torrijos return to Panama without resolving the issue. There was no way to be sure of Torrijos' reaction once he was again exposed to domestic criticism. Linowitz said that in his opinion neither an oral declaration nor an exchange of letters would satisfy the Senate. What was needed was a

written statement issued by both leaders that very day. Romulo Escobar continued to argue for an exchange of letters, although he was coming closer to our position.

To avoid the discussion petering out without a firm conclusion, Linowitz suggested that he and Romulo Escobar try to prepare a written understanding on the spot. Within an hour they had worked out a draft which Escobar took to Torrijos. Torrijos agreed, both to the text and to issuing it as a joint understanding before he left Washington. Linowitz secured Carter's approval, then rushed to a hastily convened meeting of the Senate Foreign Relations Committee to review it with the members.[120]

Several senators soon objected to the fact that the statement would only be read and not signed by the President and General Torrijos, but that was a concession Torrijos could not afford to make.

The October 14 Statement of Understanding had three sections, the first clarifying U.S. and Panamanian defense rights, the second addressing Panamanian concerns about U.S. intervention, and the third clarifying the meaning of expeditious passage.

> Under the Treaty Concerning the Permanent Neutrality and Operation of the Panama Canal (the Neutrality Treaty), Panama and the United States have the responsibility to assure that the Panama Canal will remain open and secure to ships of all nations. The correct interpretation of this principle is that each of the two countries shall, in accordance with their respective constitutional processes, defend the Canal against any threat to the regime of neutrality, and consequently shall have the right to act against any aggression or threat directed against the peaceful transit of vessels through the Canal.
>
> This does not mean, nor shall it be interpreted as a right of intervention of the United States in the internal affairs of Panama. Any United States action will be directed at insuring that the Canal will remain open, secure and accessible, and it shall never be directed against the territorial integrity or political independence of Panama.
>
> The Neutrality Treaty provides that the vessels of war and auxiliary vessels of the United States and Panama will be entitled to transit the Canal expeditiously. This is intended, and it shall so be interpreted, to assure the transit of such vessels through the Canal as quickly as possible, without any impediment, with expedited treatment, and in case of need or emergency, to go to the head of the line of vessels in order to transit the Canal rapidly.[121]

This statement was later incorporated into the Neutrality Treaty through amendments recommended by the Foreign Relations Committee and proposed by Majority Leader Byrd and Minority Leader Baker.

The DeConcini Reservation *✶ ✶✶ - make sure you understand*

A second turning point in the ratification campaign involved another clarification of U.S. defense rights under the Neutrality Treaty. Although some senators were satisfied with the amendments incorporating the October 14 Statement of Understanding into the treaty, many others were not. Several of these senators formed a coalition led by Dennis DeConcini (D-Ariz). A more complete account of this senator's role and this episode in the ratification campaign is provided in Chapter 5.

No one could have predicted in early 1977 that this little-known senator from Arizona would emerge as a significant figure during the ratification process. Senator DeConcini, to the surprise of many seasoned observers, succeeded in accomplishing what such powerful figures as Senators Allen, Dole, Laxalt, and Helms could not: wringing acceptance of a "killer" reservation from the administration. Concerning his discussion with Senator DeConcini, President Carter later said, "I had no idea that this meeting would create the single biggest threat to the treaties."[122]

The DeConcini reservation stated that if the Canal were closed, the United States could take any step it deemed necessary, including the use of military force in Panama, to reopen the Canal. Several treaty supporters, as well as many Panamanians' characterized the reservation as a permanent right of military intervention in Panama's internal affairs.[123] The administration faced a desperate situation: with only a few days remaining before the Senate was scheduled to vote on the Neutrality Treaty, it was two or three votes short of a two-thirds majority. President Carter agreed with his political advisers; the reservation would have to be accepted as the price for a few, desperately needed votes. Secretary Vance later described the events surrounding the administration's "negotiations" with Senator DeConcini:

> By March 13, DeConcini had abandoned his insistence on a treaty amendment and agreed to put it in the form of a reservation. However, [Warren] Christopher's best efforts to get him to modify his proposed language were only partly successful. Early on March 16, DeConcini telephoned Christopher to say he would not change the language . . . Carter called DeConcini to tell him that the administration would support his reservation as it stood if he would vote for the Neutrality Treaty.[124]

President Carter realized that he "had to call General Torrijos."

> He was planning to blast the Senate and reject the Panama treaties outright because of some amendment language that DeConcini insisted upon. I don't like the language either, but it doesn't change the text or the meaning of the treaties themselves. I agreed to send Warren Christopher and Hamilton Jordan down to Panama tomorrow afternoon after the votes are completed to explain the complete action of the Senate to Torrijos

rather than having him overly concerned about the one sentence in the resolution of ratification.[125]

On March 18, 1978, the Neutrality Treaty passed by a 68 to 32 vote; the first Canal treaty was saved with only one vote to spare.

Moderating the DeConcini Reservation

During the Senate debate on the second treaty, the administration launched a delicate, two-part strategy to counteract the damage created by the DeConcini reservation. Formal and informal consultations with General Torrijos were held to mute the adverse impact of the DeConcini reservation, and consultations were held with Senate leaders and Senator DeConcini to formulate a nonintervention pledge that would satisfy Panama without jeopardizing the final vote on the Panama Canal Treaty. Both strategies succeeded. According to Secretary Vance:

> Working with Byrd, Church, and Sarbanes, Christopher developed a statement that could be integrated into the DeConcini reservation . . . DeConcini objected to Christopher's language, and for several days, the leadership and Warren labored to produce something that would satisfy DeConcini and Senate conservatives, yet to speak to Panamanian sensitivities.[126]

Senate leaders suggested alternative language and a text acceptable to all was finally developed. A reservation sponsored by Senators Byrd, Baker, Church, DeConcini, and others was passed by the Senate on April 18. This reservation reaffirmed the principle of nonintervention and stated that the United States had no desire to intervene in or compromise Panama's internal affairs, its political independence, or its sovereign integrity. The Panama Canal Treaty was approved by the Senate later that day by a vote of 68 to 32. This satisfied General Torrijos, and he accepted the Senate's modifications of both treaty texts.[127] The final step in the ratification process, a formal exchange of ratifications, occurred in Panama on June 17, 1978.

Comparative Analysis of Executive Impact

This section analyzes the impact of the Nixon, Ford, and Carter administrations on the negotiations and the 1977 treaties. Assessments are based on four categories: expected executive activities, opportunities for executive action, actions taken, and impact. A profile for each administration, based on these categories and summarizing the material discussed in this chapter is presented in chart form.

Seven expected executive activities are used to assess the performance and impact of each administration: setting direction and objectives, timing of substantive initiatives, appointing personnel, setting priorities, high-level intervention (in interdepartmental conflicts), consensus building and coalition building. These activities are leadership tasks arising from the president's constitutional roles of chief diplomat and chief executive and from the treaty-making power the executive branch shares with the Senate.

A separation of powers approach leads us to expect a president and his advisors to be primarily responsible, with little congressional participation, in activities associated with treaty negotiations, with setting the general direction for U.S. foreign policy on the issue, and setting a priority for this issue among competing issues on the domestic and foreign policy agendas. The Senate's shared power under the Constitution leads us to expect consultations between the branches for two of the expected executive activities, appointing personnel and coalition building during a ratification campaign. The relative difficulty an administration encounters in gaining Senate support as it performs these activities depends largely on the nature of the issue, how the issue fits into the foreign policy consensus, and the status of executive-legislative relations at the time.

We noted in Chapter 1 that executive leadership is easier to exercise during periods of consensus on foreign policy goals and beliefs than when the world views of senators and opinion leaders conflict with an administration's. In Chapter 3, we described the divergent world views associated with support and opposition to the treaties. The presence of competing world views provides an additional basis for forming cross-cutting coalitions, which were evident during the negotiations. The possibility that competing coalitions of believers — hawks versus doves, liberal versus conservative internationalists, interventionists versus conciliators — will be formed, in addition to coalitions based on conflicting vested interests, would lead us to expect that a president can encounter great difficulties in consensus building. Similarly, we noted that executive dominance in foreign policy making has been challenged by the Congress during the 1970s. The concurrent emergence of both trends — breakdown of consensus and congressional resurgence — renders the executive's coalition building activity not only a more important determinant of the success of an initiative, but also a more difficult task to perform.

Expectations about the difficulty a president may encounter in building a consensus within the executive branch — on negotiating objectives and positions, timing, and strategy — are based on the bureaucratic approach. This approach leads us to expect organizational resistance to presidential initiatives that depart from existing policies. The more dramatic the change an administration's initiative would entail, the harder an administration

105

must work to create and maintain a consensus among executive departments and agencies. We also expect officials in different departments and agencies to build cross-cutting coalitions with other agencies, with Congress, and with interested publics, to prevent a president's initiative from succeeding. Moreover, when treaty negotiations span several administrations, this approach leads us to expect renewed organizational resistance when a change of administrations occurs or a new round of negotiations requires new guidance for the negotiating team. Prolonged negotiations entail numerous opportunities for recurring conflict within the executive branch, while formulation and reformulation processes invite organizational resistance when interdepartmental clearances must be obtained. Therefore, we expect that the president will have to intervene in interdepartmental conflict more frequently and perhaps less successfully.

Admittedly, selecting evidence of these seven activities requires judgmental decisions. Only a few activities are clear-cut. For example, an obvious case of setting objectives occurs when the National Security Council issues new guidance. But even relatively obvious cases leave the analyst woefully dependent upon available data, such as officials' public statements and press reports, which may be rightfully suspect.

The next category, opportunity for executive action, provides an important benchmark for making realistic comparisons among administrations. To assess an administration's performance, the analyst must decide whether an opportunity to exert leadership arose and evaluate how well that opportunity was used. To be meaningful, comparisons must be based on the degree of opportunity available as well as general expectations about what executives, in theory, are supposed to do. Very general qualifiers are used — low, moderate, and high — to categorize the type of opportunity that existed for each executive activity. Similarly, general terms — significant or negligible, beneficial or negative, and mixed — are used to assess an administration's impact on the treaties. Any delays or disruptions in the negotiations are also noted in this category. These modifiers are hardly precise, but they do not artificially harden necessarily soft data. A variety of sources — government documents, press reports, published statements, and interviews with participants — have been used to check and cross-check findings presented here. The assessments presented below are made with confidence but also with an acknowledgment of their limitations.

know different impacts in general Nixic Ford
Catu

Impact of the Nixon Administration

In terms of opportunity, the Nixon administration had several advantages over subsequent administrations. Since a completely new approach to

106

Canal policy was launched by this administration, it had the greatest degree of opportunity and the most significant impact on direction and policy objectives (see Chart 4.1). Organizational resistance to these changes was overcome relatively easily, at least for the duration of the first negotiating round. The accommodative direction and objectives formalized in the Kissinger-Tack Agreement marked a watershed in the evolution of Canal policy and strongly affected both the content and successful conclusion of the 1977 treaties.

Opportunities for other executive activities — timing of initiatives and high-level intervention — were also high. A flurry of significant and beneficial activity preceeded the signing of the Kissinger-Tack Agreement, but Canal policymaking then settled into a relatively invisible routine involving only the negotiating team and its advisers. The degree of opportunity for setting priorities was mixed. The Canal issue soon slipped from the executive agenda, and neither the president nor Secretary of State Kissinger were involved once formal negotiations began. However, Kissinger's initial involvement and the attention he focused on Canal policy conveyed positive signals to Panama and contributed positively to the pace and productivity of the first negotiating round.

Ambassador Bunker's appointment as chief negotiator also had a significant impact on the treaties and a beneficial impact on the negotiations. Ambassador Bunker advocated several compromises that broke deadlocks between the negotiating teams and within the administration. He advocated a short transition period in exchange for important primary responsibilities by the United States, breaking an impasse during the first negotiating round. Later, during the Ford administration, he suggested the dual-duration formula that resolved the State-Defense guidance fight during the second negotiating round. Ambassador Bunker's style and his willingness to seek new and creative concepts contributed significantly to the success of each negotiating round, and his appointment proved to be an excellent choice by the Nixon administration.

The Nixon administration's high opportunity to exert leadership through these activities can be contrasted with its relative disadvantage for consensus and coalition building. Generally, the initial stage of any negotiation affords few opportunities for building a supportive coalition in Congress or among public opinion leaders. Congress typically has a crowded agenda, and neither its members nor their staff can devote time to an issue that will not be introduced during a current session. Nonetheless, the Nixon administration made the most of its low opportunity by inviting congressional leaders to the ceremony in Panama where the Kissinger-Tack Agreement was signed.

Chart 4.1
The Nixon Administration

ACTIVITY	OPPORTUNITY	ACTION	IMPACT
setting direction, objectives, resolving formulation conflicts	high: created by Panama's rejection of 1971 draft treaty and March 1973 Security Council meeting	high-level review involving National Security Adviser Kissinger	significant: reevaluation of U.S. objectives, Panama's intentions and bargaining position; decision to take a new approach
timing of initiatives	high: provided by pressure from Panama and Minister Tack's suggestion	bilateral discussions among Tack, Bunker, and Kissinger	significant: Kissinger-Tack Agreement on Principles is formulated and signed
appointment of personnel	high: beginning new negotiations, taking a new approach	Ambassador Bunker appointed chief negotiator	significant: experienced diplomat willing to take a new approach is given wide latitude to conduct negotiations
priority set for canal issue	mixed: high priority provided by initiation of new approach, but counteracted by early stage of the negotiations	Kissinger is initially involved, but priority lapses as negotiations progress	beneficial: enough high-level attention is paid to redirect and reopen formal negotiations
consensus building	low: Canal issue only salient for short time	a few public speeches about Kissinger-Tack Agreement	negligible: fails to improve public view of merits of a new partnership
coalition building	low: congressional attention wanes as issue drops from agenda	congressional delegation invited to signing ceremony; little consultation	negligible: opponents vote for antitreaty resolutions in Congress

An even smaller opportunity existed for building a protreaty consensus at this early stage of the negotiations. Secretary Kissinger and Ambassador Bunker made a few speeches about the administration's rationale for negotiating and establishing a new partnership with Panama. Realistically, little more could be expected for this activity. Moreover, given the nature of the Canal issue, the administration did not consider it wise to engage in consensus building at that time. Whenever the issue had been debated in the past, it generated emotional slogans and rhetoric from opponents and supporters. The negotiating team feared that premature public statements would give opponents an opportunity to bias public opinion against a new treaty long before the negotiations concluded.

Overall, then, the Nixon administration's record of executive impact on Canal policy was quite strong. It successfully launched a new initiative after the UN Security Council meeting in Panama, and it set the general framework for a new relationship with Panama. Panama was equally influential in bringing about the changes embodied in the Nixon administration's new approach, because Panama's diplomatic initiative created a new bargaining situation. In fact, as we noted in Chapters 2 and 3, a true bargaining situation did not exist during the 1971-72 negotiations. Neither side was convinced that something could be gained by negotiating and that something could be lost by failing to negotiate. Each seemed to be using an intransigent position during those years as an excuse to behave differently once negotiations failed. The United States would have been content to maintain the status quo and decline further efforts to modify the 1903 treaty. Panama was obviously ready and willing to implement an alternative course of action using a diplomatic strategy to internationalize the Canal issue, and thereby pressure the United States into accepting major changes in the treaty relationship.

After the confrontation at the UN Security Council meeting in Panama, the United States revised its assumptions about the merits of a more equitable relationship with Panama. Minister Tack's initiative suggesting that further negotiations be based on a statement of principles, and the Nixon administration's positive response, reflected a major change - an emergence of a true bargaining situation. Four conditions identified by Robert Wendzel were discussed in Chapter 1 as prerequisites for the existence of a bargaining situation.

1. The parties must truly desire such an agreement (to resolve or lessen a conflict).
2. The substantive interests involved and the objectives that the parties seek must be reconcilable.
3. Both the process and the outcome of the negotiations must be such that none of the parties' prestige is unduly harmed.

4. The negotiators must have sufficient skill in the use of bargaining tactics to achieve their objectives.[128]

Minister Tack's draft statement of principles and the positive predisposition on the part of the U.S. negotiating team and Secretary Kissinger to reopen negotiations with Panama fulfilled the first and fourth conditions. Because both governments were willing to begin their initiatives with an agreement at the level of general principles rather than detailed positions, their substantive interests appeared, at this crucial time, to be reconcilable. Neither government seemed, by accepting the 1974 Statement of Principles, to lose prestige. In fact, by beginning with such general principles, both could claim to have taken reasonable and responsible steps toward meeting common goals and safeguarding national interests. The three principle figures involved at this juncture — Tack, Bunker, and Kissinger — all had operational styles and personalities that allowed them to seize the right moment to make a dramatic move.

Another factor, one emphasized in ecological approaches, was also present at this time: a change in the U.S. perception of Panama's bargaining strength. More than Panama's internationalization strategy was involved in this perceptual shift. The relative power position of the United States vis-a-vis the Third World generally, and Latin America in particular, changed dramatically between the late 1960s and 1973. In the hemisphere, regional unity was demonstrated in the 1969 statement of the Special Latin American Coordinating Committee of the Third World Group of 77. This statement, entitled the Consensus of Vina del Mar, was "the most comprehensive summation ever set forth of Latin America's position on the demands of development in the twentieth century."[129] This event marked a watershed in U.S.-Latin American relations; thereafter, the United States faced a more united hemispheric front supporting a unified position on issues of common concern. Support by that common front for Panama's demands emerged several years later and continued throughout the negotiations and ratification process. The impact of this change in the regional system cannot be underestimated. Structural changes in the hemispheric political ecosystem provided an opportunity for Panama's internationalization strategy to succeed and be perceived by the United States as a serious development that could not be ignored. Consequently, the Nixon administration's new Canal policy initiative should be seen as part of a broader, adaptive response to changing realities in U.S.-Latin American relations. These changing realities made a new approach on Canal policy seem necessary and reasonable. Without the opening of this broader bargaining window, Panama's strategy could not have gained the support of most of the delegations present at the Security Council meeting in Panama. Without such widespread support and the new realities it represented, a true bilateral bargaining situation could not have emerged. Given a history of U.S. Canal policy that consistently and adamantly rejected major changes in the 1903 treaty, the successful implementation of a new approach was a substantial achievement for Panama and for the Nixon administration.

Impact of the Ford Administration

The most disruptive disturbances that affected the 1974-77 negotiations arose during this administration. These included the guidance fight between the Departments of State and Defense, the appropriations controversy in Congress, and the 1976 election campaign. Moreover, many of the most difficult issues on the agenda were addressed during the second negotiating round. In this context, few opportunities for positive action arose, and those that did were used more effectively by treaty opponents than by the administration (see Chart 4.2).

The guidance fight had an extremely negative effect on the negotiations. The delay it caused meant that a new treaty could not be concluded until 1976, a presidential election year. If new guidance had been readily forthcoming, a new treaty might have been concluded in late 1975 and ratified in early 1976. At the end of the first negotiating round, the Ford administration had an opportunity. Attention by high-level officials could have provided the momentum and incentives needed to build support — in the Department of Defense, Congress and public opinion — for a second and final round of negotiations. Instead, the Canal issue was not given high priority; presidential intervention demanding agreement between the Departments of State and Defense was delayed; and initiatives to build public and congressional support for a new partnership with Panama were not taken during the crucial months of May and June. Instead, this opportunity was seized by treaty opponents. Congressman Snyder used his amendment to generate a public debate on the merits of changing Canal policy while President Ford and Secretary Kissinger allowed the Departments of State and Defense to wage a prolonged paper war.

A crowded agenda partly explains the administration's failure to use this opportunity, as the Canal treaty negotiations seemed much less important than other foreign and domestic issues. The relatively low priority of Canal policy was reinforced by an absence of strongly felt pressure from Panama and Latin American states. Canal policy, like many issues in the history of inter-American relations, typically receives attention only when a significant threat or crisis is perceived. Another reason for neglecting this opportunity can be attributed to high-level policymakers' lack of interest in Latin America or Canal policy. Moreover, as the appropriations con-

Chart 4.2
The Ford Administration

ACTIVITY	OPPORTUNITY	ACTION	IMPACT
setting direction, objectives, resolving formulation conflicts	high: provided by conclusion of first negotiating round and interdepartmental conflict	National Security Council meetings; President Ford demands consensus; Bunker proposes dual-duration formula	mixed: delays resumption of negotiations; temporary restoration of executive branch consensus
timing of initiatives	high: provided by conclusion of first negotiating round, appropriations controversy and 1976 primary election campaign	little pressure from high-level officials to reach consensus in executive branch or to build public or congressional support	negative: delays resumption of negotiations; allows treaty opponents to seize initiative
appointment of personnel	high: interdepartmental conflict creates opportunity to add Defense representative to negotiating team	General Dolvin appointed Deputy Negotiator for Department of Defense	mixed: in short-run, facilitates hardening of Defense position; in long-run, enhances formulation, success of negotiations and ratification
priority set for canal issue	high: provided by conclusion of first negotiating round, appropriations controversy and 1976 primary election campaign	priority set is initially low, then issue is unexpectedly politicized, then issue removed from agenda	mixed: delays conclusion of negotiations, but avoids further adverse political impact and allows working-level discussions to continue
high-level intervention	high: provided by appropriations controversy, Gov. Wallace's question, and primary elections	Pentagon promotes Snyder amendments Kissinger misstatement and comments by Kissinger and Ford	negative: delays resumption of negotiations; negative impact on Panamanian views; eventually results in suspension of negotiations
consensus building	moderate: provided by appropriations controversy and primary campaign	positions taken emphasize anticolonialism and violence themes	negative: temporarily disrupts negotiations; fails to build a positive rationale
coalition building	moderate: provided by appropriations controversy and primary campaign	Defense vs. State coalitions and lobbying some consultations	mixed: controversy resolved but negotiations delayed; negligible impact on building protreaty base in Congress

troversy and the primary election campaign proved, negotiating a new Canal treaty was a political liability for the administration. These factors — the relative unimportance of Canal policy, lack of high-level interest, and political costs of changing Canal policy — outweighed the probable benefits of pushing the negotiations to a speedy conclusion.

The administration's performance in resolving formulation conflicts and appointing personnel had a mixed impact on the negotiations. The guidance fight and subsequent breakdown of executive consensus on defense and neutrality issues illustrate how difficult it is to build and maintain a supportive bureaucratic coalition when divisive issues are under review and organizational interests are at stake. For Canal policy, these difficulties were compounded by organizational and personnel decisions made by the Department of Defense.

After talking with General Torrijos in September 1975, civilian leaders in the Department of Defense concluded that a hard-line strategy would be more appropriate than Ambassador Bunker's accommodative strategy. Maximum concessions from Panama could best be gained, these officials believed; by proposing a duration formula that exceeded their own expectations of what was possible. They felt that making an extremely tough offer would put both sides in a better position to compromise on duration and neutrality proposals. In addition, they decided to reorganize the main advisory unit for Canal policy, the Panama Canal Negotiations Working Group, and to appoint a full-time Defense Department representative to serve on the negotiating team.

In the long run, these organizational and personnel changes enhanced high-level Defense officials' trust of the negotiating team and reduced conflict between the two departments. In the short run, however, strengthening the Defense Department's role at the time that senior officials were advocating a hard-line strategy had an adverse impact on the negotiations. Panama was surprised by a major shift in U.S. proposals, and the negotiations were temporarily disrupted. Later, during the third round of negotiations, these changes produced a strong and positive working relationship between the two departments and ensured unity within the executive branch.

The dominant characteristics of consensus and coalition building during the Ford administration were avoidance and delay, and these had a negative impact on the negotiations. Several events forced the administration to take public positions on Canal policy; among these were the appropriations controversy, Governor Wallace's question at the Southern Governors' Conference, and charges raised by Ronald Reagan during the primary election campaign. The administration's response to each of these unwel-

113

comed opportunities was a steady erosion of support for the Kissinger-Tack Agreement and for the negotiations.

In addition to progressively backing away from the Canal policy objectives specified in this agreement, the Ford administration also failed to articulate a forceful and positive rationale supporting changes in Canal policy. The administration used counterproductive arguments about violence and colonialism to justify negotiating a new treaty. Assistant Secretary Rogers' few public statements attempted to build a positive rationale for a new partnership, but these did not constitute effective consensus building. Articulating a plausible and persuasive rationale for accepting partnership instead of full, unilateral control was, admittedly, an extremely difficult task. Even the Carter administration, which devoted considerable prestige and attention to changing Canal policy, found itself using these two arguments when it reacted to opponents's charges during the ratification campaign.

Given these pressures and the administration's public responses, suspending formal negotiations was a logical response. Removing the Canal issue from the agenda avoided further controversy with Panama, and the administration's decision to continue discussions at the working level allowed some additional progress to be made. In retrospect, these decisions can be characterized as a politically realistic salvage operation by recognizing that a new treaty could not be ratified before 1977. Thus, the Ford administration diffused opposition to formal negotiations and diminished treaty opponents' opportunity to debate the issue.

Impact of the Carter Administration

Opportunities for the Carter administration to take significant actions were quite high for all seven executive activities. The strong commitment made by his administration early in 1977 took advantage of each opportunity. The administration set a strongly positive direction for Canal policy, set a high priority for the Canal issue, rapidly launched a new round of negotiations, used high-level intervention to draw public and congressional attention to the Canal issue and to forge a firm executive branch consensus, and appointed personnel strongly committed to the Kissinger-Tack Agreement (see Chart 4.3). During the first few months of the year, the Carter administration's actions seemed to be succeeding.

The appointment of Ambassador Linowitz made two contributions to the success of the third negotiating round.[130] His "forceful" and "dynamic approach" had positive effects on policymaking within the executive branch, facilitating formulation, coordination, and clearance processes for issues remaining on the agenda. Sources close to the negotiations also

114

Chart 4.3
The Carter Administration

ACTIVITY	OPPORTUNITY	ACTION	IMPACT
setting direction, objectives, resolving formulation conflicts	high: provided by change of administrations and debate over defense/neutrality issues	president signals strong commitment to negotiations; negotiators suggest two-treaty formula	significant: momentum given to negotiations and two-treaty formula resolves defense/neutrality issues and enhances treaties' prospects for ratification
timing of initiatives	high: provided by change of administrations and pressure from Panama on financial issue	early resumption of, and consistent attention paid to negotiations; separate financial discussions	significant and beneficial: negotiations are concluded; separate financial package is concluded
appointment of personnel	high: provided by change of administrations	Ambassador Linowitz appointed Co-Negotiator: Ambassador Bunker is retained	significant: Linowitz facilitates formulation and negotiations processes, Bunker provides continuity
priority set for Canal issue	high: provided by change of administrations and president's interests	very high priority set for Canal issue as part of the larger program, but priority lapses	initially significant and beneficial effect on negotiations and both government's commitment to succeed
high-level intervention	high: provided by politization of canal issue and late stage of negotiations, and by Panamanian demands on financial issue	Carter comments on sea-level Canal issue; discussions for separate financial package are initiated	mixed: negotiation are temporarily disrupted by sea-level Canal issue; serious controversy is resolved by separate financial package
concensus building	high: given priority and politicization of Canal issue, late stage of negotiations and by ratification process	ratification strategy planned by White House, but delayed in implementation	mixed: treaty opponents seize the initiative and capitalize on negative themes; but delayed campaign slowly brings positive results
coalition building	high: provided by priority and politization of Canal issue, late stage of negotiations and ratification process	briefings for Senators and staff, but concerted effort not made until negotiations are concluded; acceptance of leadership amendments; last minute "deals" to gain needed votes	significant, but mixed: beneficial in that the treaties gain Senate approval, but negative in that the DeConcini reservation almost prevented an exchange of ratification

reported that despite Ambassador Linowitz's willingness to "break down obstacles to an agreement" arising from bureaucratic resistance, he "drove a very hard bargain" at the negotiating table and refused to concede to "excessive" Panamanian demands.[131] Thus, the increased momentum brought to the negotiations by the appointment of Linowitz, whose views on Latin America could have generated Defense Department opposition, actually enhanced the legitimacy of the new administration's approach. Unity within the executive branch was also facilitated by the long-term impact of personnel and organizational changes made during the Ford administration, particularly the appointment of General Dolvin as deputy negotiator.

The Linowitz appointment also facilitated the climate and progress of negotiations with Panama. Panamanian officials were aware of Ambassador Linowitz's recommendations for changes in United States policies toward Latin America and Panama, as well as his support for the Kissinger-Tack Agreement. To Panama, this appointment signaled the Carter administration's determination to conclude a mutually acceptable treaty as quickly as possible as well as U.S. recognition of Panama's legitimate grievances.

Nonetheless, the third round of negotiations proved to be more difficult than expected, partly because several important issues remained on the agenda and because treaty opponents seized the initiative on consensus and coalition building. When the negotiations were delayed over the defense and neutrality issues, the Canal issue slipped in priority. Few public statements were made by the president or other high-level officials, reinforcing a decrease in presidential concern for this policy. Then, when the president referred to Canal policy in mid-1977, he raised a formerly settled issue — building a sea-level canal; this high-level intervention caused a temporary disruption in the negotiations. The negotiating team was able to resolve this and other, more significant issues, however, by taking a flexible approach and formulating new concepts. The two-treaty formula was a particularly significant contribution to the success of the negotiations and the treaties' prospects for ratification.

During the negotiations, the Carter administration's attempts at coalition and consensus building yielded mixed results; after an arduous ratification campaign, however, the treaties did receive Senate approval. While the negotiating team attempted to consult (or, from many senators' perspectives, to inform them about the negotiations), few senators or their staff were willing to focus on Canal policy before the negotiations concluded. More damaging to the administration's ratification campaign was its failure to use opportunities for consensus building early in the year. President Carter's fireside chat on the treaties, for example, was repeatedly postponed, and the administration's ratification campaign did not begin until September. This chapter discussed several factors that undermined the plans made by the administration. As unforeseen developments occurred and strong opposition emerged, the Carter administration was forced to make several concessions during the ratification campaign. Finally, each treaty passed the Senate with one vote to spare.

Conclusions

This is the pattern that emerges from comparisons of profiles for each administration. The Nixon administration had high opportunities for all but consensus and coalition building activities, and the impact of its actions was significant and beneficial. The Ford administration's opportunities were similar, except for moderate instead of low opportunities for consensus and coalition building. This administration's impact, however, was mixed. The negotiations were repeatedly delayed and disrupted. Nonetheless, agreement with Panama on most of the specific provisions of the new treaties was achieved at working-level discussions. The Carter administration's opportunities were high for all seven executive activities. Its actions had a generally beneficial and clearly significant impact on the negotiations and the treaties. For consensus building, however, the administration's actions had mixed results. The treaties were successfully ratified but at substantial costs to the administration. The administration encountered numerous difficulties as it sought to build a pro-treaty coalition in the Senate. Nonetheless, despite the fact that the administration had to overcome several potentially disastrous turning points, the passage of both treaties rates as a significant and beneficial result.

What accounts for the different performances of each administration on executive activities associated with formulation and negotiations? Why was it relatively easy for the Nixon administration to set objectives, take initiatives, resolve formulation conflicts, and for high-level officials to personally intervene in Canal policymaking? The nature of the negotiation process largely explains why these opportunities were used relatively easily by the Nixon administration. The direction and objectives set before negotiations begin are usually vague. Therefore, conflicts among executive officials at this stage are much easier to resolve than conflicts over specific provisions. Similarly, supporting coalitions are easier to build for the type of initiative taken before negotiations begin than for initiatives that are identified with specific costs and benefits. These activities were harder for the Ford and Carter administrations to perform because they faced specific rather than general alternatives.

The Ford and Carter administrations' difficulties in performing these four activities were compounded by the emergence of vocal opponents and politicization of the Canal issue. Opposition to a fundamental change in Canal policy and to the negotiations themselves added perceived political costs to actions contemplated by these administrations. These developments also complicated implementation of executive actions.

Why were treaty opponents almost able to defeat the treaties? An ecological perspective on bargaining suggests a convincing reason for the popularity of arguments against the 1977 treaties, namely, that the bargaining window was beginning to close. When formal negotiations began in 1974, the most serious threat to the security of the Panama Canal seemed to be lack of Panamanian consent to unilateral control. Obtaining that consent through a new treaty making Panama an equal partner and eliminating the Canal Zone seemed to be a reasonable course of action for the United States. The hemisphere seemed relatively stable and Cubans were not yet fighting in Angola and Ethiopia. By 1975, however, public opinion surveys revealed that support for the type of principles included in the Kissinger-Tack Agreement had declined. An alternative world view gained increased support among opinion leaders: conservative internationalism, a view compatible with Cold War axioms, strongly competed with liberal internationalism. The breakdown of consensus on the merits of conciliatory policies was related to changes in the global system, particularly in the behavior of the Soviet Union and Cuba. A development of equal importance was a growing perception that the United States was being ''pushed around.'' An extensive discussion of the clashing belief systems held by treaty opponents and supporters during the ratification campaign was presented in Chapter 3. The views of treaty opponents reported in this chapter, during the appropriations controversy and the 1976 election campaign, confirm that the window of time during which an administration could mobilize a protreaty consensus among opinion leaders was beginning to close before the ratification campaign began.

These developments made it difficult for the Ford and Carter administrations to perform coalition and consensus building activities. These are inherently difficult tasks because they require an administration to extend its support beyond the executive branch. This difficulty is compounded when a salient and divisive issue is at stake. How well one expects an administration to perform under these conditions depends on the way this wider political context is viewed.

Two perspectives can be used to characterize the political context. One sets forth minimal expectations about executive activity in a climate of congressional assertiveness and competing views of what the interests and foreign policy goals of the United States should be. The other perspective

118

sets higher expectations and makes a more optimistic assessment of the context in which executive influence is exerted.

First Perspective *the changed role in congress from 90% just (let alone president do what he wants by lots really looks at this*

According to the first perspective, initiatives that depart from traditional Cold War foreign policies are likely to be frustrated. Three developments in the political context hamper such initiatives. One is Congress' assertive reaction to the Vietnam experience and the Nixon/Kissinger style of defining and implementing foreign policy. When Congress takes a more active role in foreign affairs, executive initiatives are more likely to be challenged. Moreover, the post-1975 reforms within Congress itself create an unmanageable set of political dynamics because greater opportunities exist for individual senators to act independently and the powers of party and committee leaders are diminished. President Carter lamented the effect of this development when he wrote in his memoirs: "I learned the hard way that there was no party loyalty or discipline when a complicated or controversial issue was at stake - none. Each legislator had to be wooed and won individually. It was every member for himself, and the devil take the hindmost."[132]

The nature of congressional challenges to executive initiatives is affected by two other developments: fragmentation of the foreign policy consensus in elite and public opinion, and the rise of the New Right as an effective coalition builder in Congress and public opinion. These two developments reflect important sources of support for Cold War objectives and opposition to accommodative gestures toward the Third World. From this perspective, the chances of getting Senate approval for a Canal treaty that substantially changed the U.S. relationship with Panama would be quite slim, and any administration would suffer politically for advocating a new Canal treaty relationship. Secretary Vance later articulated these difficulties when he stated, "The political and foreign policy risks of taking on an uphill ratification battle that might well be lost were great, and a less courageous president might have ducked the issue."[133]

The Ford and Carter administrations' experiences with treaty opponents fit this expected pattern. Increased popularity of interventionist and Cold War sentiments in public opinion created a disadvantage for all three administrations, making consensus building a particularly difficult task. The objectives stated in the Kissinger-Tack Agreement were not compatible with popular views of U.S. security; consequently, each administration found it difficult to articulate a convincing argument supporting a new relationship with Panama. When opposition emerged during the Ford administration, the president was wise, according to this perspective, to delay the negotiations. This bought time and prevented Canal policy from

119

being permanently diverted toward status quo objectives. Similarly, the Carter administration did well to assemble a narrow coalition of treaty supporters, and was wise to make concessions, particularly accepting the DeConcini reservation, needed to obtain a two-thirds majority in the Senate. By emphasizing obstacles and a competitive relationship between the branches, this perspective expects each administration to face great odds in attempting to change Canal policy and yields a positive assessment of each administration's performance.

Second Perspective

The alternative perspective is based on different factors and political dynamics. Instead of focusing on recent changes in Congress, this perspective emphasizes the formal and informal powers of the presidency that can be used to persuade Congress and the public to support new objectives and policies. In contrast to a focus on obstacles to change posed by the New Right, a perspective of executive advantages or dominance emphasizes opportunities to mobilize an elite coalition of liberal internationalist opinion to support foreign policy initiatives. It also expects an administration to shape rather than react to public opinion. An executive-oriented perspective stresses the power of leadership rather than the strength of unwilling followers. Consequently, this perspective yields a positive assessment of the Nixon administration, a negative assessment of the Ford administration, and a mixed assessment of the Carter administration.

The Nixon administration, according to this alternative perspective, successfully seized an opportune moment to negotiate an agreement in principle. The vagueness of those principles facilitated building a consensus within the executive branch and allowed treaty negotiations to begin. Naturally, when specific proposals were made during the Ford administration, conflicts within the executive and with Congress surfaced. Those conflicts provided another leadership opportunity. The administration responded, however, by prolonging debate and delaying negotiations. The Carter administration, from this perspective, faced the most difficult tasks — concluding the negotiations and gaining approval — but also the greatest opportunity. At the beginning of his administration, President Carter had an unusually high opportunity to make a few, selective changes in foreign policy. If only he had set a few, clear priorities instead of advocating changes on numerous issues without differentiating among them, an effective ratification campaign might have succeeded relatively easily. Zbigniev Brzezinski, Carter's National Security adviser, recalled that these initiatives were "to infuse new life into the paralyzed Middle East peace process, to conclude a SALT II agreement better than SALT I, to improve relations with Latin America through the ratification of the Panama Canal Treaties, to reactivate NATO, while also advancing such causes as human rights, nuclear nonproliferation, and majority rule in southern Africa.''[134] ''Inevitably,'' Brzezinski concluded, ''such widely guaged activism came close to overloading the decision-making process itself and put enormous pressure on the Presidential schedule.''[135] This perspective would praise the Carter administration's ratification plan and criticize its execution, concluding that not enough was done to mobilize pro-treaty opinion. In this view, enough support among liberal internationalist opinion could have been mobilized and sufficient time remained to counter the resurgence of cold war views with an alternative, forcefully articulated foreign policy doctrine.

The evidence presented earlier in this Chapter gives stronger support to the first perspective than the second. In his memoirs, Brzezinski reached a similar conclusion, but he also recalled the uncertainties and risks that influenced the administration's decision.

> Later on, it was sometimes said that the Panama ratification effort proved excessively debilitating and politically costly for the President. This may be the case, but it has to be remembered that at the time the negotiations were in a critical stage and we were faced with the possibility of the talks breaking down. It was generally felt that violence would then ensue, and every intelligence estimate pointed to the likelihood that it would spread to other parts of Central America. Moreover, there would be a strong wave of anti-Yankee sentiment throughout Latin America. Accordingly, the rapid conclusion of the negotiations, which still seemed on track, was thought by all concerned to be justified.[136]

During early 1977, potential political risks of a divisive ratification campaign at home had to be weighed against potential diplomatic risks in the hemisphere and potential threats to the Canal. The second perspective suggests the tasks the Ford and Carter administrations would have had to accomplish to achieve a rapid and overwhelming victory on the Canal issue. Hemispheric conditions still supported the type of changes the 1977 treaties embodied, but the domestic context was becoming less conducive to public support for a new partnership with Panama.

Events since the ratification of the 1977 treaties show how little time was left for conciliatory initiatives on Canal policy or other issues. During 1978 and 1979, implementation of the new treaties proceeded smoothly in Panama, but the House of Representatives fought the administration over passage of implementation legislation. Panama supported our boycott of the Moscow Olympics following the Soviet invasion of Afghanistan, and Panama accepted the Shah of Iran, an act that helped the United States at a difficult moment during the Hostage Crisis. These events showed Panama to be a strong ally and supporter of the United States. Nonetheless, when the Somoza regime was threatened during 1979, the House of Representatives held an extraordinary closed floor session to consider how the civil war in Nicaragua might affect implementation of the Canal treaties. Once the revolutions in Nicaragua and El Salvador were underway, perceptions of threats to U.S. interests in the region became even stronger, and Contadora Island became the site of a new and different attempt to resolve a symbolically-charged conflict through bargaining and negotiations. During the 1980s, the United States seemed to face a different hemisphere and a different world than it did when the Kissinger-Tack Agreement was signed in 1974. In a trend made clearer by its successor, the Carter administration's foreign policy premises shifted toward Cold War, conservative internationalism.

Endnotes

[1] Statements expressing administrations officials' reactions to the Security Council meeting and its implications for future Canal treaty negotiations can be found in U.S. Congress, House of Representatives, Committee on Merchant Marine and Fisheries, *Panama Canal Briefings*, committee hearing, 93rd Cong., 1st sess. (Washington: Government Printing Office, 1973); and in U.S. Congress, House of Representatives, Committee on Foreign Affairs and Committee on Merchant Marine and Fisheries, *United Nations Security Council Meeting in Panama*, joint subcommittee hearings, 93rd Cong., 2d Sess. (Washington, D.C.: Government Printing Office, 1973).

[2] "Panama and the United States: A Design for Partnership," address by Ellsworth Bunker.

[3] Interviews with members of the negotiating team and its advisers, 1977-78, Washington.

[4] Henry Kissinger was appointed Secretary of State, replacing William P. Rogers, in September 1973; he continued to hold the position of National Security Adviser.

[5] *New York Times*, January 6, 1974.

[6] Henry Kissinger, "U.S. and Panama Agree on Principles for Negotiation of a New Panama Canal Treaty," address by Secretary of State Kissinger.

[7] *New York Times*, February 8, 1974, p. 2.

[8] In addition to Ambassador Bunker and his deputy, S. Morey Bell, the U.S. negotiating team was advised by John P. Sheffey, who had worked with the 1965-67 negotiating team; Michael Kozak, from the Department of State; and Richard Wyrough, from the Department of Defense and its Panama Canal Negotiations Working Group. During subsequent negotiations during 1974-76, input from the White House and the National Security Council was minimal, except during the guidance fight of summer 1975.

⁹ For example, the transfer of old France Field was selected as the first visible action because key congressional treaty opponents, notably Congresswoman Leonor K. Sullivan (D-Mo) had already made a similar proposal; nonetheless, she and other members of the House opposed this and other visible actions taken unilaterally by the executive branch; see, for example, U.S. Congress, *Congressional Record*, Vol. 121, pt. 16, House, pp. 20947 and 20951; for a description of visible actions that were considered, see U.S. Congress, House of Representatives, Committee on Merchant Marine and Fisheries, *Panama Canal Finances*, committee hearings, 94th Cong., 2d Sess. (Washington; D.C.: Government Printing Office, 1976), pp. 431-32.

¹⁰ Connecticut Walker, "Ellsworth Bunker's Toughest Mission: Can He Solve the Explosive Panama Canal Issue?" *Washington Post*, *Parade Magazine* (August 31, 1975),pp. 4-6.

¹¹ *Congressional Record*, October 6, 1975, p. 9661.

¹² Ibid.

¹³ Ibid.

¹⁴ Ibid. -

¹⁵ Ibid., pp. 9661-62.

¹⁶ Ibid., p. 9663.

¹⁷ Ibid.

¹⁸ Franck and Weisband, "Panama Paralysis," *Foreign Policy* 21 (Winter 1975-76): 175.

¹⁹ U. S. initiating team advisors, interviews with author, Washington D.C., 1977-1978.

²⁰ *New York Times*, 21 August 1975.

²¹ Atlantic-Pacific Interoceanic Canal Study Commission, *Interoceanic Canal Studies 1970* (Washington; D.C.: Government Printing Office, 1971).

²² Interviews; some of the concerns expressed by officials in the Department of Defense were made public during hearings on the 1977 Canal treaties; see U.S. Congress, Senate, Committee on Armed Services, *Defense, Maintenance and Operation of the Panama Canal, Including Administration and Government of the Canal Zone*, committee hearings, 95th Cong., 2nd Sess. (Washington; D.C.: Government Printing Office, 1978), especially pp. 62-64 (hereafter cited as *Defense Maintenance*).

²³ Ibid., pp. 202-203.

²⁴ Marilyn Berger, "House Rejects Funds for Canal Zone Talks," *Washington Post*, 27 July 1975.

²⁵ U.S. Congress, *Congressional Record*, House, vol. 121, pt. 16, June 26, 1975, p. 20945.

²⁶ Ibid., p. 20947.

²⁷ Ibid.

²⁸ Ibid., p. 20948.

29 Ibid., p. 20951.

30 Ibid.

31 Rosenfeld, "The Panama Negotiations," *Foreign Affairs* 54 (October 1975):10.

32 *Washington Post*, 17 July 1975.

33 *Washington Post*, 19 July 1975.

34 Jeremiah O'Leary, "Panama Talks Face Crucial Hill Test," *Washington Post*, July 21, 1975.

35 *Washington Post*, 17 July 1975.

36 *Washington Star*, 27 July 1975.

37 TRB, "A Panama Canal Blow-Up Could Rock the World," *Los Angeles Times*, 26 July 1975.

38 Carl T. Rowan, "Danger Brews in Panama," *Washington Star*, 25 July 1975.

39 Harry F. Byrd, "We're Going to Need that Waterway for Many, Many Years," *U.S. News and World Report*, 6 October 1975.

40 William D. Rogers, "The Big Ditch in Panama: Get Out," *Denver Post*, 25 May 1975.

41 *Baltimore Sun*, 4 August 1975.

42 Rosenfeld, *Panama Negotiations*, p. 11. The major participants in the guidance fight at the level of the National Security Council were Deputy Secretary of Defense Clements and Secretary of the Army Calloway, Deputy Secretary of State Ingersoll, Assistant Secretary of State Rogers, Ambassador Bunker, and Assistant Secretary of Defense for International Security Affairs Ellsworth.

43 David Binder, "Pentagon Yielded," *New York Times*, 16 September 1975, p. 11.

44 *Defense Maintenance*, p. 30.

45 David Binder, "Bunker to Seek Compromise on Panama Canal," *New York Times*, 2 September 1975, p. 3.

46 *New York Times*, 5 September 1975.

47 *Defense Maintenance*, p. 201.

48 Murray Mauder, "Kissinger's Statements Heat Canal Zone Talks," *Washington Post*, 19 September 1975.

49 Henry Bradsher, "Bunker Tries to Soothe Panamanians," *Washington Star*, 18 September 1975.

50 *New York Times*, 28 November 1975.

51 *Washington Post*, 21 September 1975.

52 *New York Times*, 29 February 1976.

53 Ibid.

54 Gerald R. Ford, *A Time to Heal: The Autobiography of Gerald R. Ford* (New York: Harper and Row and Reader's Digest Association, Inc., 1979), p. 374.

55 *New York Times*, 15 April 1976.

[56]*New York Times*, 7 October 1976.

[57]Interviews.

[58]Joseph W. Aragon, Remarks made at Roundtable Discussion, "Public Opinion and the Panama Controversy," 19th Annual Meeting of the International Studies Association, Washington, D.C., February 23, 1978.

[59]For the 1975 Commission report, see Commission on United States-Latin American Relations, *The Americas in a Changing World* (New York: Quadrangle 1975); see also *New York Times*, 19 December 1976, p. 23.

[60]Zbigniew Brzezinski, *Power and Principle: Memoirs of the National Security Adviser* (New York: Farrar, Straus, Giroux, 1983), p. 81.

[61]Ibid., p. 38.

[62]Vance, *Hard Choices*, p. 141.

[63]Ibid., p. 44; see also Brzezinski, *Power and Principle*, p. 81

[64]Jimmy Carter, *Keeping Faith: Memoirs of a President* (New York: Bantam, 1982), p. 65.

[65]Brzezinski, *Power and Principle*, p. 81.

[66]Carter, *Keeping Faith*, p. 156.

[67]Edward Walsh, "Applying the Canal Lessons to SALT," *Washington Post*, 19 March 1978, p. A7.

[68]Vance, *Hard Choices*, p. 33.

[69]Canal policy did, in fact, consistently receive high-level attention, but the review of Canal policy (PRM 1) preceeded the "wide-ranging review of U.S. policy toward Latin America" ordered by Brzezinski in January and completed in March; see Brzezinski, *Power and Principle*, pp. 134-35.

[70]Brzezinski, *Power and Principle*, p. 51. Present at the January 5, 1977 meeting were: Vice-President-Elect Mondale, Secretary of State designate Cyrus Vance and his designated deputy, Warren Christopher; Secretary of Defense-designate Harold Brown and his designated deputy, Charles Duncan; Ambassador to the UN-designate Andrew Young; Director of the CIA-designate Ted Sorensen; Charles Schultz, head of the Council of Economic Advisers; and National Security Adviser Zbigniew Brzezinski and two of his staff assistants, David Aaron and Rick Inderfurth.

[71]Vance, *Hard Choices*, p. 144.

[72]Carter, *Keeping Faith*, p. 156.

[73]Vance, *Hard Choices*, p. 145.

[74]This negotiating session had been postponed because of a change in personnel on the Panamanian negotiating team; Romulo Escobar replaced Aquilino Boyd as Panama's Chief Negotiator.

[75]Vance, *Hard Choices*, p. 145.

[76]*New York Times*, 14 February 1977 and 6 March 1977, p. 10.

[77]Carter, *Keeping Faith*, p. 157. In this passage, President Carter stresses defense against external threats; however, a distinction between U.S. rights to

defend the canal against external threats and Panamanian rights to counter internal threats was not made by the negotiating teams until early May.

[78] Secretary Vance reports that Linowitz and Bunker suggested the two-treaty formula (Vance, *Hard Choices*, p. 146); participants interviewed during 1978 stated that the formula was first derived at a working session held by advisers to the Chief negotiators.

[79] *New York Times*, 18 May 1977.

[80] Vance, *Hard Choices*, p. 146.

[81] Carter, *Keeping Faith*, p. 157.

[82] Vance, *Hard Choices*, p. 146.

[83] *New York Times*, 29 May 1977.

[84] *Washington Post*, 22 June 1977.

[85] Carter, *Keeping Faith*, p. 157.

[86] *Washington Post*, 22 June 1977.

[87] Ibid.

[88] *Baltimore Sun*, 7 August 1977.

[89] Carter, *Keeping Faith*, p. 158.

[90] *Washington Post*, 15 June 1977.

[91] Vance, *Hard Choices*, p. 146.

[92] Ibid.

[93] U.S. Congress Senate, Committee on Foreign Relations, *Panama Canal Treaties: Hearings*, Exec. N, 95th Congress, 1st Session, Washington D.C., 1977, pt. I, pp. 374-401. (Hereafter cited as Senate Committee on Foreign Relations, *Hearings*). The date June 8 was given by a participant interviewed during 1977; in his memoirs, President Carter dates the Panamanian financial proposal as being made on May 30 (Carter, *Keeping Faith*, p. 158).

[94] Carter, *Keeping Faith*, p. 518.

[95] *New York Times*, 10 August 1977.

[96] *New York Times*, 20 August 1977.

[97] William J. Lanouette, "The Panama Canal Treaties — Playing in Peoria and in the Senate," *National Journal*, October 8, 1977, pp. 1556-62.

[98] Philip M. Crane, *Surrender in Panama: The Case Against the Treaty* (New York: Dale Books, 1978), p. 16.

[99] Ibid., p. 17.

[100] *New York Times*, 28 September 1977.

[101] Vance, *Hard Choices*, p. 140.

[102] Ibid.

[103] Carter, *Keeping Faith*, p. 156.

[104] *New York Times*, 2 February 1978.

[105] Joseph Kraft, "Double Snow Job," *Washington Post*, September 11, 1978.

[106] Brzezinski, *Power and Principle*, p. 136.
[107] *Washington Post*, 23 July 1977.
[108] Carter, *Keeping Faith*, p. 162.
[109] Lanouette, pp. 1556-62.
[110] Carter, *Keeping Faith*, p. 162.
[111] *Washington Post*, 19 August 1977.
[112] Carter, *Keeping Faith*, p. 162.
[113] Washington Post, 23 July 1977.
[114] Brzezinski, *Power and Principle*, p. 137.
[115] Carter, *Keeping Faith*, p. 162.
[116] Vance, *Hard Choices*, p. 149.
[117] Ibid.
[118] Ibid.
[119] Ibid.
[120] Ibid., pp. 149-150.
[121] *Background Documents*, No. 187, October 14 statement, p. 1620.
[122] Carter, *Keeping Faith*, pp. 169-70.
[123] *Washington Post*, 11 April 1978, p. A1.
[124] Vance, *Hard Choices*, p. 154.
[125] Carter, *Keeping Faith*, p. 172.
[126] Vance, *Hard Choices*, pp. 155-56.
[127] Robert G. Kaiser, "Strategy: The Engineering Feat Behind Canal Treaties Began on a Bleak Day," *Washington Post*, 20 April 1978, pp. A1 & A3.
[128] Robert L. Wendzel, *International Relations: A Policymaker Focus* (New York, Wiley, 2nd ed., 1980), p. 179.
[129] Frederico G. Gil, *Latin American - United States Relations* (New York: Harcourt, Brace, Jovanovitch, 1970), p. 272.
[130] Brzezinski claims credit for recommending that Carter appoint Linowitz to be co-negotiator and that Linowitz was willing to accept "only as a co-negotiator with Bunker" (Brzezinski, p. 143).
[131] Interviews
[132] Carter, *Keeping Faith*, p. 80.
[133] Vance, *Hard Choices*, p. 140.
[134] Brzezinski, *Power and Principle*, p. 81.
[135] Ibid.
[136] Ibid., p. 51.

CHAPTER 5

CONGRESS AND THE TREATIES

The Senate of the U.S. Congress must act upon all treaties before they are ratified. The Senate does not actually ratify a treaty, but instead gives its "advice and consent" to ratification. If it fails to do so, the treaty cannot be ratified. After Senate consent or approval is obtained, the president is then responsible for the formal ratification. The Senate's role in this process is defined in Article II, Section 2 of the Constitution. A treaty only becomes legally binding in the United States after the following sequence is completed: the advice and consent is given by the Senate, and it is submitted to the president who ratifies, then the other party(ies) also ratify according to their legal processes, and finally there is an exchange and/or deposit of the ratification.

Several historians contend that when the Constitution was written, our Founding Fathers intended that the Senate should participate in the full treaty-making process. They envisioned the Senate formulating instructions for the negotiators and acting as counsel during the course of negotiations. The only major exception to this role would be when secrecy required the president to act otherwise.[1]

Despite the original intention of the Founding Fathers, President George Washington's first attempt to seek counsel and advice from the Senate in August 1789 was not as successful as he had hoped. President Washington personally presented a treaty on the Senate floor and requested their advice and consent. Instead of giving advice, the Senate referred this matter to a committee. ". . . No President of the United States has since that day ever darkened the doors of the Senate for the purpose of personal consultation with it concerning the advisability of a desired negotiation."[2] From then on, the practice developed whereby the president negotiated treaties, and the Senate exercised a veto or approval power over such settlements. The Senate seldom became directly involved in the negotiating process or in giving advice to the executive during such negotiations.

Under current procedures, the executive submits a treaty to the Senate after it has been negotiated and signed. In considering a treaty, the Senate can do several things besides approving or disapproving. If it chooses to approve it as it is written, then a two-thirds vote is required. If it chooses to disapprove, the Senate can reject the treaty by voting against it; but the Senate usually indicates its dissatisfaction through inaction and postponement rather than by a direct vote against the treaty. When postponement occurs and defeat appears imminent, the president usually withdraws the treaty from consideration before the Senate votes it down. Even when the

Senate is in basic agreement with a treaty, it does not have to accept it exactly as written. It still has at least four options to clarify, restrict, or otherwise make its views known during the "advice and consent" phase.

The first of these options is to state its views before the treaty comes to the Senate floor in the committee report recommending approval. This procedure, however, only gives the whole Senate the committee's instruction and sentiment and has little legal impact. In the second option, the Senate may include in its treaty approval resolution, language expressing its "understanding" or "interpretation" of certain aspects of the treaty; but again this action does not have a binding legal effect. In order to have a legal and continuing impact, the Senate may exercise its third option by including reservations that would be binding and might affect the terms of the treaty. These would need to be communicated to the other parties involved, which might require new negotiations. Finally, the Senate may specifically "amend" the terms of the treaty itself. This fourth option could require renegotiation of the treaty or at least acceptance of the changes by the other nation or nations involved.[3]

The Senate approval procedure can also be broken down into two stages: (1) the committee stage and (2) the floor stage. The first stage can include a through investigation and a long hearing process. Upon completion of investigations and hearings, the committee reporting on the treaty can follow the first option explained above and direct its comments to the whole Senate. It can include suggested changes to the treaty and any other recommendations, reservations, and clarifications it deems necessary by attaching these to the official "Resolution of Ratification" of the committee report. In the case of the Panama Canal Treaties, this option was not followed. Instead the Senate Foreign Relations Committee used an innovation in its report to the full Senate. Instead of including its recommendations in the resolution of ratification, the committee merely included them with the rest of the report. This left the way open for complete and open debate on these issues on the floor.

After the committee makes its report, the treaty is placed on the executive calendar. The Senate then by Rule 37, acts as a "Committee of the Whole" and considers the treaty article by article. After this procedure is completed, the Senate considers the entire treaty. A vote of "unanimous consent" is required to bypass the Committee of the Whole stage.[4]

The practice in the Senate since the early 1920s — which was partially a result of the defeat of the Treaty of Versailles — was to bypass this Committee as a Whole stage and to consider the ratification resolution only. This streamlined procedure forced a consideration of the entire treaty at once and bypassed the article-by-article consideration. Since the early 1940s, the Senate has rarely amended or changed treaties. On a few occasions it has insisted on some understandings, reservations, and clarifications, but the overall trend, has been for the Senate to approve complete treaties without major alterations and without an article-by-article consideration. In contrast, treatment of the Panama Canal Treaties ratification deviated from this fifty-year-old practice.

Because this process is complex, cumbersome, and slow, most presidents in the twentieth century have reduced their use of treaties as a major tool for conducting foreign policy and have instead turned to executive agreements. Most executive agreements need not be approved in an advice and consent procedure by the Senate. For the first fifty years of U.S. diplomatic history there were twice as many treaties made as executive agreements. Since World War II, there have been approximately twenty times as many executive agreements made as treaties.

Substantive Issues

The issues discussed in the congressional hearings and on the Senate floor were many of the same issues that the negotiators faced in working on the treaties. The president, The Defense Department, and the Congress, in general, and specifically the Senate were concerned about U.S. interests, traditions and needs regarding the treaties. Many arguments made during the floor debates and public statements of many politicians were, however, aimed more at constituents rather than improving or changing the treaties. The Panamanians had their own interpretations of what the important issues were and what the treaties meant. Most of the information in this chapter, however, is related to the perceptions, arguments, and disagreements that occurred in the United States over specific aspects of the treaties. Some mention is made of the Panamanian side of some issues throughout the book, but an indepth analysis of the Panamanian viewpoint will have to be left to another study and other authors.

Sovereignty

The main issue between the United States and Panama in the negotiations and much of the argument in the Senate focused on the question of sovereignty and political jurisdiction over the Canal Zone. These questions had successfully been ignored by the United States in nearly all previous negotiations with Panama since 1903. Yet without earnest consideration of this issue, Panama could not take U.S. positions on any other issues seriously. Any consideration of changing U.S. interpretation of its rights, however, raised great opposition in the U.S. Congress and Defense Department and with the public in general.

130

The sovereignty problem was central to the treaty. Treaty proponents contended that the United States had rights but not sovereignty in the Canal Zone, while opponents maintained that the United States was the owner and sovereign of the Zone just as much as they were in Alaska and other such places.

The question concerning sovereignty had been the focal point of disagreement between Panama and the United States since 1903. There were good arguments that the United States had obtained sovereignty by the 1903 Treaty. Equally good justification exists to indicate that sovereignty had been retained by Panama and that the United States could exercise use and control of the Zone, acting as if it were sovereign, while in actuality retaining no territorial sovereignty.

It was argued by opponents to negotiations, that it would be impossible to defend and control the Canal if the United States did not have complete sovereign power within the Zone. One spokesman stated: "If we are to retain the Canal, there cannot be any compromise on the issue of sovereignty . . . We must not retain responsibility without authority."[5]

The Canal Treaty, nevertheless, resolved the question of sovereignty over the Zone. Without this agreement, no administration in Panama could survive long and no new treaty could have been ratified in Panama. The United States had to eventually relinquish all claim to sovereignty over Panamanian land. Article III of the Canal Treaty simply states, "The Republic of Panama, as territorial sovereign, grants to the United States of America the rights to manage, operate, and maintain the Panama Canal . . ." Thus, rights not sovereignty were granted to the United States until December 31, 1999 by the Canal Treaty.

Defense

The defense issue was associated directly with the sovereignty issue. Many military people as well as political leaders believed that without American control of the Zone, defense of the Canal would be extremely more difficult and costly, and perhaps impossible. Senator Robert Griffin (R-Mich), the lone dissenter on the Senate Foreign Relations Committee, strongly feared that the treaties were "fatally flawed."[6] The defense issue was one of his major concerns. He was worried that the rapidly expanding Soviet navy would try to control the "choke points" of the world such as the Panama Canal. He also quoted from Admiral Thomas Moorer stating that "a large majority of our war and contingency plans are totally infeasible unless one assumes that full and priority use of the Canal will be available."[7]

Both James Allen (D-Ala) and Sam Nunn (D-Ga) agreed on many defense issues, although they ended up on different sides of the ratification vote. Senator Allen believed that one of the major defects of the treaties was the failure to provide adequate defense during the twenty-three year term of the Canal Treaty. Senator Nunn was more concerned that the Neutrality Treaty did not assure the United States that it could continue to have military and defense bases within Panama after the year 2000.

Senator Nunn, however, in his speech on the Senate floor before he cast his vote to support the treaties, commented that without the treaties the risk to the Canal would be much greater than if the treaties were ratified. He claimed that the threat of guerrilla war, the possibility of a hostile local population, and the potential of internal domestic violence to the Canal would be very high if the treaties were not approved.[8] He further stated:

> I believe that rejection of the treaties by the Senate is likely to cause serious consequences. These consequences include attempts to disrupt the Canal. They include an expansion of U.S. Forces in the Canal Zone. They include a substantial increase in defense spending with no increase in overall U.S. power measured against our principal adversary. They include the emergence of new opportunities for the Soviet Union and its Cuban henchmen to fan the flames of anti-Americanism throughout Latin America and the Third World.[9]

The communist threat was raised a number of times during the hearings and debates. There was a continual barrage by opponents that either Cuba or Russia would benefit directly from the treaties and/or that General Torrijos was, if not a Communist himself, at least a sympathizer. Retired military officers like former chairman of the Joint Chiefs, Thomas H. Moorer, Gen. Maxwell Taylor, and Admiral Elmo R. Zumwalt Jr. maintained that the treaty would give the Cubans and the Russians a political and military advantage over the status quo.[10]

In contrast to the fears expressed by the opponents that the defense of the Canal would be weakened by the treaties, many military leaders on active duty, and especially those responsible for the direct defense of the Canal, argued that the treaties actually increased the defensibility of the Canal. Foremost among these Defense Department spokesman was Harold Brown, the Secretary of Defense. Secretary Brown stated: "I see three elements which together make up our national security concerns relating to the Canal. These are, first unimpeded use; second, effective operation; and finally, physical security of the Canal."[11] He went on to explain that all of these elements were enhanced by the new treaties. On the last issue — the physical security of the Canal — he commented: "Our armed forces now control and they will continue to control with overwhelming force, the sea approaches to the Canal, on both the Pacific and the Caribbean ends. This is not affected by the treaty.'"[12] The ability of the United States to defend the Canal against foreign threats will continue unabated, according to his testimony.

He was equally adamant that the treaties would reduce the potential within Panama for domestic violence and internal threats to the Canal. He stated that the problems of terrorism and guerrilla actions were far less under the new treaties than the status quo. He went on to say, "I am convinced that approval of these treaties will best provide for our national security.'"[13]

Unresolved defense issues after December 31, 1999 included the possibility for the U.S. to maintain at least one military base in Panama, the problem of priority passage for U.S. warships in time of emergency, and the problems of keeping the Canal open during internal disruption or political instability within Panama. In an attempt to resolve these issues, several reservations, conditions and amendments were introduced in the Senate.

Economic Issues

Economic issues were about the most varied aspect of the new treaties. They included such items as the cost of construction and maintenance of the Canal, the value of property purchased by the United States in the Zone, the value of military bases, defense costs, employee housing, and other such employee costs. They also included the question of tolls, and how much they could be increased without significantly reducing traffic, and how revenues from tolls should be distributed between Panama and the United States. Payments for services such as culinary water, sewage disposal, garbage collection, street maintenance, as well as health and mail services were also on the agenda. The transfer costs for control of the Canal and the implementation of the treaties were discussed. Numerous other economic issues pervaded the negotiations and the Senate debates.

The so-called give away of the Canal and all of its facilities under the treaty raised the most emotional of the economic issues. The State Department estimated that the original value of the Canal and its auxiliary buildings and machinery was roughly $1 billion, but their replacement value was over $8 billion.[14] This figure, when added to the value of other properties, defense bases and buildings in and around the Zone, made the economic costs appear much higher than they actually were. However, this figure does not reveal any of the economic and military advantages and benefits that the U.S had derived from the Canal and the military bases in Panama for over seventy years during which no significant amount of money was paid to recompense Panama. For example, although gross revenues for the Canal exceeded $250 million in 1977, only approximately

133

$2.3 million were paid to Panama that year. In contrast, the United Brands Fruit Company paid $15 million that same year to lease forty-seven square miles of land, while the rent-free Canal Zone covered over 647 square miles.[15] In other countries where the United States maintains military facilities, it must pay annual fees, rentals, provide military weapons, and in addition, it must leave buildings and other structures in place when they depart.

Congress was also concerned by implementation costs. The best estimates suggested that they would be somewhere around $1 billion. Congressman George Hansen (R-Idaho) however, held that they would be closer to $4 billion. Senator John Stennis (D-Miss) claimed that the loss to the U.S. Treasury would be between $1.0 and $3.4 billion.[16] The Senate and the House attempted to assure that all such payments would come from tolls and not from the U.S. taxpayer. They accomplished this by adding conditions to the treaties and such specific provisions to the implementation legislation.

Although questions were raised concerning the costs of public services and police protection for the new Canal area, Congress did little to modify this economic aspect. However, there was a great deal of debate on the $10 million contingency payment to be made to Panama when the Canal makes a profit. Amendments and conditions were proposed by the Senate to restrict or delete this concession from the treaty. The House also tried to prevent it from taking effect when formulating the implementation legislation. The provision however, was not deleted nor clarified on either occasion and continues to create misunderstanding and contention between Panama and the United States.

Other Issues

Several other issues also arose during the treaty-making process. Among these other issues were the improvement of relations between the United States and Latin America in general, the continuing general usability of the Canal given the growth in size of ships and the patterns of trade, the suspected differences between the Spanish versions of the Treaties and the English versions, the proposed sea-level canal, and the granting of military aid and technical assistance loans to Panama outside the treaties themselves. A number of nontreaty issues also arose such as the alleged bugging of the negotiations by the CIA, the supposed connection between General Torrijos's brother and drug traffic, suspected communism in Panama, the alleged corporate connections of negotiator Sol Linowitz, and myriad other such nontreaty accusations.

Congress Begins Deliberation

As stated in Chapter 2, the House tried to enter the stage early and influence any action taken on the Panama Canal. Actions by Congressmen Gene Snyder, Daniel Flood, and others from 1974 to 1977 were only a foreshadowing of the actions and attitudes that were to follow.

In 1975, 1976, and 1977, the House either considered or passed amendments to the State Department appropriations bill requiring that no money be spent to support treaty negotiations with Panama that might alter U.S. status there. The latest use of this tactic occurred in May 1977, when Congressman Robert K. Dorman (R-Calif) offered a similar amendment to the Foreign Relations Authorization Act of 1977-78. It stated that no funds could be used "... for the purpose of negotiating the surrender or relinquishment of the Canal Zone or the Panama Canal."[17] This amendment was subsequently defeated, and a compromise amendment was approved.

Opposition to negotiations took another tactic as six members of Congress and a private citizen initiated a suit in the federal courts to halt treaty negotiations on the grounds that only Congress, not the executive, could dispose of U.S. property and territory, citing article IV, Section 3, Clause 2 of the Constitution: "The Congress shall have Power to dispose of and make all needful Rules and Regulations respecting the Territory or other Property belonging to the United States . . ." In late May 1977, a federal court refused to issue a restraining order on the suit. On June 20, the Supreme Court dismissed the suit by allowing the lower courts refusal to stand.[18]

Committee Hearings

On July 25, 1977, the Senate Judiciary Subcommittee on Separation of Powers, chaired by Senator James Allen (D-Ala), began hearings on the legal and constitutional question mentioned above. Not to be outdone, the House Merchant Marine and Fisheries Subcommittee on the Panama Canal met the same day and began hearings on U.S. vital interests in Panama.[19] It is very unusual that hearings were held *before* the treaties were even completed. Both of these committees held subsequent hearings after the treaties were finished and signed.

On August 10, 1977, the U.S. negotiators announced that agreement on the treaties had been completed and that although the official texts were yet to be drafted, the United States and Panama now agreed on all major provisions of both treaties. This announcement triggered more action in both houses of Congress. Many individual congressmen and senators publicly announced their positions, but most senators chose to remain uncommitted. The first of forty-two senators began visits to Panama when three opposition senators, Thurmond, Helms, and Hatch left for Panama on August 18.

On September 16, 1977 before the treaties were officially submitted to the Senate for consideration, the Senate Intelligence Committee began to investigate reports that the United States had wiretapped the negotiations and that the Panamanians had discovered this and had in turn blackmailed the United States negotiators. By October 6, however, the investigation, which had proven nothing, disintegrated and treaty opponents began looking elsewhere for an explosive issue to kill the treaties. They were not long in coming up with a more convincing ploy. On October 13, 1977, Senator Robert Dole presented information to the Senate that implicated General Omar Torrijos's brother in the drug smuggling business in Panama. After special investigations and an unprecedented closed session of the Senate, this issue also faded into the background due to the lack of solid evidence.

In the meantime, the Senate Foreign Relations Committee, to which the treaties had been referred, began to hold their hearings on September 26. This committee held the most extensive hearings on the treaties, lasting for seventeen days, where sixteen administration witnesses testified and seventy-five congressional and public witnesses testified. The committee filled five volumes with testimony, transcripts, and supporting materials.

Before the hearing process was completed, numerous committees and subcommittees had participated in a total of forty-two days of hearings. In the House, the Panama Canal Subcommittee of the Merchant Marine and Fisheries Committee held hearings in July and November 1977. The full committee held its hearing in August 1977. The House International Relations Committee held hearings in September and October while the House Armed Services Committee held theirs in late October. In the Senate the Foreign Relations Committee held the most extensive hearings of all the committees from September 26 to October 1977 and resumed again in January 1978. The Senate Judiciary Subcommittee hearings in July, September, October, and November 1977. The Senate Armed Services Committee held the last series of hearings from January 24 to February 1, 1978.[20]

Referral to the Courts

During this time, two different law suits were filed in the federal courts by opponents to the treaties. On October 3, 1977, fifty-one — later to become sixty — members of the House of Representatives initiated a court action requesting that the courts require the House to play a role in the disposal of U.S. property in Panama and the Canal Zone. On October 13, Senators Helms, McClure, Thurmond, and Hatch, along with Con-

136

gressman Daniel Flood and the attorney generals of Idaho, Iowa, Louisiana, and Nebraska, and private citizens Mr. William Drummond and Mr. Sendak filed a similar suit claiming that Article IV, Section 3 of the Constitution required that the House participate in any disposal of U.S. property.[21] In May, June, and September 1977, the Supreme Court had dismissed similar suits.[22]

This issue was finally decided at the federal appeals level on April 6, 1978 in a 2 to 1 decision in *Edward v. Carter*.[23] The court held in this case that U.S. property could be ceded by a ratified treaty and that the House would have their chance for input on the issue during the implementation stage. On May 15, 1980, the Supreme Court refused to hear the case and allowed the lower court decision to stand.[24]

Although the courts finally settled this problem, this constitutional question became one of the most contentious issues in Congress concerning the treaties. Many congressmen and most of the opposition senators supported the concept that the House had to participate in the decision to transfer United States property in the Canal Zone. The opposition also believed that this tactic would kill the treaties as they were convinced that the House would never approve them. Many other senators, not necessarily opponents, were concerned with this constitutional question. A great amount of antagonism grew between the two houses of Congress over this issue. It frequently plagued the deliberations and debates on the Senate floor and flourished in the House until the implementation legislation on the treaties was finally passed in September of 1979.

Misinterpretations

Interpretation as to the meaning of the specific details of the treaties in each country was another major problem that emerged during this early period. After Panama and the United States signed the treaties in September 1977, each administration attempted to explain the treaties to their respective citizens in the most nationalistic terms possible, stressing concessions gained and minimizing compromises made in the negotiations. According to Secretary of State Cyrus Vance, we as well as the Panamanians were trying "to 'sell' the treaties to skeptical constituences." He went on to say that the Panamanians were ". . . trying to deflect domestic criticism in Panama, but in doing so, . . . had created a major problem for us in the Senate."[25] These campaigns to gain domestic support in one country were also transmitted by the news media to the other. This in turn raised suspicions that each nation was giving different interpretations to various aspects of the treaties. These suspicions led to the accusations that the English and Spanish versions were different or that the other side had negotiated in bad faith. A good example of this problem was stated by

137

Senator Robert Griffin (R-Mich). During the floor debate on very critical issues of Canal defense, he said:

> The chief Panamanian negotiator Dr. Romulo Escobar, declared publicly that: "The draft neutrality pact . . . does not make the U.S. a guarantor of (the Canal's) neutrality . . . ." Panamanian spokesman have insisted that the United States would be able to respond militarily only if a foreign power attacked or threatened the Canal. Just as often, our own negotiators and others have publicly asserted that the United States has the right to protect the neutrality of the Canal against any threat, including a Panamanian threat.[26]

These types of claims and counterclaims led to misunderstandings, to harsh statements by U.S. opponents, and to demonstrations by treaty opponents in Panama. In an effort to clarify some of these misunderstandings, a joint statement was mutually negotiated between President Carter and General Torrijos on October 14, 1977, an event described in Chapter 4 as a turning point in the ratification campaign. The Statement of Understanding dealt with the defense of the Canal and priority passage of warships as these items were related to the Neutrality Treaty. This statement eventually was incorporated into the treaties through the amendment process on the floor of the Senate and was later accepted by Panama as a clarification of meaning and not as an alteration of the original treaties.[27]

The Senate Foreign Relations Committee

While all of these activities were taking place, the Senate Foreign Relations Committee continued to hold hearings. On January 25, 1978, the public hearings were completed, and after three more days of internal hearings and a mark-up session, the final committee report was agreed upon, by a 14 to 1 vote.

The committee submitted their report to the full Senate on February 3, 1978. It included the admission that they were following an unusual procedure due to the unique nature of, and the strong opposition to, the treaties.

> Because the Committee firmly believes that ratification of the treaties will best serve our national interest, it agrees to depart from standard practice and to include its recommendations in the Committee's report instead of in the resolutions of ratification . . . In the Committee's opinion, the likelihood of securing this vote (the ⅔'s necessary to approve) will be enhanced substantially by permitting the full Senate to work its will on the treaties and the resolution of ratification without any formal encumbrances on them.[28]

The committee then recommended that two amendments be added to the Neutrality Treaty incorporating the Statement of Understanding into the treaties, and it further recommended four understandings to clarify some of the vague wording of the treaties. With these changes, the committee then recommended the adoption of the resolutions of ratification and defined the treaties' major objective.

> The basic purpose of the Treaty concerning the Permanent Neutrality and Operation of the Panama Canal (the Neutrality Treaty) and the Panama Canal Treaty is to assure the continued use and neutrality of the Panama Canal. In fulfilling this purpose, the two treaties serve and protect the vital interests of the United States.[29]

The report also recognized the fundamental nature of the treaties that had required significant compromises and concessions. It asked the Senate to consider the treaties within this reality. "In requesting this support, the Committee urges that one consideration be kept uppermost in mind — the pending agreements are first, foremost and fundamentally, political documents, based on political decisions and grounded in political logic."[30]

What the committee was trying to tell everyone was a basic fact of political reality. Treaties such as these are results of long negotiations between two sovereign powers. In this case, negotiations that had proceeded over a fourteen year period. The final product of this long process was one that had to give concessions as well as receive them.

These treaties included aspects that were offensive to Panamanians and other concessions that were equally offensive to the United States. In a very real sense, the treaties gave Panama about as much as the United States could give and still obtain serious ratification consideration in the U.S. Senate. On the other hand, the Panamanians gave up about as many concessions as they could and still obtain approval in Panama through an honest plebiscite and at the same time quell the ultranationalists who wanted the United States out of Panama immediately.

The committee was well in tune with these problems of nationalism in both countries and tried to make the Senate aware of them.

> Overhanging and interlacing all of these issues and sub-issues is a fervent nationalism. Panamanian nationalism on one side and American nationalism of the other. From the United States comes the rallying cry, "We bought it. We built it. It's ours. It's as American as the Liberty Bell or the Fourth of July." From Panama comes a different rallying cry, "Yanqui, go home. An end to Colonialism. Freedom and Independence now." The nationalist sentiment on both sides is as understandable as it is potentially dangerous . . .[31]

139

This nationalistic sentiment clouded the entire debate in the Senate on the treaties, and later the debates in the House on the implementation legislation. It was also to arise continually in Panama as the Panamanians heard the Senate debates translated into Spanish over their own radios. Expressions of nationalism were, however, more evident on the floor of the Senate, than on the streets of Panama.

U.S. government officials, particularly opposition senators and congressmen, made extreme nationalistic comments openly, and they continually depreciated and disparaged Panama and the Panamanian people. There was no parallel activity on the part of Panamanian government officials. This is surprising because the Panama Canal and Zone created the most nationalistic issues in Panamanian politics and had done so ever since the construction of the Canal.

The Senate Goes to Panama

Nearly one half of the Senate membership traveled to Panama to explore the Canal, the Zone, and the surrounding area; to meet with Panamanian officials and Canal administrators; and to obtain information to use in the debates or to help themselves decide which way to vote. These trips also served a rather unique and innovative function in the treaty-making process. In some instances, such as with the group led by Howard Baker, the senators actually engaged in a second phase of treaty negotiations. The senators worked out deals and compromises with General Torrijos in order to improve the chances the Senate would pass the treaties. Senator Baker clearly revealed this in his January 1978 report to the Senate.[32] Senator Baker explained to General Torrijos that the treaties were in real trouble. In response, the General agreed that if the Statement of Understanding were added to the Neutrality Treaty by amendment, then Panama would still accept the treaties without requiring additional negotiations or a second plebiscite. In turn, Senator Baker indicated that he would support the treaties with such a change.[33]

President Carter also recorded the results of this trip in his diary on January 16, 1978. He wrote: "I met early with Senator Baker, who wanted to give me a report on his trip to Panama, Mexico, Colombia, Brazil, and Venezuela. He's decided to support the Panama Canal Treaties."[34]

Other groups of senators went to Panama to reaffirm their own convictions for or against the treaties. Others went to answer questions they had and to gain more insight into the political and economic realities of Panama and the Canal. Ten of the fifteen members of the Senate Foreign Relations Committee were among those who visited Panama and also met with General Torrijos.

The turning point for Senate Majority Leader Robert Byrd, like that of Senator Baker, seemed to occur after his trip to Panama. Before the trip, he remained uncommitted to the treaties, but after his November 1977 visit, his commitment to the treaties crystallized. For the first time, he indicated to the administration that he would lead the treaties through the Senate. The majority of the members of the Foreign Relations Committee who traveled to Panama were also influenced positively by the trip. President Carter later claimed that many uncommitted senators had been "won over" by their trips to Panama and their meetings with General Torrijos.[35]

Even before the treaties were signed, groups of senators began to coalesce on both sides of the issue. Before debate began on the Senate floor, the *Christian Science Monitor* polled and reported on November 9 that fifty-one senators supported the treaties, thirty-three opposed, and sixteen undecided.[36] A few days later, Senator Dole claimed that there were fifty-five in favor, twenty against, and twenty-five undecided.[37] Later in November, a UPI poll counted only twenty-four senators committed to approval, while twenty-three were committed to opposition and four were leaning towards opposition. The UPI poll listed a total of thirty-seven who were still uncommitted, including much of the leadership on both sides of the aisle.[38] Despite the great disparity in these results, each poll indicated that there was a core of senators on each side of the question and that those opposed were much closer to the thirty-four votes they needed to block the treaties than the supporters were to mustering the sixty-seven supporters they needed for passage.

Mobilization of the Public

Both the opposition and the White House began a campaign to influence public opinion and thereby bring pressure to bear on the Senate to reject or pass the treaties. The "media blitz" of the opposition was well funded by various conservative organizations. Over $1.4 million were raised by the American Conservative Union and the Conservative Caucus alone.[39] Their campaign was aimed at mobilizing the more than 50 percent of American adults who opposed the treaties. They sent out 4 million pieces of mail requesting assistance to prevent the passage of the treaties.[40]

The White House had a much harder task. It had to try to educate the people and alter their opinions. Only about 30 percent of the public supported the treaties during much of the process.[41] Of this, President Carter said: "I had to do something to seize the initiative, because the antitreaty forces had been active for more than three years. . . . During the fall of 1977, I spent a lot of my time planning carefully how to get Senate votes."[42] The administration task force and other proponents made more than 1500 appearances throughout the nation in order to win support for the treaties and reduce public pressure in uncommitted senators so that they could vote for the treaties.

The opposition was more effective in its mobilization efforts. Hundreds of thousands of letters and telegrams were received by the members of the Senate. Even at best, the mail ran 2 to 1 against the treaties and in some instances it was as high as 100 to 1 against.[43] In many cases, the letters were extreme in their comments and occasionally they were quite threatening. Senator McIntyre revealed that some letters "were very vitriolic and abusive" and some charged him and other treaty supporters with treason and promised severe retribution.[44]

In January 1978, President Carter made the passage of the Canal treaties one of his principle goals for the New Year. He commented in his State of the Union message that approval would "directly contribute to the economic well being and security of the United States."[45] The president went on to add that our relationship with Latin America would improve and that we needed to demonstrate our good faith to the world.

An ABC poll taken after the speech indicated that if two key provisions were added to the treaties — the U.S. right to defend the Canal after 2000 and priority passage for U.S. warships — that Senate support might increase. The poll showed that with these additions fifty-two senators would vote for the treaties; nineteen would vote against them, and twenty-seven were still undecided.[46] This poll had the fewest senators in opposition to it.

Just a few days before the treaties went to the Senate floor for debate, the Senate Armed Services Committee held their hearings on the defense, maintenance, administration, and operation of the Canal. The hearings were held on January 24, 31, and on February 1, 1978. They called thirteen witnesses, most of whom were military and Defense Department personnel to give their expert opinions. This was the last set of hearings before debate on the floor of the Senate. During the hearing process, three full committees in the House and one subcommittee had held hearings on the treaties, while in the Senate four full committees and one subcommittee had held hearings. Hence the Canal hearings were among the most extensive in recent congressional history.

Senate Deliberation and Major Resolutions

Senate debate on the treaties opened on February 8, 1978. Senator James Allen, a brilliant parliamentarian, posed seventeen parliamentary procedural inquiries to presiding officer Vice President Mondale even before debate on substantive questions began.[47] For over fifty years, debate had taken place on the ratification resolution of a whole treaty and the article-by-article approach had been discontinued. Senator Allen, however insisted on reinstituting the "Committee of the Whole Senate" procedure in order that each article of the treaties could be debated and amended on a one-by-one basis. Unanimous consent of the Senate was required to bypass the article-by-article treatment of the treaties, which, of course, Senator Allen refused to give. In his words, "Mr. President, I will object to any consideration other than the consideration that the rule requires that they be considered article by article."[48]

Having won this battle, Senator Allen attempted another procedural tactic. The Foreign Relations Committee and the Senate leadership scheduled debate on the Neutrality Treaty first. It was the least controversial and had the best chance of passage. It also provided for present and future defense of the Canal even after Panama gained control in the year 2000. Senator Allen and other opposition senators tried to reverse the order of consideration by having the Canal treaty come to the floor first. However, they failed in this effort.

Having disposed of these procedural matters, the Senate began its longest foreign policy debate since the debate over the Treaty of Versailles after World War I. There were thirty-eight days of continuous Senate debate that practically excluded consideration of any other policy problems or issues. While the debate was going on, no committee was able to meet for more than two hours after the debating began.[49]

President Carter indicated that a similar phenomenon also occurred at the White House. He stated that "the Panama issue had almost everything else bogged down."[50] In the last few days before debate ended, the situation became even worse. Many varied and extremely important issues had to be placed lower on the agenda. He said, "It's hard to concentrate on anything except Panama."[51]

Although many changes were proposed during the debating process, they may be placed into three major categories. First, there were the changes to improve or clarify the treaties. Second, there were changes designed to appeal to constituents and reduce their antagonism to the treaties. Third, changes were proposed in order to destroy the treaties. Some senators who supported the treaties but wished to reduce constituent opposition offered changes and reservations to appeal to audiences back home. Others who wanted to support the treaties but felt that there were flaws and ambiguities in them, submitted changes. Many of these first two types of additions were approved and were finally added to the treaty. The third major type of change was presented by those who opposed the treaties on principle and were thus determined to prevent their adoption. This group of senators, led by Senator James Allen, offered scores of "killer" amendments proposed to make the treaties unacceptable to Panama. Before

143

the end of the thirty-eight days, these three groups of senators had proposed and submitted for consideration 145 amendments and amendments to amendments, twenty-six reservations, eighteen understandings, and three declarations. Of these 192 proposed changes, the Senate actually voted on eighty-eight of them.[52]

An interesting tactic was used by the opponents in order to increase their chances of winning approval of one of the "killer" amendments. Many of these changes were proposed on the floor and were not written up and printed beforehand. This prevented the treaty supporters from preparing arguments in advance, and in some cases, it reduced their ability to see the "hooker" in the proposed change.

In order to combat this tactic, the treaty proponents countered with their own strategy. Four special staff members, including a representative from the State Department and another from Defense were placed in a small private room in the Capital. They listened to the debate on the radio and senatorial pages delivered written copies of amendments as soon as they were proposed on the floor. In this manner, the special staff could react, analyze, and suggest arguments and rebuttals for supporters. These materials were then sent back to the Senate floor via the pages. In this fashion, the proponents were able to counter some of the more subtle charges proposed by the treaty opponents.[53] This strategy also illustrates how cross-cutting coalitions can cooperate in order to succeed.

In addition, the administration placed Warren Christopher, deputy secretary of state, in a position to coordinate with Senate leaders in order to assist them in blocking the "killer amendments." Christopher also had a direct channel to the U.S. ambassador in Panama, William Jordan. General Torrijos assigned several Panamanians to work and coordinate with Ambassador Jordan to assure that changes in the treaties would be acceptable in Panama.[54]

The treaty proponents, in addition, used parliamentary tactics against the opposition. Instead of trying to defeat many of the unwanted changes and so-called "killer" amendments, the proponents would request a vote to table them. Although, this standard parliamentary tactic allows the change to be reconsidered, it seldom is; thus, the proposal would be defeated without a direct vote against it. This procedure was used quite effectively, much to the distress of opposition senators who desired that treaty supporters go on the record and later pay a political price for that support.

Over fifty-five amendments and amendments to amendments were voted on by the Senate. Of these, only the two which were sponsored by the Senate leadership were adopted. These two amendments incorporated the Carter-Torrijos Statement of Understanding into the Neutrality Treaty. In

144

addition to these amendments, over thirty conditions, reservations, and understandings were voted on, and twenty-one of them were adopted.

It has often been noted that this activity regarding the Panama Canal Treaties was one of the most active roles of advice and consent that the Senate had played, since rejecting the Treaty of Versailles in 1919-1920. It was through this procedure that the Senate played a significant role in changing the treaties, although many of these changes were not substantial. Furthermore, this role can be seen as beneficial, since many of those who finally voted for the treaties indicated that they would not have supported them if the changes had not been made.[55]

Senatorial Changes in the Treaties

Of all the treaty changes, those related to defense were among the most critical. The only two amendments to be approved by the Senate and attached to the treaties were the aforementioned leadership amendments. These two amendments were cosponsored by Senators Byrd and Baker and over seventy-five other senators. The first amendment provided that each country could defend the Canal against any threat to it or to the Canal's neutrality in accordance with each nation's constitutional process. On March 9, 1978, this amendment was adopted by a vote of 84 to 5.

The second amendment, although not itself directly concerned with the defense of the canal, was related to the concept of U.S. military needs. This change in the treaty language allowed for emergency and expeditious passage through the Canal by U.S. and Panamanian warships and auxiliary vessels, which permits such vessels to proceed to the head of the line.

DeConcini Reservation

The change that caused the greatest concern to the senate leadership and also brought the strongest reaction from Panama was not the passage of these two amendments, nor was it the approval of a so-called killer amendment, since none were passed. Instead, it was the DeConcini reservation[56] which almost killed both treaties. This reservation provided that

> In the event the Canal is closed or its operations are interfered with, that the United States and Panama would each independently have the right to take the steps it deemed necessary, including *the use of military force in Panama*, to reopen the Canal or to restore its operation.[57] (emphasis added)

The controversial and explosive language including "the use of military force in Panama" was the problem. This reservation was added to the Neutrality Treaty in the Senate by a vote of 75 to 23 on March 16, the same day that the Neutrality Treaty was approved.

Everyone blamed others for the strong language of the reservation. Some personnel in the State Department blamed other State Department personnel and the White House, the White House blamed the inability of the Senate leadership to deliver the sixty-seven needed votes, DeConcini's staff and others blamed the State Department and the Senate leadership blamed the White House and its staff.

According to State Department critics such as Franck and Weisband, the State Department was so relieved that they had convinced DeConcini to introduce his change as a reservation instead of an amendment that they failed to see the explosive nature of the language.[58] State Department personnel claimed that despite approval by their colleagues in State, Robert Beckel and Warren Christopher, that other treaty staff members in the department were not consulted before the reservation was approved. According to this source, if the legal counsel or the negotiating team had been brought into the discussion with DeConcini, the interventionist language may never had been tolerated, either as a condition or an amendment.[59] Some White House critics claimed that the White House itself was to blame, as Vice President Mondale and others had also been involved in the negotiations with DeConcini. The president, himself, had also given DeConcini his approval.[60] Some Senate staffers indicated that the White House had not consulted the Senate leadership and they claimed that the concessions to DeConcini were not necessary because Robert Byrd had the necessary number of votes without DeConini and his reservation.[61] On the other hand, the White House did not accept this claim and contended that with less than one week to go before the vote on the Neutrality Treaty, they might be as seven votes short of the sixty-seven needed to pass the treaty.[62]

The White House and staff defended itself from these attacks and claimed that they had had numerous contacts with DeConcini and his staff. They claimed to have warned him that the language of the reservation was offensive and probably was unacceptable to Panama. Members of the White House staff suspected that DeConcini had one or two motives for the severe wording of the amendment and his evident unwillingness to alter it or compromise on the Senate floor. Either DeConcini was trying to impress his constituency and take some of the heat out of the opposition forces in his state, or he really was trying to kill the treaties through this subtle and less than frontal attack upon them. Regardless of his motives, some White House people believed that DeConcini exactly knew what he was doing and that the language of the amendment was not a result of naivete and ignorance but was deliberately offensive and unacceptable to Panama.[63]

President Carter also made similar claims. He claimed that Senator Byrd had admitted that he did not have sufficient votes to pass the treaties. Even by March 14 — two days before the vote — the president still did not have the votes and he was convinced that Byrd did not have them either.[64] Regarding the language of the reservation, Carter is even more direct: "... we tried to induce DeConcini to delete the words 'in Panama,' but he adamantly refused. Two or three other Senators informed me that their votes, too, were contingent on this language being adopted. We finally yielded to save the treaty."[65]

The White House staff claimed it was aware of the problems this change would create with the Panamanians. According to President Carter and the White House staff itself, DeConcini had been completely intransigent. Therefore, according to them, in order to secure passage of the Neutrality Treaty on March 16, the DeConcini reservation had to be approved despite the offensive language and Panamanian opposition.

After other State Department staff members and the Panamanian ambassador to the United States[66] saw the reservation language, Warren Christopher, deputy secretary of state, and the White House realized the impact that the explosive response its language might cause in Panama. One day before the vote —March 15— they tried again and again to work out a last-minute change with the Senate leadership. But still DeConcini refused to alter the wording. General Torrijos was so upset by the wording of the reservation that he called President Carter on March 15 to discuss the problem, but the call did little to placate the General or the Panamanians.[67] As previously mentioned, the DeConcini reservation was approved by a vote of 75 to 23. Later that same day, the Neutrality Treaty was also approved. Support for the reservation included both opponents who hoped to thereby kill the treaties and by proponents who hoped to convince the uncommitted senators to vote with them.

Not only did the language of this reservation threaten Panama's ability to accept the treaties, but the negotiation with DeConcini by the State Department leadership and the White House nearly caused Majority Leader Byrd to lose some of the early supporters of the treaties. Few White House concessions had been given to these early supporters despite the fact that many of them were being highly criticized in their home states. Yet, the White House went out of its way to placate the junior senator from Arizona, while ignoring the political needs of many others. This may have been a mistaken tactic, and it could have destroyed the treaties if one of the early supporters had changed because of this and decided not to vote for the Neutrality Treaty.[68]

Public and official reaction from Panama was restrained and slow in coming. One of the reasons for this was the skill with which Romulo Escobar, who had been Panama's chief negotiator on the treaties, went to the Panamanians and requested calm and reasoned reflection on the issue until the problem could be resolved in Washington. He was also well

147

known in Panama for Marxist leanings and as an ardent nationalist. These left-wing and nationalist credentials gave his statement credibility, and Panama remained momentarily calm.[69] But by the end of March, the Panamanian's reaction could no longer be restrained and it became vehement and extremely critical. Panamanians of all political persuasions perceived the reservation as a direct threat to their sovereignty, and an imperialistic and a very offensive tactic. General Torrijos said that he did not believe that the United States would expect Panama to exchange its sovereignty to get the new treaties.[70]

Before the passage of this reservation, experts suggested the principal issues that the Senate would debate on the second Panama Canal Treaty would involve defense questions, military bases, the transfer of property, and implementation costs. Although the debates dealt with these issues, they were constantly clouded by the DeConcini language and Panama's reaction to it.

The Senate leadership, the State Department, and the White House concentrated their efforts on working out a compromise reservation to the Panama Canal Treaty that would soften the DeConcini wording without losing Senate votes and at the same time make it palatable to the Panamanians.[71]

This action, in some instances, placed the Senate leadership in direct negotiations with the Panamanians. Some of the frantic negotiations between the United States and Panama also included the good offices of a Washington lawyer, and former assistant secretary of state for Inter-American Affairs, William D. Rogers.[72]

By the end of March, pressures in Panama against the reservation began to gather strength. From the first of April until the passage of the Canal treaty on April 18, the newspapers of Panama discussed the DeConcini reservation far more than any other issue, and always in a negative manner. Groups and political parties which had heretofore supported the treaties began to withdraw their support.[73]

The reservation provoked political, business, and religious groups on the left, in the center, and on the right to call upon the Torrijos government to reject the treaties unless the reservation was revoked or neutralized. Students demonstrated against it, denounced it, and warned that if it were imposed upon Panama, it would "bathe our people in blood and mourning.'"[74]

General Torrijos went so far as to send letters to 115 heads of state throughout the world and to the secretary general of the United Nations revealing his deep concern over the reservation and its implications on Panamanian sovereignty.[75] He also threatened to hold a new plebiscite on the treaties if the situation were not altered. He indicated that he did not believe that another plebiscite would obtain approval.[76]

Between March 16 and April 18, the Senate leadership with William Rogers and Panamanian Ambassador Gabriel Lewis Galindo were able to propose a reservation to the Panama Canal Treaty which would neutralize the DeConcini reservation. During this delicate act of diplomacy, the White House stayed out of the negotiations and the Senate leadership was the focal group.[77] Senator DeConcini, while defending his reservation, aided in the negotiations with the Senate leadership to find an acceptable solution to this problem. He claimed that it was never his intention to kill the treaties.[78] When the final compromise was worked out, he supported it and helped to work for Senate acceptance of it.

The compromise stated that any U.S. effort to reopen the Canal or return it to operation would not be used as an excuse for intervention in the internal affairs of Panama or to interfere with its ''political independence or sovereign integrity.'' This new resolution was adopted by the Senate with a vote of 73 to 27 on April 18. This language was accepted by Panama and was sufficient for the Senate to still insure the passage of the Canal Treaty which took place later that same day.

Other Changes

The Nunn-Talmadge condition was the other defense oriented change added to the Neutrality Treaty. It stated that nothing in the treaties would preclude the United States and Panama from making other agreements that might allow the United States to maintain military bases in Panama or to station troops there after the year 2000.[79]

Nondefense changes added to the treaties included such things as battle monuments and cemetery clarifications, prisoner exchanges, limitation on toll increases, the right of each country to waive its authority to block the other from building a sea-level canal with a third country, a denial of a commitment on the part of the United States to provide economic assistance to Panama, and some procedural clarifications. A couple of other minor changes related to economic and local maintenance services were also made. One very important procedural change was added by Senator Brooke of Massachusetts. It stated that the implementation of the ratification of the treaties could not be effective before March 31, 1979, but would be no later than October 1, 1979. This was done to allow the administration time to introduce implementation legislation to the Congress, and allow Congress time to deliberate and alter that policy as it might see fit. As it turned out, this was a critical time period, and Congress took advantage of the extended deadline, as it did not approve implementation legislation until September 26, 1979.

Having made these many changes, a majority of senators were ready to support the treaties. But even the day before the final vote on the Panama Canal Treaty, no one was certain that the proponents could muster the sixty-seven votes needed. It will be recalled that the Neutrality Treaty had been approved with only a one-vote margin (68 to 32), with all 100 senators voting. Another month of debate on the Panama Canal Treaty followed that vote and finally on April 18, 1978, the final vote was taken and the second treaty was approved by the same 68 to 32 vote.

Prior to the final vote, the Senate leadership and the White House were concerned that four of the senators who had voted for the Neutrality Treaty might not vote for the Panama Canal Treaty. Senators James Abourezk and S.I. Hayakawa were concerned about nontreaty issues. Senator Abourezk was unhappy about energy legislation and the White House effort to deregulate natural gas prices and some other legislative procedural matters. Senator Hayakawa, on the other hand, was unhappy about the president's policy decisions on the Neutron Bomb and the SALT talks. Senators Howard Cannon and Edward Brooke were concerned about specific elements of the treaty. The administration and the Senate leadership agreed to consider their proposed changes, which were minor and were eventually approved.[80] The deals made to win these senators back, led Senator William Scott to say "it was disgusting how the leadership was accepting proposed amendments in an obvious effort to win last minute votes for the treaty."[81] Nevertheless, Senator Robert Byrd admitted that during this last count, there were no votes to spare.[82]

President Carter, after winning Senator Cannon back to the support of the treaties, still was unsure about the final vote. He recalled: "All during the day we were anticipating massive violence in Panama if the treaties were defeated. When the vote started at 6:00, we were *finally* sure that we would have all three of the doubtful senators with us . . ."[83]

Accusations aimed at the White House about vote trading began as early as February 1978. Some senators were pressured while others were given the chance to discuss their favorite projects with the president.[84] After the Neutrality Treaty vote, Senator Packwood accused the president of making deals to win votes for the treaty.[85] According to another source, Senator Talmadge obtained an administration switch on a $2.3 billion emergency farm bill, Senator DeConcini was promised that the government would purchase $250 million worth of copper, and Senators Jennings Randolph and Huddleston received more general promises.[86] Additional IOU's were reportedly given to a number of other senators as well.[87]

Despite these accusations and rumors, Senate staffers who were interviewed for part of this study consistently denied that any of these deals were made, or if they were, they really did not make much difference.[88] Douglas

150

Bennett, assistant secretary of state for congressional relations, also claimed that not one vote was decided on issues not directly related to the treaties and that no significant vote trading existed.[89] As the debate progressed, the White House ignored many of the original treaty supporters; earlier, it had claimed that it would not make deals. As pressure built and as time grew short, the inability of the White House to play politics skillfully and to give the original supporters some type of political rewards or at least recognition nearly jeopardized the treaties. The perception, whether correct or not, that many last-minute deals were made to sway the uncommitted, and angered those who had supported the treaties all along.[90]

The vote taken on April 18, 1978, on the Resolution of Ratification of the Panama Canal Treaty did not end congressional consideration of the treaties. The implementation legislation, which is analyzed in Chapter 6, still had to be introduced into both houses of Congress, where the House would have the opportunity to deliberate and resolve this policy in its own due time. This would give the House members their chance to react to the treaties and to exact their revenge on the Senate and the White House.

The Senatorial Actors

The major senatorial actors consisted of three general groups. The first group included the strong proponents of the treaties and the Senate leadership who were committed to treaty passage. The second major group was composed of the opponents who were determined that the treaties were a threat to United States national interests and were determined to prevent approval. A third major category included the senators who were really undecided; nevertheless, some took active roles in the debates and in proposing changes to the treaties. Many other senators were not active on either side of the issue, and remained relatively uncommitted throughout most of the process. As earlier stated in this chapter, close to 50 percent of the Senate supported the treaties soon after they were signed. Approximately 20 percent were opposed to the treaties from the beginning to the end. The remaining 30 percent maintained various levels of commitment, some of whom did not decide until just before the final votes were taken.

Treaty Supporters

Even before negotiations were completed, four important senators indicated their support for treaty negotiations in February 1977. Senators Hubert Humphrey (D-Minn), Jacob Javits (R-NY), John Sparkman (D-Ala), and Clifford Case (R-NJ) expressed their support for a successful conclusion of the negotiations as soon as possible.[91]

151

When the treaties finally made it to the Senate floor, however, Senators Robert Byrd and Howard Baker were the ones who played the most important roles for the proponents. Senator Byrd helped to head off situations that could have prevented passage of the treaties. He was forced to negotiate directly with the Panamanians over the DeConcini reservation; he also worked with the White House staff in their efforts to obtain support from key senators and provided suggestions for building public support.

Senator Baker was able to convince a number of Republicans to support the treaties who otherwise would not have. He negotiated directly with General Torrijos over the inclusion of the Statement of Understanding into the treaties. He and Senator Byrd cosponsored the two leadership amendments to the Neutrality Treaty to accomplish it. Without Senator Baker's leadership and ability, it is doubtful that the treaties could have been approved. The president and the White House and staff were aware that Baker's support was essential for treaty passage, but it was difficult for them to work with the leader of the opposition party, and a potential challenger who could run against the president in 1980. It was therefore difficult to keep constant communications open. They did not consult with him on some of the major issues, and they could not offer him much political or moral support. Some State Department advisors and Senate staffers believed that the White House had not treated Senator Baker with the care and attention he deserved. White House staffers countered that they did all they could within the framework of the two-party system and the separation of powers.[92] This illustrates how difficult it is to cross party lines, coordinate institutions, and work with your potential political opponent. President Carter was thus caught in this political dilemma.

Despite this dilemma, Carter had this to say about Byrd and Baker: "After several weeks of our working closely with [them] . . . both endorsed the treaties in mid-January, giving us our biggest boost. They were formidable allies on the Senate floor, and their support made it easier for other doubtful or timid senators to join our forces."[93]

The floor leaders for the debate were Senators Frank Church (D-Idaho) and Paul Sarbanes (D-Md). Although Senator John Sparkman was chairman of the Senate Foreign Relations Committee and had already indicated his support for the treaties, for health and other reasons he assigned these other senators to manage the floor debate for the proponents. Frank Church played a very active and vocal role. He participated extensively in the debates on many of the major issues and made many of the tabling motions to defeat the oppositions amendments. On the other hand, Paul Sarbanes played a more subdued role. Through his dedication and his thorough examination of the issues he became a central figure in the hearings and the debates. His consistent work earned praise from Senator Robert Byrd and

152

other leaders. Senators Mike Gravel (D-Alaska), Ernest Hollings (D-SC), Jacob Javits (R-NY), Edward Muskie (D-Me), and George McGovern (D-SC), also contributed to the proponents tasks and the debates. Senator Hollings is a good example of an interested supporter who received little credit for his role from either the White House or the press. He produced a newsletter for his constituents explaining why he supported the treaties, that was said to be the best produced in the Senate.[94] He participated in the debates and gave reasoned, well organized speeches favoring the treaties. Unfortunately for the proponents, Senator Hubert Humphrey died on January 13, 1978. This was a significant loss to their ranks, but Muriel Humphrey stepped in gallantly to finish her husband's term and strongly supported the treaties.

Outside the Senate, the proponents received some very influential support for the treaties from a surprising source. While members of the Senate Foreign Relations Committee were visiting Panama, they attended a luncheon given by General Torrijos. The surprise guest was actor John Wayne, who was familiar with Panama and was an old acquaintance of General Torrijos. After the meeting, Wayne's public support for the treaties gave them more credibility with the conservatives. He wrote several letters to the Senate and spoke out in favor of the treaties on many occasions. In one letter to Senator Humphrey in October 1977, Wayne stated:

. . . I have carefully studied the Treaty, and I support it based on my belief that America looks always to the future and that our people have demonstrated qualities of justice and reason for 200 years. . . . The new Treaty modernizes an outmoded relation with a friendly and hospitable country. It also solves an international question with our other Latin American neighbors, and finally the Treaty protects and legitimates fundamental interests and desires of our Country.[95]

In another letter to Senator Charles Percy in January 1978, Wayne took opponents to task for their negative comments on Panama and its leader.

I am embarrassed by the political rhetoric and abuse to our neighboring country, which regardless of internal political turmoil, at all times has been our most friendly ally. It is certainly not deserving of the inconsiderate and fallacious comments made by our prominent politicians.[96]

Treaty Opponents

Treaty opponents, like the whole Senate, may be broken into three groups. One group included those who did not favor the treaties, but took only minor roles in the hearings and debates. The second group was opposed only specific weaknesses and ambiguities in the treaties. However, some of the senators in this group were eventually persuaded to vote

153

for the treaties because of the reservations and clarifications that were added. The third group of senators adamantly opposed the treaties both as a concept and as a reality. They believed that the treaties were fundamentally flawed and that under no condition should the United States give up the control of the Canal Zone, relinquish the exercise of sovereignty, or turn operations of the canal over to Panama. The solid core of this group was composed of the leaders of the active opposition who were determined to kill the treaties.

The first group of the opposition was not very active and did little except vote against the treaties. For example, Senator Wendell Ford(D-Ky) reportedly had little knowledge or experience in international affairs and was not well informed on the treaties. He was an example of many other senators whose specialities lay mostly in domestic affairs. He believed that the costs for implementation would be excessive and that the administration had tried to deceive the Senate about those costs; he therefore voted against the treaties.[97]

Senators Abourezk, Cannon, Hayakawa, DeConcini, Randolph, and Zorinsky were representative of the senators from the second group. Most remained uncommitted until the vote was finally taken. Some voted for the treaties and some against. Three of these senators voted for the Neutrality Treaty yet threatened not to vote for the second treaty. Of those who voted against the treaties, some came very close to changing their vote at the last minute. It had been said that Jennings Randolph (D-WVa) would have voted for the treaties if his vote had been needed.[98]

Senator Edward Zorinsky (D-Neb) epitomizes the senator who remained uncommitted to the end. He apparently supported the concept of the treaties but had some specific problems with them, and he was also being very strongly pressured from constituents at home. Senator Zorinsky maintained an uncommitted posture throughout the whole debate. The senator was contacted by both sides and his vote was sought with considerable persistence. The news media paid careful attention to him and covered his case in more depth than nearly any one else.[99] According to his staff, the senator tried to remain open and objective until the final vote was taken. He studied the facts and the debates. He primarily objected to the treaties because there was no guarantee for military bases in Panama after the year 2000. His vote would also have cost him critical support in Nebraska. It was one of the most important issues to surface there in years, and Zorinsky received very strong antitreaty sentiment from his constituency. Although he understood the Panamanian side of the sovereignty issue and strongly preferred improved relationships with Latin America, he believed that the Canal was so important to the United States both economically and for defense purposes, that he ultimately rejected the treaties.[100]

154

Out of the third group of senators came the real leaders of the opposition who were against the whole idea of the treaties and against altering the status quo in the Zone. They held that the waterway was too important to the United States to be defended or controlled by anyone else. They used the argument that we bought it, we built it, we owned it, and it will always be ours. This group used a number of sophisticated strategies in order to block the treaties. Their favorite ploy was to introduce a "killer" amendment in popular and descriptive language that did not appear to be capable of destroying the treaties. They also introduced many amendments in handwritten form in order to catch the proponents by surprise. These activities led Senator Church to say on one occasion that this looked like a "Godfather tactic": "I'll make him an offer he can't refuse."[101] Although some of these amendments received significant support, none were approved and most were rejected by more than thirty-four senators, the number required to block the treaties in the final vote.

Senator James Allen (D-Ala) was the principal spokesman for this group. He received assistance from several colleagues. Senator Paul Laxalt (R-Nev) who organized and participated in the "truth squad," which traveled throughout the country mobilizing public opposition to the treaties, was also a leading opponent. He was joined by Senators Robert Griffin (R-Mich), Orrin Hatch (R-Utah), Jesse Helms (R-NC) and Robert Dole (R-Ks). All were adamantly opposed to the treaties and participated in the debate on almost every issue. Each one also had a specific aspect of the treaties that they attacked with extra vigor.

Senator Dole emphasized several points in opposing the treaties, including a reduction of payments to Panama, the constitutional right of the House of Representative to have input on any transfer of property, unilateral U.S. military intervention to assure usage, neutrality and the continued functioning of the Canal, the proposed sea-level canal, the human rights violations of the Torrijos regime, the drug question, and a number of other issues. Senator Dole introduced amendments and reservations to the treaties on all of these as well as on other issues.[102]

Senator Helms stressed defense-related issues more than the others. Senator Hatch, like Senator Dole, was concerned about many of the major aspects of the treaties, but he seemed to stress the constitutional right of the House to be involved when U.S. property was being transferred. He also objected to what he saw as disagreement between the Spanish and English versions of the treaties.

Barry Goldwater's role in the opposition is an interesting one. During the primary election campaign of 1976, Senator Goldwater disagreed with Ronald Reagan on the treaty negotiations.[103] Because of this strong disagreement with Reagan, the Carter administration assumed that Senator

155

Goldwater would support the treaties. As late as August 1977, Goldwater indicated that the Canal should be handed over to Panama.[104] Yet in January 1977, Senator Goldwater had raised questions concerning the negotiation team; and when the treaties were agreed to, he began to raise questions concerning the costs of the treaties and the Canal's crucial role in U.S. defense. In September 1977, he revealed that he would oppose the treaties.[105] Some people thought that the senator had changed sides because the Carter administration seemed to take his support for granted or had handled him in a politically inept fashion. The Goldwater staff stated emphatically, however, that as soon as the texts of the treaties were available for scrutiny, he had objected to many of its concessions and costs.[106]

Like the proponents who had received unexpected help from John Wayne while he was in Panama to pass the treaties, the opponents also expected to receive support from some of the people in Panama to defeat the treaties. They counted upon major input from the Zonians including criticism, threatening to strike, and actively lobbying against the treaties. The opponents hoped that the Zonians would use their contacts in the Defense Department and the House Committee a Merchant Marine and Fisheries to prevent ratification. However, though adroit actions of the administration and treaty supporters in the Pentagon, these antitreaty activities were kept at a minimum. The Zonians did much less to prevent treaty approval than had been predicted earlier and anticipated by congressional opponents.[107]

In addition to attacking specific aspects of the treaties, the opponents used the tactic of vicious attacks on the personality and government of President Torrijos.[108] President Torrijos was called many names, from "Tin Horn dictator" to "communist puppet." His rise to power was questioned and attacked, as were his military background, his education, and his ability and right to rule. Human rights violations of the regime were revealed and strongly criticized. Of all the major opposition tactics that were unrelated to specific treaty issues, this one was most difficult to counter. Treaty proponents reminded the Senate that the Torrijos regime would not be around when the Canal was finally turned over to Panama and that the treaties would be with the Panamanian people and future governments not just this particular regime. All of these tactics, along with the media blitz, the so-called Truth Squad and one of the best organized letter-writing campaigns in recent history, failed to prevent the approval of the treaties and their ratification and implementation.

The House Deliberations and Implementation Legislation

The antagonism between Congress and the White House was evident in many of the conflicts over specific provisions in the treaties. Many senators like Robert Griffin believed that the treaties were flawed and blamed the president for accepting them without insisting on further negotiations to improve and clarify them. Many also believed that the United States gave up too much. On the process side of the question, it was broadly reported that the president and his staff failed in many instances to give the treaties the positive support they needed. The most striking examples of this are the charges of frantic vote buying in the few days just before March 16 vote when the Neutrality Treaty was passed, and the subsequent confusion the administration created about the DeConcini reservation.

This antagonism was amplified in the White House treatment of the House of Representatives. Many congressmen were very bitter about their lack of input and inability to influence the treaties. This was also reemphasized when the courts rejected their claim that the House had to vote on any disposition of U.S. property in Panama. On the other hand, one cannot blame the administration for not including the House on the treaty vote, for it was widely believed that it would have rejected the treaties by a significant margin.

What becomes evident regarding the implementation legislation is the depth and breadth of the gap separating the House from the Senate, which was partly a result of the strong committment built up in the House Subcommittee on the Panama Canal over the decades of oversight it exercised. There was no parallel committee in the Senate. The cross-cutting coalition between this committee and opponents to change in the Defense Department also accounts for part of this antagonism. Many Senate staffers commented on the degree of animosity that existed between the two houses and how this hearty dislike surfaced so often during the Panama Canal treaties deliberation and resolution phases.[109]

Although the House did not participate directly in the events of 1978, it did get its chance to act in 1979. The administration finally put together the implementation legislation package in January and had it introduced into the House. Now the representatives had their opportunity to exact their revenge upon the Senate and the administration. Congressman John Dingell (D-Mich) epitomized the sentiment of the House when he stated:

> We in the House are tired of you people in the State Department going over to your tea-sipping friends in the Senate . . . Now you good folks come up here and you say you need legislation, after you ignored the House. If you expect me to vote for this travesty you're sorely in error.[110]

157

Even before House action on the implementation legislation began, the representatives chose to show their displeasure with the treaties by cutting off all foreign military assistance to Panama in March 1979. On April 5, they went one step further and voted to prohibit nearly all economic aid to Panama. Representative Robert Bauman (R-Md) was one of the main opposition leaders in this battle against aid to Panama.[111] The administration was aware of the strength of the opposition and who its leaders would be in the House.

Nevertheless, the White House missed the opportunity to work with Congress and some of these opposition leaders on the implementation legislation. Now that the treaties had been approved, it would have been very advantageous to have had members of the House play a role in writing the implementation legislation and working out the details and the problems. Instead, the legislation was introduced without real House support or input.

Unlike the Senate, the House does not have the luxury of drawn out floor debates. Much of its work takes place in committees. This is especially true when one compares the thirty-eight days of floor debate in the Senate on the treaties to the three to four days of floor debate in the House on the implementation legislation. It is true that the topic came up during several occasions in the House, but very few days were given to relatively exclusive consideration of the Panama Canal issues.

The House committees became the center stage for the implementation legislation in the spring of 1979. The administration bill for the treaty implementation (HR1716) was assigned to four House committees: Foreign Affairs, Merchant Marine and Fisheries, Judiciary, and Post Office and Civil Service. The administration bill was attacked, amended, and strongly criticized in the various committees. The Merchant Marine and Fisheries Committee, which had the heart of the bill assigned to it, went even one step further. Congressman John Murphy (D-NY), committee chairman, replaced the Administration bill with his own (HR111). This bill contained several provisions that the White House claimed were in direct conflict with the treaties. The committee, however, turned back a bill presented by Congressman George Hansen (R-Idaho), which required that Panama reimburse the United States for all costs associated with the Canal transfer and also required Congress to approve of all payments and property transfers to Panama.[112] On April 3, the committee adopted the Murphy Bill by a vote of 20 to 17.

In the meantime, the Post Office and Civil Service Committee altered the administration bill (HR1716) by requiring that all Canal users, rather than the United States, pay early retirement and other Canal employee benefits. The House Foreign Affairs Committee wanted control and operation of the

Canal turned completely over to the U.S. military during wartime or other such emergencies for the life of the Canal treaty. The Murphy bill had also included such a provision.[113] The Judiciary Committee deleted a section that would have allowed over 1,000 Panamanian Canal employees who were not U.S. citizens to immigrate to the United States and altered a few other minor matters.

The opponents in the House, like those in the Senate, used several tactics to kill the implementation legislation. They tried to alienate Congressman John Murphy from the White House and thus increase differences between the administration's proposal and Murphy's bill, which was the only bill that had a chance to pass. They tried to kill the legislation with the Hansen Bill and later the Hansen Amendment. They tried to obtain sufficient pressure from constituents to make a vote for the legislation too costly, and they tried to offend Panama and make the Panamanians react in such a way as to cause a backlash in the House and defeat the legislation. With all of these efforts, the opponents nearly succeeded.

Everyone knew that the administration's bill was in trouble, but it suffered the final blow on April 26, 1979, when the House Rules Committee rejected the administration's bill in favor of the Murphy Bill (HRlll). The Rules Committee did, however, also reject the third proposed bill (HR3656) sponsored by Congressman George Hansen (R-Idaho).[114] The administration suffered a further setback, when floor debate on the Murphy Bill, which the White House strongly disliked but had to support, had to be postponed from mid-May to June due to lack of House support even for this bill. In a test vote on May 17, on setting rules for debate on the Murphy Bill, the rules were approved by only two votes — 200 to 198. In one of the few instances of floor debate, on May 21, both treaty opponents and supporters debated the Canal issue and attacked the administration and accused President Carter and his aides of misleading them and even of lying to Congress about the impact of the treaties and particularly about the costs of implementation.[115]

One gets the impression while studying the House actions in 1979 that somehow the congressmen thought that by delaying or rejecting the implementation legislation, the treaties would not take effect on October 1, 1979 as stated in the ratification agreement. Yet despite any action by the House, the treaties would have gone into effect with or without implementing legislation because so many provisions in the treaties were self-executing.

Letters and postcards going to Congress during this period also indicated a similar lack of understanding. Most of the communications were the result of an obvious antitreaty campaign and accused congressmen who voted for implementation legislation of "giving the Canal away to a

Marxist oriented Panama."[116] The implication of these letters and post-cards was that the House could somehow prevent the treaties from taking effect. This belief was obviously inaccurate.

The publicly declared position of Congressman Murphy was one of support to implement the treaties. This stand was suggested by his statement concerning one of Congressman George Hansen's amendments: ". . . it is my position that we are duty-bound under international and domestic law to honor our commitments, however distasteful they may be. The treaty is the law of the land and we cannot and must not attempt to violate unilaterally our obligations . . ."[117] Despite this statement his bill probably violated the treaty in a number of ways which will be discussed in detail in Chapter 6.

The House finally got around to floor consideration of the Murphy Bill on June 20 and 21, 1979. The debates included a rare event, when on June 20, the House held its first closed session in 149 years. The Senate had also held a closed session on the treaties. During the secret session, Representative Robert Bauman presented classified testimony on Panama's involvement in the Nicaraguan civil war on the side of the Sandinistas.[118] Although this issue raised many questions, it was not pursued at this time and from the reports studied and interviews it did not appear to alter the final vote.

Although several amendments were presented to the House, most were defeated. The opposition concentrated on their attempt to pass the Hansen Bill by amendment to the Murphy Bill. The Hansen Bill required Panama to pay for most of the costs of transfer and implementation. It would also have altered some of the payments that the treaty had committed to Panama. This amendment clearly violated the treaty and was an attempt to kill the implementation legislation in the same way killer amendments were introduced in the Senate to kill the treaties. A Murphy substitute amendment, which read much like his original bill, was passed by a vote of 220 to 200.[119]

Representative G.V. Montgomery (D-Miss) came the closest to adding a very destructive amendment to the legislation. It would have required Panama to pay $75 million for relocating U.S. military facilities within the Canal Zone. It was defeated by a very close vote of 210 to 213.[120]

A number of other amendments that would have violated the treaty were also narrowly defeated. The House finally passed the Murphy Bill (HR111) by a vote of 224 to 202 on June 21. Voting for the bill were 189 Democrats and 35 Republicans; 80 Democrats and 122 Republicans voted against the bill.[121]

President Aristides Royo of Panama reacted to the Murphy Bill by sending a very lengthy letter to President Carter. The letter accused the United States and the Murphy Bill of being extremely offensive to Panama.

He claimed that the bill directly conflicted with the treaties and cited nearly thirty articles of the bill that he believed disagreed with the treaty or directly contradicted it. He criticized the bill in detail and discussed it article by article. He stated that if it were adopted, it would raise important legal questions that might force Panama to reject it thus creating real problems with implementation on October 1, 1979.[122]

Unlike the House, the Senate believed that they had had their opportunity to influence events when they debated the treaties. Few senators wanted a repeat performance of the previous year.[123] In contrast to the House, the Senate assigned the administration bill (S-1024) to only one committee, the Senate Armed Services Committee. On June 26 and 27, hearings were held and then the committee reworked the bill to include some of the less offensive provisions of HR111. In a very close and completely partisan vote on July 17, the committee reported the compromise bill out by a vote 9 to 8. The whole Senate quickly disposed of the bill by approving it by a vote of 64 to 30 on July 26.

Senator Carl Levin (D-Mich) with some assistance from Senator J.J. Exon (D-Neb) drafted the final legislation that passed the Senate. It was closer to the administration version and was in less conflict with the treaties. These two freshmen senators greatly assisted in the quick approval of the legislation by the Senate. The fact that a majority vote was all that was needed for approval, and not the two-thirds vote that had been required to pass the treaties, helped to expedite the passage of this legislation.

The House reacted rapidly to the Senate version and on July 30 by a vote of 308 to 98 agreed to instruct its members who would attend the conference committee that they not deviate from House language on the key issues.[124] This move offended the Senate and brought a quick response from conference committee Chairman Senator John Stennis (D-Miss). He told the House conferees that he would not be intimidated by instructions from the House. If they were not going to negotiate and attempt to resolve the differences between the bills, he would cancel the conference committee.[125] In a private meeting between Senator Stennis and Representative John Murphy on July 31, they decided to try to resolve their differences after the summer and Labor Day recess. Their aides were given the task to work out the specific compromises during the recess.[126]

By mid-September, the conferees achieved what had seemed impossible in July. They completed their task and produced a compromise bill. The Senate immediately approved of the compromise, but the House continued to act in its uncompromising fashion as the representatives rejected the conference report on September 20 by a 203 to 192 vote.

The conferees hastily returned to the conference table and on September 24 produced another compromise. The new compromise included some of the House requirements and was symbolically made more palatable to them on few issues. The Senate again immediately approved the committee's conference report on September 25 by a vote of 63 to 37. The House finally approved of the second compromise on September 26 by a vote of 232 to 188, just four days before the legislation had to take effect on October 1, 1979.

Representative John Murphy, like many other proponents, lectured the House on their responsibility to pass the final conference compromise.

> We no longer have the luxury of giving vent to our anger. A time bomb is ticking away and the hour is short . . . a defeat of this bill would be unthinkable, and would not only mean the shutting down of the Panama Canal, but could very well result in the loss of American lives.[127]

House Speaker Thomas O'Neill and Majority Leader Jim Wright also warned the House and argued that the legislation was in the national interest of the United States.

On October 1, 1979, in a festive ceremony in Panama, the treaties went into force and the Canal Zone was turned over to President Aristides Royo of Panama. The ceremony was also attended by Vice President Walter Mondale. The first step in the twenty-year process to turn the Canal and its operation over to Panama began.

Despite the festivities of October, Panama found reason to strongly criticize U.S. policy before the end of 1979. In December, President Royo communicated with Washington complaining that delays in establishing the Panama Canal Commission was a violation of the spirit and the letter of the treaties.[128]

In early January, President Royo continued his criticism by writing another letter to President Carter complaining that the implementation legislation contradicted the treaties. He specifically took issue with the way the commission was to be established as a U.S. government agency; this meant that it would need to seek annual funds from Congress and remain under the jurisdiction of Congress. Instead, the Panamanians would have preferred an organization like the old Panama Canal Company which was a quasigovernment corporation. Royo stated that this structural arrangement placed too many restrictions on the commission. Finally, he concluded that the law passed did not correspond with the "fundamental principles and objectives of the treaties."[129]

The United States continued to delay the organization of the commission due to White House slowness and to continued opposition to the treaties by a few die-hard senators. Early in 1980 President Carter finally submitted the five names for the commission to the Senate for its approval. Senator

Harry Byrd (I-Va) was able to delay their approval by the Armed Services Committee until April.[130]

Finally in early April of 1980, the U.S. Senate confirmed the five U.S. nominees to the board, but not without a brief floor fight. Senator Jesse Helms attempted to prevent the confirmation but failed, and the five were confirmed by a 77 to 15 vote.[131] The Board of Directors was established to help advise the commission, and was sufficiently organized to convene for the first time in June 1980. Finally, three years after the treaties were signed in September 1977 they were fully implemented in June 1980.

The deliberation and resolution phases of this policy had been long, arduous, and politically painful. The disagreements over the treaties are not dead but will continue to be reasserted as Congress discusses annual funding for the commission as well as other economic problems of the Canal. Property transfers that occur before the year 2000 will also cause political conflicts in both Houses of Congress.

Conclusions

Just as the substance and results of the treaty and the ratification battle are significant, so too are the decisional procedures and the treaty approval process. Two main procedural changes occurred during the deliberation of these treaties that will undoubtedly influence the Senate's considerations of treaties for some time to come. First was the procedure adopted for article-by-article consideration of the treaties on the Senate floor. Second was the Senate's assertiveness. This case study showed the Senate to be more than willing to become involved in a second, or ratification stage of treaty negotiations, and to be unrestrained in offering and adopting changes and conditions to the treaties.

Whereas it could be argued that the Senate's actions on the treaties strengthened, clarified, and improved them, the actions of the House on the implementation legislation clearly created antagonism, controversy, and misunderstandings. The two amendments made by the Senate to the Neutrality Treaty incorporating the Carter-Torrijos Statement of Understanding helped clarify important language. They also strengthened the defense component by allowing U.S. warships "first of the line" privileges in time of crisis or emergency. The Nunn addition to the Panama Canal Treaty also strengthened the defense element by allowing the United States and Panama to negotiate retention of U.S. military bases in Panama after December 31, 1999. The Brooke addition allowing more time for implementation was important and did not detract from the treaties. The DeConcini reservation, however, came close to destroying them. The subsequent modifications, nevertheless, were able to defuse the crisis and

163

consequently the reservation somewhat strengthened the defense capability without damaging the overall agreement.

These alterations by the Senate however, took an inordinate amount of time. They prevented both the Senate and the administration from consideration of other issues and crises. This time was disproportionate to the relative world importance of the Canal issue. We do not want to suggest, however, that consideration of treaties by the Senate should be hasty and *pro forma*. The case of the canal treaties provides an opportunity, however, to examine how the Senate's constitutional role could be performed with less negative impact on the treaty process and the institution itself. One way to avoid undue senatorial delay and stalling would be to include more of the senators, their staffs and committee staffs in the actual negotiation process. This suggestion was frequently made by critics of the Carter administration. The main problem with this suggestion from the point of view of treaty negotiators is that senators have a need to maximize their electoral benefits; they might allow "leaks" that could damage sensitive negotiations and even do harm to the international relations of the parties involved. The more senators know during the early stages of negotiations, the more likely they are to demand that specific items be included in the treaty, as a condition for their support of the final product. Problems of this sort occurred with regard to the Salt II negotiations and Senate approval process. From the point of view of senators, whose daily calendars are already crowded, preliminary consultations are hard to arrange for an issue that may not reach the floor or committee for several months, a years, or ever.

In the case of the implementation legislation, these reservations do not hold. A set deadline for the action was imminent. Against the prospect of House members bargaining for better terms, the administrations could have effectively countered with the ultimate argument: the treaties will go into effect with or without implementation legislation. The administration could and should have involved House leaders much more than it did in the creation of the implementation package and its guidance through the House process. Treaty opponents in the House could also have been involved at this stage.

One of the findings of this study is how difficult it is for the president to work with a leader of the opposition party, and a person who might possibly run against him in the next election, but without whose support the president's policy has no chance of passage. Consequently, the White House found it difficult to encourage and reward Senator Baker, but it needed his support.

The Senate Leadership was not cultivated either. So much effort went into convincing the uncommitted senators and some of the opponents that

164

early treaty supporters and strong proponents were somewhat ignored by the White House. They were thus forced to suffer the heat from angry constituents alone. Had better communications and understandings been made with Senator Byrd and other Senate leaders, problems such as the DeConcini disaster may have been diminished.

Despite the lack of White House support and recognition of long term treaty supporters, the White House eventually became too blatant in its last-minute attempts to woo the fence straddlers. Perceptions of concessions to DeConcini and Talmadge, and promises to Randolph, Huddleston and others were somewhat detrimental, and nearly caused a loss of some of the early proponents. In addition, this also reinforced the anti-Carter attitudes of some of the other supporters. It also lost their commitment on future issues.

The separation of powers approach helps to explain much of the difficulty in obtaining passage of the treaties. There were major problems between the executive and legislative branches. Some created misunderstandings, miscues, power struggles, and accusations of mismanagement during the whole process. The nature of the issue added to these problems because it was so emotional, nationalistic and at times elicited extremist rhetoric. The separation of powers approach helps to clarify the reasons for some of the the animosity between the administration and the Senate, but does not explain the severe competition between the Senate and the House of Representative that was evident throughout the ratification process and the passage of the implementation legislation. Despite the existence of this antagonism and competition, there is little in the literature to suggest it. The cross-cutting coalition approach deals with the condition somewhat. Interinstitutional rivalry also lends some explanation.

The bureaucratic approach helps to answer the question of why it took so long to obtain a new set of treaties. The Department of Defense, which had the most tangible interests at stake, was, at least initially, adamantly opposed to altering the defense and sovereignty arrangements under the 1903 treaty. Similarly, the Department of State had the greater organizational predisposition to respond favorably to Panama's grievances and to seek a negotiated solution to bilateral differences. The cross-cutting coalition approach is also needed to understand some of the activities of the Departments of State and Defense in the 1960s and 1970s. This is especially true when considering the tactic used by proponents during the Senate floor fight. The four advisers who aided the proponents were from the State Department, the Defense Department, the White House, and a Senate committee staff.

The bargaining perspective also aids in understanding how someone like Senator Baker could travel to Panama and actually participate in a type of treaty negotiation with General Torrijos. The separation of powers approach cannot account for such an activity as it is completely outside the constitutional framework and the ratification process. The Senate leadership's participation in undoing the damage of the DeConcini reservation through direct participation in negotiations with the Panamanians would also be inexplicable within a separation of powers approach.

A bargaining approach, on the other hand, defines actors in terms of their motivation and responses to the bilateral or international situation rather than in terms of their institutional or organizational position. Therefore, Senator Baker is not limited, according to bargaining theory, in his role as minority leader. What accounts for his behavior is his commitment to the negotiation process itself, his belief that a compromise is better than no solution, and his belief that Panama's and the U.S. interests could, in fact, be reconciled. As an expert reconciler, a skill be perfected in his institutional role as Minority Leader, Senator Baker had the expertise and the credibility to insert himself into the negotiations with Panama. A bargaining approach uses the concept of personality — some individuals being predisposed to initiate rather than react — to explain why some individuals enter bargaining situations while others do not.

The use of varied approaches helps to explain some of the very complex actions that occurred in order to obtain passage, ratification, and implementation of the treaties. The interrelationships between the executive, the bureaucracy, the houses of Congress, the electorate and the political parties are more completely described through this eclectic method.

This study also reveals the difficulty of obtaining a two-thirds majority vote in the Senate on a highly controversial foreign policy issue. It is much easier to build public antagonism to change in the status quo than to build support for an altered policy. James Symington stated it more eloquently when he said that treaty opponents could ". . . win standing ovations. The best its supporters can expect to achieve is adequate reflection. It is easier to bring a crowd to its feet than to its senses."[132]

Endnotes

[1] Edward S. Corwin, *The President*, (New York: New York University Press, 4th rev. ed, 1957), pp. 204-212.

[2] Ibid; p. 210.

[3] U.S. Congress, Senate Committee on Foreign Relations, *The Role of the Senate in Treaty Ratification: A Staff Memorandum*, 95th Congress, 1st session, Washington, D.C., 1977, p. 45-46.

[4] U.S. Congress Senate Committee on Foreign Relations, *Senate Debate on the Panama Canal Treaties: A Compendium of Major Statements, Documents, Rec-*

ord Votes and Relevant Events, 96th Congress, 1st Session, February 1979, p.4. (Hereafter cited as *Compendium*).

[5] Hanson Baldwin, "A New Treaty for Panama?" *AEI Defense Review*, No. 4, 1977, pp. 21-22, 30-31.

[6] U.S. Congress, Senate Committee on Foreign Relations, *Panama Canal Treaties Report*, Executive Report No. 95-12, 95th Congress, 2nd Session, Feb. 3, 1978, p.177-200. (Hereafter cited as *Report*).

[7] Ibid.

[8] U.S. Congress, *Congressional Record*, March 14, 1978, pp. S-3614-17 (Daily Record).

[9] Ibid. p. S-3617

[10] Senate Foreign Relations Committee, *Hearing*, Pt. III.

[11] Ibid., Pt. I, p. 96.

[12] Ibid., p. 97

[13] Ibid., p. 98

[14] *Report*, p. 99

[15] *Compendium*, p. 209.

[16] U.S. Congress, *Congressional Record*, Feb. 23, 1978, pp. S-2116-2121, (Daily Record).

[17] *CQ Weekly*, May 7, 1977, p. 884.

[18] U.S. Congress Senate Committee on Foreign Relations, *A Chronology of Events Relative to Panama Canal*, 95th Congress, 1st Session, Washington, D.C. 1977, pp. 29-30 (Hereafter cited as *Chronology*).

[19] Ibid., p. 32.

[20] *Compendium*, p. 6.

[21] Ibid., pp. 509-510.

[22] *Washington Post*, 4 Sept., 1977; *Washington Post*, 7 Sept., 1977; and *Chronology*, pp. 29-30.

[23] 580 F 2d 1055 (D.C. Cir.) 189 U.S. App. D.C., Certiorari denied 436 U.S. 907 (1978).

[24] *Compendium*, p. 541 and *Harvard Law Review* "Transfer of the Panama Canal by Treaty Without House Approval" Vol. 29, No. 2, Dec. 1978, pp. 524-35.

[25] Vance, *Hard Choices*, p. 148.

[26] *Compendium*, p.70.

[27] President Carter discussed this action in similar terms in his memoirs; see *Keeping Faith*, p. 162.

[28] *Report*, p. 4.

[29] Ibid., p. 1.

[30] Ibid., p. 16.

[31] Ibid.

167

[32] U.S. Senate, *Report of Delegation Studying the Panama Canal Treaties and Other Matters of Interest to the U.S. in Latin America*, 95th Congress, 2nd Session, Senate Document No. 95-80, Washington, D.C., 1978, p. 5-6.

[33] Vance, *Hard Choices*, pp. 152-152.

[34] Carter, *Keeping Faith*, p. 224.

[35] Ibid., p. 164.

[36] *Compendium*, p. 513.

[37] Ibid.; p. 514.

[38] *Congressional Quarterly Weekly Report*, December 10, 1979: p. 2578.

[39] Thomas J. McIntyre, *The Fear Brokers*, (New York: The Pilgrim Press, 1979), pp. 122-23.

[40] Ibid.

[41] Bernard Roshco, "The Polls: Polling on Panama — Si, Don't Know; Hell No?" *Public Opinion Quarterly*, Vol. 42, 1978, p. 562.

[42] Carter, *Keeping Faith*, pp. 161-162.

[43] Interviews.

[44] McIntyre, *The Fear Brokers*, p. XXIV and p. 19 and pp. 154-55.

[45] Graham Hovey, "Carter in State of Union Address, Appeals for Canal Pact's Approval," *New York Times*, 20 January, 1978.

[46] Ibid.

[47] *Compendium*, p. 523.

[48] U.S. Congress, *The Congressional Record*, 95th Congress, 2nd Session, Vol. 124, No. 14, Feb. 8, 1978, p. S-1498. (Daily Record).

[49] Wendell Rawls, "Senate Panel Opens Hearings on Civiletti" *New York Times*, 22 February, 1978.

[50] Carter, *Keeping Faith*, p. 176.

[51] *Ibid.*, p. 171.

[52] Cecil V. Crabb and Pat M. Holt *Invitation to Struggle: Congress, the President and Foreign Policy* (Washington, D.C.: CQ Press, 1980), p. 75.

[53] Interviews.

[54] Vance, *Hard Choices*, pp. 152-153.

[55] Interviews.

[56] Although it was called the DeConcini amendment or reservation during the Senate debates and in the press, it is officially added to the treaty as a Condition to the Resolution on Ratification and not to the treaty itself.

[57] *Compendium*, pp. 403-404.

[58] Thomas M. Franck and Edward Weisband. *Foreign Policy by Congress* (New York: Oxford University Press, 1979), p. 276.

[59] Interviews.

[60] *Congressional Quarterly Almanac*, "Panama Canal Treaties: Major Carter Victory," Vol. 4, 1978, p. 393.

[61] Interviews.

[62] Franck and Weisband, *Foreign Policy by Congress*, p. 278.

[63] Interviews.

[64] Carter, *Keeping Faith*, pp. 168-177.

[65] Ibid., p. 173

[66] Interviews.

[67] Carter, *Keeping Faith*, p. 172.

[68] Interviews.

[69] Ibid.

[70] *New York Times*, 10 April, 1979.

[71] Interviews and *Congressional Quarterly Weekly Report*, April 22, 1978, p. 952.

[72] Crabb and Holt, *Invitation to Struggle* pp. 78-79.

[73] *Matutino*, April 1978.

[74] Alan Riding, "Panama Indicates It Can Not Accept Canal Treaties," *New York Times*, 18 April, 1978, p. 6.

[75] *U.S. News* "Now There's Treaty Trouble in Panama" April 17, 1978, p. 59.

[76] *Matutino*, 8 April, 1978, pp. 1-A and 4-A.

[77] Frank and Weisband, *Foreign Policy by Congress*, pp. 281-284.

[78] Adam Clymer, "Key Senator Yields to Party's Leaders on Pledge to Panama" *New York Times*, 18 April, 1978, p. 1.

[79] *Compendium*, pp. 398-399.

[80] Clymer, "Key Senator," p. 1, and the *Congressional Quarterly Weekly Report*, April 22, 1978, p. 954. Crabb and Holt, *Invitation to Struggle*, pp. 81-82.

[81] *Congressional Quarterly Weekly*, April 22, 1978, p. 954.

[82] Ibid., p. 951.

[83] Carter, *Keeping Faith*, pp. 176-177. Professor Furlong was also concerned about the possibility of violence. He was in his hotel room in downtown Panama City listening to the vote on a portable radio.

[84] *U.S. News & World Report*, "Panama Canal Fight: Senators Feel the Heat" February 13, 1978, p. 37-38.

[85] Adam Clymer, "Canal pact Support Still Short of Goal," *New York Times*, 15 March, 1978, p. 6.

[86] Martin Tolchin, "White House Woos Holdouts on Canal," *New York Times*, 14 March, 1978, p. 1 and 7.

[87] *U.S. News & World Report*, March 27, 1978, pp. 27-28; Time, March 27, 1978, p. 8; and Crabb and Holt, pp. 80-82.

[88] Interviews.

[89] Crabb and Holt, *Invitation to Struggle*, p. 80 and *Congressional Quarterly Almanac*, 1978, Vol. 34, p. 392.

[90] Interviews.

[91] Graham Hovey, "Senators Hopeful on Canal Treaty" *New York Times*, 3 February, 1977, p. 8.

[92] Interviews.

[93] Carter, *Keeping Faith*, p. 164.

[94] Interviews.

[95] U.S. Senate, Committee on the Judiciary, Subcommittee on Separation of Powers. *Panama Canal Treaties: U.S. Senate Debate 1977-78*. 95th Congress, pt. 1, Washington, D.C., 1978, p. 603. (Hereafter cited as *Debates*).

[96] Ibid. Pt 2, p. 2569.

[97] Interviews.

[98] Ibid.

[99] *Time*, "The Wooing of Senator Zorinsky," Vol. III, March 27, 1978, p. 12-13.

[100] Interviews.

[101] *Debates*, Pt 2, p. 2270.

[102] *Debates*, Pt 1, pp. 200-231.

[103] *New York Times*, 3 May, 1976, p. 1.

[104] *Time*, August 22, 1977, p. 10.

[105] *New York Times*, 10 September, 1977, p. 2.

[106] Interviews.

[107] Interviews.

[108] *New York Times*, 5 May, 1976, and 10 May, 1976.

[109] Interviews.

[110] *Congressional Quarterly Weekly Report*, February 17, 1978, p. 306.

[111] *New York Times*, 6 April, 1979.

[112] *Congressional Quarterly Weekly Report*, April 7, 1979, p. 668.

[113] Ibid., pp. 667-668.

[114] *Congressional Quarterly Weekly Report*, April 28, 1979, p. 806.

[115] *Congressional Quarterly Weekly Report*, May 26, 1979, p. 1008.

[116] Interviews.

[117] U.S. Congress, *The Congressional Record*, 95th Congress, 1st Session, Vol. 125, June 20, 1979, H-4833.

[118] *Congressional Quarterly Weekly Report*, June 23, 1979, p. 1208.

[119] *Congressional Quarterly Weekly Report*, June 23, 1979, p. 1208.

[120] Ibid., p. 208.

[121] Ibid., p. 1207.

[122] *Matutino*, 16 de Julio, 1979, pp. 8-A and 9-A.

[123] Interviews.

[124] *Congressional Quarterly Weekly Report*, August 4, 1979, p. 1584.

[125] Interviews.

[126] *Congressional Quarterly Weekly Report*, August 4, 1979, p. 1584.

[127] Ibid., Sept. 29, 1979, p. 2120.

[128] *Washington Post*, 8 Dec., 1979.

[129] *Los Angeles Times*, 10 January 1980.

[130] Ibid., 16 March 1980.

[131] Ibid., 3 April 1980.

[132] James W. Symington, "The Canal: Use Not Territory is the Issue," *Washington Post*, September 2, 1977.

CHAPTER 6
IMPLEMENTATION LEGISLATION AND IMPACTS

Introduction

The implementation of a treaty may be simple or it may be complex. Normally, there are at least four general different types of congressional situations following the advice, consent, and ratification stages of a treaty. First, a treaty may be fully self-executing and need no further congressional action. Second, some minor aspects of the treaty may require additional implementation legislation. Third, major aspects of the treaty may need major legislation before implementing actions can begin. And finally, a treaty may incur costs. When this happens, Congress must make appropriations. The U.S. Constitution clearly states that bills related to money matters must originate in the House of Representatives; therefore when funding is required, Congress and especially the House, continue to play a critical role in the treaty-making process.

The Panama Canal Treaty contained a number of provisions that were self-executing, but it also had important portions that required additional legislation. In addition, there were and are costs associated with the treaty and the transition period that require appropriations subject to congressional approval. Because of these conditions, the House of Representatives was assured a role in the passage of the treaty implementation legislation and in any appropriations needed for the twenty-year life of the treaty.

During the battle for ratification in 1978, members of the House of Representatives demanded an opportunity to participate in the ratification process. They argued that because the treaty transferred U.S. property, both houses of Congress, not just the Senate, would have to approve the treaty. This argument was rejected by the Senate, the Carter administration, and the courts.[1]

Subsequently, such a rejection guaranteed that the administration could expect a major confrontation when the House received the implementation legislation. Earlier chapters have discussed this political context in some detail. In addition to this confrontation, the House was historically and consistently opposed to any changes that would significantly alter the status quo on defense or sovereignty related to the Panama Canal.

Given these facts, it is surprising that the Carter administration did not more actively cultivate the House leadership, the relevant committee and subcommittee chairmen, and the known treaty proponents in the House.

The president also could have worked with some of the less adamant opponents. It would have been a wise strategy to have at least approached John Murphy, chairman of the Merchant Marine and Fisheries Committee, and Carroll Hubbard, chairman of the Subcommittee on the Panama Canal, and request that they participate in formulating the legislation. Other House leaders and proponents could also have been involved, but were not.[2]

The Senate had had its opportunity to handle the treaties and wanted to expedite the implementation legislation. The House, on the other hand, was determined to make its will known. The general attitude was almost one of preventing the treaties from taking effect. This option was not open to them, but the House opponents were determined to significantly damage the treaties and to restrict them as much as possible. Some opponents hoped to goad Panama into a reaction that might cancel or postpone the treaties. The administration had hoped that the 1978 elections would place fewer opponents into the House and that some of the animosity of the 1977 and 1978 period would be reduced. Neither of these conditions occurred and action on the implementation legislation became necessary. The administration had hesitated for over eight months to reveal its program for the legislation and had been frequently accused of delaying its own submission for political reasons.

As it turned out, Congressman John Murphy submitted his own bill for implementation legislation to the House fifteen days before the administration submitted its version, January 15, 1979, and January 31, 1979, respectively. In addition to election hopes, the Carter administration assumed that because the Senate had ratified the treaties, it would assist in pressuring the House into approving the administration's implementation program.[3] They could not have been more mistaken. Both the executive and the Senate were attacked by the House.

As noted in the preceding chapter, the battle to pass the legislation in the House was bitter, vitriolic, and marked by harsh recriminations against the administration and the Senate. The House accused the Carter administration of lying, especially about the costs of implementation, of incompetently handling the legislation, and of giving away the Canal.[4] The Senate, too, was the recipient of considerable rebuke as it was criticized for cooperating with the administration and the State Department and for refusing to allow House participation in the ratification process. Rivalry and competition between the two houses was accentuated by bitterness, accusations, and personal attacks generated by the implementation process as well. It was evident that the conservative internationalist philosophy prevailed in the House.

President Carter indicated that the House of Representatives was being misguided and receiving incorrect information. The battle for votes was difficult, but the fight against incorrect assumptions, perceptions, and the conservative internationalist philosophy was even worse.[5] In reviewing this period, the president later stated,

> The House members were being told that their vote could prevent control of the Canal being turned over to Panama, that we would have to pay Panama billions of dollars from United States tax revenues, that Torrijos was controlled by communist forces, that our military leaders had been forced by me to support the treaties against their will, and that the Panamanians would be blackmailing us for the rest of this century by threatening to destroy the Canal.[6]

These charges were simply not true. Opponents had emotion on their side but few facts. This battle for approval of the treaty implementation legislation ranged across party lines, between the administration and the House, and between the House and the Senate. Because of changes in the international environment and disagreement on some implementation issues, the united front that had existed between the Departments of Defense and State on ratification also collapsed. All of this political wrangling prevented early resolution of the main issues. Not only was the administration's bill defeated, but all the implementation legislation almost met a similar fate.

Despite the tearing and pulling, the campaign rhetoric, the mutual accusations, and the harsh debates, the legislation was finally passed; but the process took months, with frequent delays, and many near failures. Two conference committee sessions had to be held and each house had to vote on numerous occasions before the legislation was finally passed on September 26, 1979. Final presidential approval was given on September 27, 1979, just three short days before it had to take effect. The House fought the Senate on many of the main issues. The Senate attempted to honor the letter and spirit of the treaties whereas the House was attempting to alter the treaties as much as possible. The final legislation therefore contained aspects that appear to be contrary to the treaty and were definitely detrimental to U.S.-Panamanian relations.

The legislation revolved around six key points. First, the type of organization that would run and maintain the Canal until the year 2000 was of paramount importance. Both the administration and the Senate wanted an autonomous business enterprise similar to the old Canal Company. The House wanted an appropriated-type agency that would be more susceptible to congressional oversight and that would need annual budget appropriations. This would force the agency to be more directly responsible to the House. Second, the costs of the treaties to the United States were a major issue. Representatives in the House held that the United States should pay very little towards the costs of implementation and most of the costs should be paid from toll revenues. The Senate also attempted to keep employee cost increases at a minimum. Third, the transfer of property became an important issue as the House attempted to reduce executive flexibility and attempted to make the treaty-mandated property transfers subject to a veto by Congress. Fourth, ultimate responsibility for the operation of the Canal was an issue and the roles of the Department of Defense as well as the president were debated. The House wanted State Department influence to be minimal and the Defense Department to play the central role. Fifth, defense of the Canal was extremely important. How the Canal was to be defended by the United States both against internal and external threats until the year 2000 was debated. Means for increasing U.S. defense capability were explored. The continued role of the U.S. military in the defense of the Canal against all external enemies was one of the few issues that was agreed upon by all sides. Sixth, economic and social benefits, and job protection for all U.S. employees of the Canal became major aspects of legislation, but there was major disagreement on specific elements of these issues between the administration, the Senate, and the House.

Public Law 96-70, the Panama Canal Act of 1979, is the final product of this legislative duel. This duel had forced compromises in both houses and with the executive as well. And as a result, the legislation is not as clear and precise as its stated purpose might appear. Under the provisions of the treaty, the legislation went into effect on October 1, 1979. The treaty of 1977 also went into force on the same day and many of the self-executing provisions became effective.

The purpose of the legislation was stated at the outset. "It is the purpose of this Act to provide legislation necessary or desirable for the implementation of the Panama Canal Treaty of 1977 between the United States of America and the Republic of Panama and of the related agreements accompanying that Treaty."[7] Despite this declaration, there were many provisions in the legislation that could be interpreted to be in violation with the treaty.

The legislation was principally designed to insure that the United States could manage and maintain the Canal in order that it would remain open and operating, and that it would defend the Canal in order to prevent its closure due to hostile action. The act included protection for U.S. citizens working on the Canal and attempted to assure that the levels of services and support for these employees did not deteriorate.[8]

Canal Administration

The bill establishes the Panama Canal Commission to run the Canal until December 31, 1999. The commission is an appropriated agency rather than

175

the earlier Panama Canal Company, which was a government corporation, and the appropriations process allows the Congress to maintain a certain amount of influence over its activities. All funds collected by the commission were to be deposited in the Treasury and all expenditures must be authorized by Congress. The president of the United States is to exercise his authority over the commission through the secretary of defense.

The bill also establishes the three top positions in the commission: administrator, deputy administrator, and chief engineer (see Chart 6.1). On October 19, 1979, the Senate confirmed Dennis P. McAuliffe, the Commander of the U.S. Southern Command based in Panama, as the first commission administrator.[9] The administrator thus became the Department of Defense's representative and the individual through whom the president exercises his authority over the commission.

In accordance with the treaty, the act also established a Board of Directors to advise the commission. This board was to be composed of nine members: five U.S. citizens and four Panamanians. All members of the board, including the four Panamanians, had to be appointed by the president of the United States and confirmed by the Senate. One of the U.S. members had to be designated by the secretary of defense, one had to possess experience with commercial shipping, one had to have had past port and harbor experience and the fourth had to have been active in labor affairs in the United States.

Although the four Panamanians were to be designated by Panama, they had to be officially appointed by the president of the United States. This provision raises some important questions. A number of constitutional experts have indicated that the president has no constitutional authority to appoint foreigners (non-U.S. citizens) to a U.S. executive agency. Despite this contention, the Senate confirmed all of the members to the Panama Canal Commission Board of Directors, and the board held its first meeting on June 2, 1980.

Thus, the principal organization at the focal point in this new relationship with the United States and Panama contained elements of contention. The commission, which is less independent of Congress than the old Panama Canal Company, has much less financial and decision-making flexibility. Revenues and funding were completely separated, thus making it more difficult to meet changing demands for services and shifts in traffic patterns. More than one accounting system was also required. Finally, the organizational nature of the commission created legal strains between the commission and the Panamanians that would be absent in a more flexible, more business-like, government corporation.[10] This type of bureaucratic structure has created more problems between the United States and Panama than any other issue related to the treaties and the implementation legislation.

Chart 6.1
COMPARISON OF CORPORATE FORM versus APPROPRIATED-FUND AGENCY

Appropriated Agency		Corporation
Strict congressional control with budgetary limitation.	LEGAL FORM	Legal and financial autonomy and operating flexibility through fund reallocation.
Treasury funding without reference income from operations.	FINANCING	Sustained by its own to operating revenue.
Reflects agency's expenditures within budgetary limitations.	ACCOUNTING	Uses standard means to reflect profit and loss.
Requires congressional approval to meet emergency reallocation of funds.	FLEXIBILITY	Resources may be reallocated at management discretion to meet unexpected demands.
With expenses budgeted annually agency has no incentive to reduce expenses as revenue declines.	PRUDENCE	Management must live within its income.
As demand for services increases funds are not available to expand scope of the operation.	EXPANSION	As demand increases added revenue is available to the provide additional services.
Congress may be politicatlly motivated to provide services not economically justified by operating revenues.	BALANCE	Only financially justified services will be provided.
Government accounting methods when applied to business operation may be subject to differing interpretations.	STANDARDIZATION	Corporate accounting procedures use standard, generally accepted methods.

Source: General Accounting Office, *Background Information Bearing Upon Panama Canal Treaty Implementing Legislation*, No. IE-79-33 (Washington, D.C.: General Accounting Office), June 4, 1979, p. 52.

177

Canal Commission Administrator McAuliffe stated to the Senate Armed Services Committee in June 1980 that despite many built-in hazards and chances for failure, the management of the Canal and the transition to the new administrative organization had been successful and without major difficulty. He attributed this success to extensive planning and a high level of cooperation and coordination.[11]

Despite this positive statement, there have been and continue to be heavy criticisms of the commission and problems with many aspects of the legislation. Since the beginning of the transition period, President Aristides Royo had complained that the legislation contained portions that conflicted with the spirit and letter of the 1977 Panama Canal Treaties. In 1979 and early 1980, he listed his criticisms article by article as he reviewed the whole legislation. He made over twenty major points and criticized numerous minor ones. President Royo specifically indicated that the structure of the commission created too many restrictions and hampered the Panamanians.[12] As an appropriated agency, the commission was bound by rigid procedural requirements imposed by those who controlled the purse strings, namely the U.S. House of Representatives.

The Senate, the Carter administration, and the General Accounting Office had all recommended that the commission, like the Panama Canal Company, be a government corporation. The House of Representatives, however, had insisted that it could exercise more control if the commission were an appropriated agency. In this way, the House could more closely oversee the expenditures of the commission and keep complete track of its revenues. Consequently, it refused to pass the implementation legislation if any other form were given to the commission.

A number of tensions continue to exist between the commission and the House. The lack of financial flexibility forces the commission into an impossible budgetary game. For example, Canal traffic must be predicted for thirty months in order to predict toll revenues. This is difficult at best and close to impossible with major changes in the world economic conditions and trading patterns. Second, the budget must be balanced. This is difficult as most of the budget depends on tolls. There are also treaty payments to Panama that must be met. Costs for maintenance problems, accidents, and emergencies cannot be forecasted accurately. In addition, continued animosity exists on the Hill toward the treaties. Many House members would still like to turn the clock back and rescind or cancel the treaties. This type of sentiment increased significantly on Capitol Hill in 1981 through 1983 due to the turmoil in Central America. There are few sympathetic voices who are willing to defend the treaty and the needs and goals of the commission.[13]

If the United States insists on maintaining this type of agency for the duration of the treaty, it will be a major source of continuing conflict with Panama; this disagreement has the potential of creating problems hampering the smooth functioning of the Canal. Hence the House of Representatives may have created more problems than the possible benefits of close supervision might give them.

Employees and Administration

A major portion of Public Law 96-70 defined employment practices and delineated administrative guidelines. The act provided for detailed protections for Canal employees and their dependents. Salaries and fringe benefits were outlined; job security, rotation, and recruitment practices were defined; a number of employment procedures and other employee safeguards were established. Immigration to the United States of 15,000 past employees was also included. Administrative structures and patterns were outlined in detail and job protection was provided. Hence, continuity as well as security were guaranteed to U.S. workers in the Zone during and after the transfer period.

This aspect of implementation has progressed with only minor problems but without the previously anticipated major difficulties. In June 1980, the new Panama Canal Commission formulated draft recommendations on the Panama Canal Employment System that would replace the Canal Zone Merit System. Through the efforts of this commission, a number of the new employment practices and procedures began to take effect in 1980.[14] Preference for hiring Panamanians increased their participation in Canal operations, the establishment of Defense civilian personnel policies ensured that eventually 90 percent of the work force will be Panamanian; other employee changes were progressing favorably and on schedule.[15]

One of the greatest impacts of the treaty was on the Canal's 12,200 employees. Administrator McAuliffe stated:

> One of the most significant problems involves personnel turbulence. The personnel movements which occurred in October 1979 were substantial. Some 5,500 individuals were affected by involuntary separations, transfer of functions, resignations, retirements, internal reassignments, and grade changes. Prior to that, the uncertainties of the impending treaty were manifest in a relatively high rate of resignations and retirements.[16]

Despite many dire predictions, fewer U.S. civilian personnel voluntarily quit their jobs or left Panama in 1979 and 1980 than was expected. Nevertheless, over 2,300 people out of a work force of 12,200 were transferred to other positions and 460 employees were terminated.[17] The work force began to stabilize after the treaty went into effect, despite the disruptions of the first year. From October 1979 to November 1980, only seventy-five people resigned, or about 1 percent of the commission's labor force.[18]

There were also significantly fewer employee disruptions, strikes, slow-downs, or other difficulties than had been anticipated. Granted, the morale problem and the transition created tension among personnel, but work continued. The only major work problem to occur was due to increased traffic through the Canal, not to employee dissatisfaction. The increased traffic caused a major slowdown in October 1980, but this would have occurred with or without the new treaties. By the end of 1980, personnel conditions seemed to have stabilized and were nearly back to normal.[19]

Administrator McAuliffe claimed in April 1981 that most of the personnel unrest had been overcome but that low morale and continuing "pockets" of employee dissatisfaction would receive consistent administrative attention.[20] In 1983, he reiterated his commitment ". . .to maintain a strong sensitivity for the moral and quality of life of our employees."[21]

Obviously, the transition was a traumatic experience for the work force. Employee morale was low during the ratification proceedings and the long debate over the implementation legislation. Morale declined further at the beginning of the implementation phase, but began improving as many anticipated negative consequences failed to materialize. As implementation continued smoothly, morale improved. However, employee problems are certain to continue, as inconveniences resulting from the treaty persist in affecting everyday life and life-styles.[22]

John Augelli's findings support the negative aspects of the transition on the Zonians. After interviewing over three hundred people in Panama, he found that many had suffered significantly because of the transition beginning on October 1, 1979.

> . . . Americans were affected by low morale and a lack of motivation, and they frequently complained about a growing shortage of experienced workers in their area of operation. . . . Virtually everyone tended to be pessimistic about the future. . . . Thus, much of the grousing revealed by the survey was merely a way of expressing nostalgia for the "good old days."[23]

They had lost group identity, job and personal security, and continuity in their lives and interpersonal relationships. Apprehension, pessimism, and uncertainty seemed to pervade most of those interviewed. They were in a state of cultural shock: demoralized and insecure. They also indicated that a number of benefits had been discontinued and that life in general became more inconvenient and more threatening. Their sense of mission was gone

180

and most agreed that the situation could worsen significantly. An entire life-style and culture had been destroyed, and many became very angry and unhappy about it.[24]

Transfer of Functions

The Panama Canal Company and/or the Canal Zone government had been responsible for a number of public services and functions that had to be transferred to the Panamanian government under the provisions of the treaty. Four major agencies as well as several of their subcommittees began working out the details of this transition as soon as the treaty was ratified. The major agencies were the U.S. diplomatic mission led by the Ambassador Ambler Moss, the now defunct Canal Zone government and the Panama Canal Company, the U.S. Southern Command based in Panama, and the government of the Republic of Panama. Each agency had its individual assignments as well as its own specific responsibilities. They began planning and coordinating efforts in order that the transition would be orderly and without any major disruptions in service.

The treaty enumerated several functions to be transferred to Panama on October 1, 1979.

1. Postal services
2. Customs and immigration
3. Partial fire protection
4. Commercial operations on any commercial activity not related to the Canal (such as a bowling alley, movie houses, or retail stores)
5. Port operations
6. Panama railroad
7. Commercial vessel repair

At the same time other services were also transferred to Panama for which the United States or the Panama Canal Commission will make payment.

1. Garbage and trash collection
2. Street cleaning and maintenance
3. Partial fire protection
4. Police protection

The Panama Canal Company and the Zone government, in October 1979, also transferred some functions to the Department of Defense, including services such as health and educational activities. Some commercial activities were also given to Defense, such as the commissary for U.S. employees and their dependents.

181

Most functions were transferred by the end of 1980. During the transition period, the United States and Panama had made considerable progress in implementing changes mandated by the treaty and by the implementation legislation. The port facilities, the railroad, vehicle licensing and registration, certain health and sanitation services, and some of the utility functions and billing were transferred. These are operating smoothly. According to the General Accounting Office, no apparent degradation of services or major negative impacts had been reported.[25] However, John Augelli disagreed with the GAO report and stated that some services, especially garbage collection and street cleaning operations, had deteriorated significantly.[26]

Public Services

The transfer and operation of public services presents a distinct problem, not with the services themselves or with the ability of Panama to provide them, but with determining the quality and cost. The treaty provides that Panama will receive $10 million a year reimbursement while the implementation legislation requires that Panama be reimbursed for the actual cost of garbage collection, street maintenance, and fire and police protection, but only up to a maximum of $10 million a year.

By the end of 1980, Panama had not developed the bureaucratic procedures or acceptable bookkeeping methods for cost accounting. The Panamanian government may wish to dispute this provision in the implementation act and claim that the treaty does not require such specific and sophisticated verification procedures. Also, according to the act, the U.S. Comptroller General is supposed to audit the costs and the U.S. payment for these services annually. Without sufficient data, this audit will be extremely difficult to perform.[27] Nevertheless, the $10 million has been paid to date. The level of payment is also open to renegotiation every three years in order to deal with inflation and other increased costs.

The determination of quality of services and its verification also present problems to be resolved. No agreements have been reached on how the quality of services can be evaluated. Thus, there is no assurance that service quality will remain at the previous levels. Mutually accepted procedures for quality determination and basic standards need to be developed.[28] Both the problem of payment and the question of quality need to be resolved or they could lead to confrontations in the future.

A thirty-month transition period to March 31, 1982 for legal and juridical matters was granted, and a number of general legal conditions were also stated by the act; thus, police protection became a joint venture from October 1979 to May 1982. While reports continued on the deterioration of services, such as road and street maintenance, housing, commissary and medical coverage,[29] police protection between October 1979 and March 1982 was generally much better than expected. According to Administrator McAuliffe, the transition was both smooth and effective.[30] A number of people who worked closely with the Canal were interviewed in Washington in September 1981, and nearly all agreed that this aspect of the transition had been both smooth and effective. There were concerted efforts on the part of the police force to make the former Zonians feel comfortable. For example, the typical Volkswagon police car found throughout Panama was replaced with cars of similar make and model as used by the former Zonian police.[31] The new combined police protection was so efficient in the U.S. residential areas that the incidence of crime was actually reduced in 1980.[32] On the other hand, in neighborhoods and suburbs where Canal employees of West Indian extraction resided, crime increased during the same period because police protection in those areas deteriorated significantly.[33]

On April 1, 1982, total police, judicial, and legal functions were completely transferred to Panama without incident. In a nationalist celebration to commemorate this transfer, Foreign Minister Jorge Illueca noted that "for the first time in 5 centuries, at the end of 48 decades of Spanish, Colombian and U.S. jurisdiction, Panama is acquiring full jurisdiction in its territory."[34]

Defense Services

The Department of Defense also assumed a number of public functions under the treaty. This had a greater immediate impact on the department than any other aspect of the treaty. The functions included in this expansion of responsibility are education, health services, postal services and some reail outlets. These functions are to be provided to U.S. military personnel, civilian dependents, U.S. citizens employed by the Panama Canal Commission, U.S. contractors and any dependents of these and other persons that the United States and Panamanian governments might agree to employ.[35] These new functions increased defense operations and responsibilities and added 2,300 employees to the department's personnel staff. The department had to recruit and hire hundreds of new personnel. The department also had to expand and renovate a number of buildings and other facilities, and provide services and support for these new employees. Nearly $35 million in facilities and equipment were also transferred to its jurisdiction (see Table 6.1). It also had to take change of new construction and other new projects.

Four minor difficulties have been related to these functions assumed by the Defense Department. First, are disagreements over the procedures for air mail deliveries and cost. Second, is the problem that Panama does not recognize mail privileges for nonprofit organizations. Third, there is no

Table 6.1
NET BOOK VALUE OF PROPERTY TRANSFERS TO PANAMA ON
OCTOBER 1, 1979

	(thousands)
PANAMA CANAL COMPANY	
Channel, Harbors	$ 8,201
Thatcher Ferry Bridge	12,911
Marine Bunkering	4,193
Harbor Terminal	5,938
Employee Housing	34,985
Supply Division	2,738
Railroad Division	2,298
Other	2,793
Subtotal	$74,098
CANAL ZONE GOVERNMENT	
Roads, Streets, and Sidewalks	4,542
Street Lighting System	1,198
Miscellaneous Government Buildings	2,552
Other	1,837
Subtotal	$10,129
Total	84,187

GAO note: Values as of Feb. 5, 1980

Source: Comptroller General, *Report to the Congress of the United States*, "Implementing the Panama Canal Treaty of 1977 — Good Planning But Many Issues Remain," No. ID-80-30. Washington, D.C., General Accounting Office, May 15, 1980, p. 83.

mutually accepted criterion for billing for certain health services. Finally, some of the benefits and privileges promised to Panamanian health care professionals have not been given. These minor inconveniences will be resolved as implementation proceeds.[36]

Property Transfers

The transfer of property to Panama was one of the other issues of grave concern to the House during its debates on the implementation legislation. This issue had also been the basis for the House's contention that they be involved in the treaty ratification process in 1978. The Murphy Bill (HR111), which passed the House in June 1979, mandated congressional approval before any U.S. property could be transferred to Panama. This section of the law implied that Congress could have virtual veto power over any property exchanges, including the Canal itself in December 1999. The provision clearly violated the letter and the spirit of the treaty, and the Senate was able to remove most of it from the final legislation.

This act, as passed, authorized the secretary of state and our ambassador to Panama to coordinate treaty-mandated transfers. However, Congress retained some role in property transfer, because the president must submit a report to Congress at least 180 days before transferring U.S. property to Panama. The act also prohibited the president from transferring the Canal to Panama before December 31, 1999.

Sections 1503 and 1504 of the Panama Canal Act are the final product of the legislative compromise between the House and the Senate. Section 1503 requires that no U.S. property in Panama can be disposed of "except pursuant to law enacted by the Congress." Section 1504 requires that the president inform Congress at least 180 days before any transfer can take place. But Congress does not have veto power over the disvestment that can occur according to the original treaty provisions. In a sense, the implementing legislation itself complies with section 1503 and is the law enacted by Congress to permit such property transfers.

As of 1983, all property transfers have proceeded without any major interruptions or difficulties. On October 1, 1979, Panama assumed control of about 60 percent of the old Canal Zone. In addition, $84.2 million worth of assets were transferred to Panama. Panama will acquire $4.2 million in other assets, which are to be turned over to Panama during the first phases of the implementation.[37] Table 6.2 indicates the different transfers that constitute these totals.

The transfer of ports and railroad facilities was one of the most complicated aspects of the property transfers, yet it has proceeded smoothly and services continued. One minor problem surfaced regarding some of the port facilities, as Panama has not yet determined their future use. But this is a minor aspect of the whole transfer that has been accomplished in a surprisingly simple and effective fashion. The railroads, however, have deteriorated significantly. Service has been reduced and rolling stock and railbeds are in serious need of repairs.

The question of ultimate transfer of the Canal and the remaining Canal property in the old Zone arose in 1982. There were rumors in Washington that if Central America and/or Panama were in turmoil, as Central America is presently, that final exchange of property and of the Canal might be

Table 6.2
NET BOOK VALUE OF PROPERTY TRANSFERS TO DEPARTMENT
OF DEFENSE ON OCTOBER 1, 1979

	(thousands)
CANAL ZONE GOVERNMENT	
Division of Schools	$16,736
Other Civil Functions	823
Gorgas Hospital and Clinics	11,553
Coco Solo Hospital and Clinics	2,504
Other Health & Sanitation Facilities	1,985
General Facilities: Completed	91
General Facilities: In Progress	506
Subtotal	$34,199
PANAMA CANAL COMPANY	
Supply Division	330
Motor Transportation Division	164
Other	222
Subtotal	$ 717
Total	34,916

GAO note: May not add due to rounding:
Values as of Feb. 5, 1980

Source: Comptroller General, *Report to the Congress of the United States*,
"Impletmenting the Panama Canal Treaty of 1977 — Good Planning But Many Issues
Remain," No. ID-80-30. Washington, D.C., General Accounting Office, May 15, 1980,
p. 84.

postponed. Such talk eighteen years prior to such action can only cause problems in present relations and does nothing to resolve issues that might arise in some indefinite future.

The fears of massive land invasions by peasants and/or land speculators when Panama assumed control of approximately 60 percent of the Canal Zone territory never materialized. Instead, in such places as the Free Trade Zone in Colon, the acquisition of additional property will allow the Zone to expand and grow. This has led to major investments in the area and a World Bank $35 million loan for needed construction of additional facilities and small industry and assembly plants.

Others disagree with this positive evaluation of the use of Zonian land. One study indicated that although the use and benefits from the land should have been for the benefit of the poor and unemployed, this did not occur. Instead, according to the study:

> . . . government had no intention of fulfilling its earlier pledge to use the Canal for social benefit. Instead, the lands slated for recovery were already being carved up among the various fractions of transnational finance and the export-oriented bourgeoisie.[38]

The acquisition of parts of the former Zone will be helpful to both Panama City and Colon. Both cities have had trouble with urban growth within the old Zone and at the same time suburban growth had to take place outside the Zone, five or six miles away. Some of the problems faced can be overcome with rational urban development in areas previously inaccessible to Panama.

Costs

Before the treaty was ratified and during the implementation fight, implementation cost was a major concern for both the Senate and the House. It had been estimated that over the twenty-year period of the treaty that the costs of implementation would range between $600 million and $1.2 billion. Treaty and implementation opponents on the Merchant Marine and Fisheries Committee placed the costs much higher — over $4 billion. In addition, they placed the overall value of the total properties and Canal to be transferred to Panama as high as $20 billion. These figures, however, were generally rejected by Congress and by the administration.[39] A significant portion of the lower predicted costs are to go to Canal employees, many of whom are U.S. citizens. Nevertheless, the legislation attempted to minimize the costs of implementation. Four approaches were used to reduce costs. First, many of the expenses will be borne by Canal users by requiring that they be taken from tolls. Second, interest payments to the U.S. Treasury on U.S. capital investments in the Canal and in Panama are to continue through the life of the treaty. In 1978, this payment amounted to $19.4 million, and $11.3 million in 1981.[40] Third, the Congress stated in section 1344 of the bill that no U.S. tax revenues can be used to fulfill obligations of the treaties. Finally, section 1302 requires that no more than $666 million be appropriated to cover other treaty costs over the twenty-year period.

In addition, Congress attempted to reduce costs by strictly controlling two treaty financial agreements; the Panamanians claim that both directly violate the treaty. The first is related to the $10 million a year payment for the services while the second deals with the treaty's $10 million contingency payment. This was to be paid to Panama when the profits of the Canal exceeded expenditures sufficiently to do so. Under the legislation, however, it can only be made after a long list of requirements are first met, including a number of payments to the United States. These payments include the interest payment on original capital investment in the Old Zone and other maintenance and improvement costs. The 1979 GAO Report indicates that this provision may be in violation of Article XIII, Section 4C of the Treaty.[41] According to a State Department source, the Panamanians view this provision as a method to deprive them of this contingency payment when a surplus occurs. Undoubtedly, they are correct. The House maintains, on the other hand, that all capital improvements, costs, and purchases must be met before this contingency payment can be made. Panama contends that such costs as capital improvements and major purchases of new equipment should be made without regard to the contingency fund. Therefore, there is a constant, low level of disagreement that creates unnecessary animosity between Panama, the commission, and the House of Representatives. In 1980, $2.7 million were paid despite the fact that some of the conditions of the implementation act were not met.[42] The 1982 payment was still under review in June 1983. If the House would have been less adamantly opposed to the treaties, much of this structural and financial tension could have been avoided.

The actual out of treasury costs above revenues are very difficult to determine. Many of the costs are not directly related to the Canal and its maintenance and operations, but include such items as defense expenditures, employee payments and benefits, support for military dependents costs, etc.

The Comptroller General estimates that the Department of Defense will incur 98 percent of the overall treaty costs to the United States. The rest will be divided among eight other agencies. The army will incur the largest portion of this 98 percent. If the defense costs, property transfers, and capital improvements on the Canal are not considered, the United States actually saved money in fiscal year 1980 due to the implementation of the treaties. Despite these savings, the overall expense of operating and defending the Canal increased after implementation took effect.

Most costs accruing to the United States over the next twenty years, other than defense, will be in the category of capital improvements. In order to keep the Canal open and operating, it will have to be maintained at an even higher level than before the new treaties were implemented. This condition exists for two main reasons. First, much of the original equipment is still in place; and as it continues to age, maintenance costs will increase. Second, the ships using the Canal are approaching maximum size limitation (110' x 1000'). For example, as recently a 1976, less than one third of the ships using the Canal had an 80 foot beam or greater. By 1981, nearly 50 percent of the ships were in this size category.[43] These larger ships will strain the Canal's present facilities and thereby create higher maintenance costs.

Ex-Congressman Robert Bauman expressed typical House antitreaty sentiment when he criticized increases in capital improvement costs. He stated, "One of the objectives of Public Law 96-70 was to restrict new capital expenditures unless necessary since any such improvements will accrue to the benefit of Panama as opposed to the operation of the Canal itself."[44] This short-sighted concern hampers the efficient and effective operation of the Canal, and reveals the fear that Panama might benefit from these improvements twenty years from now.

This xenophobic and ill-conceived view is not only counterproductive but inaccurate as the Untied States continues to be the major commercial user of the Canal. Similarly, the military, should it need to use the Canal, needs a facility that can work at peak performance. In order to assure these types of continued use, the United States should be willing to continue capital improvements at a high level and not let the facility deteriorate despite the fact that Panama may someday enjoy some small benefit from it.

Along with capital improvement costs, employee salaries and benefits will continue to increase costs. Most of these increases, however, will be borne by higher toll rates. The costs of defense will be the other category that will increase cost to the U.S. taxpayer. This cannot be avoided and is a natural cost of a major sea-going nation, and one determined to remain a principal power in the region.

In order to meet these increased expenses and the other treaty-mandated payments to both Panama and the United States, tolls had to be increased. This was to assure that the users paid for these costs and that they not be paid by the U.S. taxpayer. On October 1, 1979, the average costs for Canal transit increased by almost 30 percent. Despite an anticipated reduction in Canal traffic due to this price hike, an increase in traffic actually occurred.[45]

Overall, financially the Canal did very well in its first year of operation under the new circumstances. There was a 9 percent increase in tonnage and nearly fifty ships more a month traversed the Canal. Toll revenues increased by about 40 percent from $210 to $293 million. Part of this was due to the increased traffic, but most of it was due to the 29.3 percent increase in toll rates that became effective on October 1, 1979.[46]

Canal Operation

The number of ships using the Canal, as well as their size, increased in 1980, 1981, and 1982. General Secretary of the Panama Canal Commission Michael Rhode, Jr., indicated in the spring of 1983 that the Canal was operating better and more efficiently than any time in the past.[47] Average daily transits had increased from thirty-six to nearly forty by 1982, the most successful year in the Canal's history. More tonnage transited the Canal and more toll revenues ($325 million) were collected than ever before.[48]

Nevertheless, the economic recession and the opening of a trans-Panamanian oil pipeline in October 1982 reduced Canal usage in 1983. Although Canal improvements made in 1981 and 1982 allowed for between forty-two and forty-four ships to transit per day, only approximately thirty-five were doing so. This short-fall will cause the Canal to operate in the red in 1983, despite a number of budget-cutting maneuvers made by the Panama Canal Commission to avoid a deficit. This also forced the commission to raise tolls again by 9.8 percent in March 1983.[49]

Dealing with financial problems is much more difficult for the commission than for the previous Panama Canal Company. In the past, the company, with its flexibility and different rules, could have resolved these problems more easily. In a very real sense, the House sent a message to the commission and to Panama by the restrictions placed in the legislation. The implication is that neither Panama nor the commission can be trusted. Therefore, Congress must exercise a continual oversight of the commission and the Canal operations. It seems clear that this paternalistic sentiment is a strongly entrenched attitude in the House, an attitude that the House wishes to underscore in its relations with Panama. The record established by the Panama Canal Company was one of the most admirable in the United States government. Unfortunately, the House refused to recognize past success and determined that they could do better themselves with more interference and control.

Defense

Basically, the treaties provided for the defense of the Canal before and after the year 2000. The implementation legislation further provided that in the event of an armed attack against the Canal, or if the president of the United States determined that the security of the Canal is threatened, the administrator of the commission will comply with any directives that the U.S. military officer in charge of Canal protection may consider necessary. In essence, this is a watered-down version of the House request that the U.S. military assume control of the commission and the Canal under such circumstances.

One of the most critical issues during the treaty negotiations was the use of the Canal Zone lands and water for the defense and operation of the Canal. It was extremely difficult to obtain agreement on exactly what land was *necessary* for U.S. defense of the Canal until treaty termination. Approximately 60 percent of the Zone lands were ultimately turned over to Panama on October 1, 1979. Most of the remaining 40 percent was held for defense bases, training and military housing (see Map 6.1).

During the debates on the treaties, defense was major issue. Opponents were convinced that the treaties would surely weaken defense and make the Canal even more vulnerable. This main fear of the treaty opponents has not materialized and in a very real sense just the opposite has occurred. Admiral Thomas H. Moorer (USN Ret.) stated in his testimony against treaty ratification before the Senate Committee on Foreign Relations that "we have, in fact, in my view a Torrijos-Castro-Moscow axis . . . do not be surprised if this treaty is ratified in its present form, to see a Soviet and/or Cuban presence quickly established in the country of Panama.' "[50] Not only has such a presence not been established, but Panama has remained a strong ally and a strong, stable nation in a Central American region of discontent, violence, revolution, and anti-U.S. sentiment.

Since October 1979, defense fell under a cooperative military arrangement. Although the Untied States retained primary responsibility for defense, the Panamanian National Guard will gradually increase its responsibility and capability. Although it is possible that the United States may not have any bases on Panamanian soil after the year 2000, it will still defend the Canal from external threats.

The National Guard of Panama is primarily a police force, but its training, equipment, and capabilities will be improved over the twenty-year period in order to provide adequate national defense. Until December 31, 1999, the United States and Panama will hold joint responsibility for the defense of the Canal from internal and external threats. The United States will train and help equip the National Guard and coordinate activities and defense with them through programs established in the treaties and the legislation. U.S. military aid will continue at higher levels than in pre-treaty years. After January 1, 2000, the U.S. military will continue to cooperate to maintain Canal neutrality and operations. In addition, the implementation legislation mandated that the president negotiate an agreement with Panama to allow for a U.S. military base or bases to remain in Panama after January 1, 2000.

After implementation, the U.S. military and the Panamanian National Guard held joint maneuvers, cooperated in training and patrolling activities, and began working out the details for joint defense and security activities. Several agreements were also made resolving specific problems and issues that arose as the treaties began to be implemented.

The domestic threat to the Canal has diminished tremendously due to the new treaty. Since the U.S. military and the Panamanian National Guard

MAP 6.1 CANAL ZONE AFTER 1977 TREATY

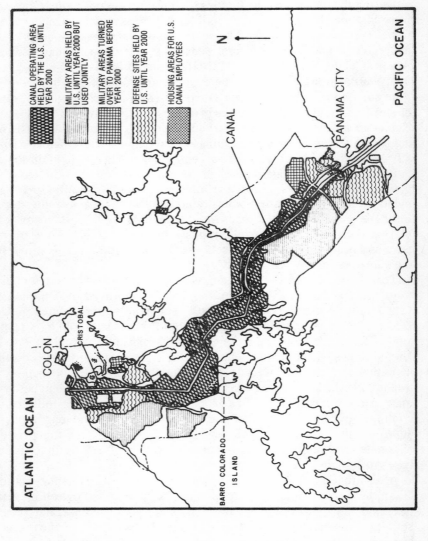

CANAL OPERATING AREA HELD BY THE U.S. UNTIL YEAR 2000

MILITARY AREAS HELD BY U.S. UNTIL YEAR 2000 BUT USED JOINTLY

MILITARY AREAS TURNED OVER TO PANAMA BEFORE YEAR 2000

DEFENSE SITES HELD BY U.S. UNTIL YEAR 2000

HOUSING AREAS FOR U.S. CANAL EMPLOYEES

N

ATLANTIC OCEAN

COLON

CRISTOBAL

BARRO COLORADO ISLAND

CANAL

PANAMA CITY

PACIFIC OCEAN

began working together on Canal defense, there is much less threat now from domestic violence and civil unrest. If the treaties had not been ratified before the fall of Anastasio Somoza in Nicaragua or he political crisis in El Salvador, surely Panama would have experienced similar political unrest. This would have been especially true after Torrijos's death on July 31, 1981.

Unresolved Issues

Some interagency rivalry has surfaced as implementation has occurred. This is not surprising, as four major agencies, as well as over twenty different subcommittees, are attempting to coordinate and accomplish the changes that the treaty and the legislation have mandated. The major conflict is between the Departments of State and Defense. This competition is reminiscent of the pre-1975 period. The State Department has been generally removed from direct representation on the binational working groups, and the joint working committee and its subcommittees who were responsible for working out the details and specifics of the treaties and the implementation legislation. Defense, on the other hand, moved to center stage and was completely immersed in the implementation of the treaties, the operation and defense of the Canal, and in the resolution of many of specific small issues among the government of Panama, the new Panama Canal Commission, the U.S. Defense Department, and the U.S. Embassy. With so many other entities involved and so many details to be worked out, it is surprising that there is not more duplication, misunderstanding, and lack of coordination and cooperation in the many areas of jurisdiction. For the most part, the transition and implementation have gone well and without major conflict. Nevertheless, the embassy is still not an active member of either the Coordinating Committee or the Joint Committee established after October 1979 to work on treaty and implementation problems.[51]

One of the most bizarre of the unresolved issues is that Congress has yet to pass authorization legislation for the Panama Canal Commission. Instead, the budget continues to be added as a line item to the general Department of Transportation budget.

Liability for vessel and cargo damage in the Canal and the locks remains unclear. Congress has been requested to clarify this matter through additional legislation, which has been introduced, yet still not been passed. This question has caused significant financial insecurity to the commission and serious problems to some of the Canal's customers.[52]

One of most important aspects of Canal operation has become more obvious due to the economic slowdown of the early 1980s and the initiation

193

in October 1982 of the trans-Panamanian oil pipeline. The pipeline itself has captured nearly 80 percent of the Alaska North Slope oil trade that transited the Canal and which accounted for $50.8 million in toll revenues in 1982.[53] This loss of toll revenues and the continuing world economic problems caused a reduction in tonnage shipped through the Canal, resulting in a decline of toll revenues of approximately 10 percent during the first half of fiscal year 1983. This loss of revenues will probably cause the Canal to run a deficit for the year.

The Canal operates on a very narrow financial margin. Although a nonprofit operation, it must not generate a deficit that requires the U.S. taxpayer to balance the budget. The window of profitability for the commission is very narrow because of the restrictions placed on the commission by PL 96-70, the cost of maintaining and operating the Canal and the costs of capital expenditures. This narrow margin of profit could cause some difficulties in the future, and raise some important questions concerning proposed modifications of the Canal or the construction of a sea-level canal. The implementation legislation provided for presidential authorization of a joint committee to study the possible construction of such a sea-level canal.

The question of different Canal options was studied in detail in late 1982. A conference on "Future Trans-Isthmian Transportation Alternatives" was organized by the *Futures Group* and held in Washington, D.C. Although it came to no conclusions, it did examine the major suggested alternatives and raise important questions concerning any options to the currently utilized system of locks and lakes. These included, who will benefit? How will the changes be paid for and how will they be financed? Are changes justified given the adequacy of the Canal, the costs of changes, and projected demands on the Canal? Table 6.3 reveals some of the cost-related problems of any alternatives.[54]

In an interview with one of the participants of this conference in June 1983, it was suggested that a number of financial problems must be resolved before any of the physical alterations in the Canal are seriously considered. He also stated that the idea of a sea-level canal was dead for the foreseeable future, because of the enormous costs, the uncertainty of need and demands, the problems of construction, and the questions relating to environmental impacts.[55]

Whereas alterations of the present Canal could run as high as $4 billion — $7 to 8 billion if interest charges are included — the costs of a sea-level Canal range from $15 to 20 billion, including interest charges.[56] In view of these facts, plus the fact that construction may encounter unforeseen problems causing significant cost overruns, environmental damage, and

Table 6.3
COMPARATIVE COSTS OF ALTERNATIVES
TO THE PRESENT CANAL

Option	Cost	Capacity	Cost/Ton
1. Pipeline	$200 million	50 m tons	$ 4 m/ton
2. Widening of Gaillard Cut	$500 million	40 m tons	$12.5 m/ton
3. Lopez-Moreno with interest costs	with $8.0 billion	250 m tons	$32 m/ton
4. Sea-level canal with interest costs	$20 billion	250 m tons	$80 m/ton

given the inelasticity of current financial margins, it is difficult to justify an expense of this magnitude.[57]

Given the current Canal capacity and the improvements already scheduled for the Canal, the present facility should be adequate until the early 1990s and perhaps even later. Also because of the attitude of Congress towards the Canal and capital improvements, it is doubtful that the U.S. government will be able or willing to finance any significant changes in the Canal in the foreseeable future.

A number of other minor issues remain unresolved. Although they will require some discussion and cooperation, they should not result in any major negotiations or difficulties. Consequently, they will present some inconveniences, but with patience and cooperation they will be resolved as new processes and procedures are developed and other problems solved.

During much of 1980, 1981, and 1982, the United States and Panama concentrated their efforts as well as their criticisms on all of the minor details and small unresolved problems instead of the major difficulties, such as commission type, public services, economic disagreements, the contingency fund, and employee concerns. This approach was dysfunctional and will not help to resolve these major conflicts. Panama and the United States must attempt to solve the major problems first and many of the minor details will work themselves out.[58]

In any interaction and agreement as complex as this, there are bound to be myriad problems, negative impacts, and misunderstandings concerning specific issues, functions, jurisdictions, and responsibilities. With the level of politicking that went into the ratification of the treaty and the drafting and passage of the implementation legislation on the part of the United States, it is surprising that the issues were not more conflictual and the unresolved problems much greater.

U.S.-Panamanian Relations After Carter

The ratification of the treaties created a new era in relations between Panama and the United States. The principal gain for Panama was psychological. The treaties reduced tensions, frustrations, and the image of colonialism. In addition, the treaties promised a new orientation of equality and partnership. The Panamanians would like the new relationship to evolve into one of equal partnership, cooperation, and respect for one another's sovereignty.[59]

After the treaties were ratified, relations between the Untied States and Panama in general and between General Torrijos and President Carter in particular improved. Nevertheless, there were times when relations were less than favorable. One instance, in particular, occurred in the summer of 1979 when the House of Representatives debated the implementation legislation. Fears grew and confrontation seemed inevitable, when by mid-September the implementation legislation was still not passed. Once legislation passed, relations improved and implementation began on October 1, 1979. Relations remained cool, however, as President Aristides Royo attacked aspects of the legislation as contrary to the spirit and letter of the treaties.

In marked contrast, when the Shah of Iran was in trouble and hospitalized in the United States, to whom did we turn? Panama was willing to suffer the domestic political consequences of allowing him to enter during his recuperation period.

Other incidents such as the following occurred, before the transfer of Canal and Zone property on October 1, 1979, that placed a strain on U.S. - Panamanian relations. In late spring 1979, a group of U.S. businessmen and government officials negotiated with the Panama Canal Company for the return of the only remaining steam locomotive that had been used during the construction of the Canal. Engine 299 had been on display at the Balboa Station, but was shipped from Panama to the Paterson Museum in New Jersey without the Panamanian's knowledge. This action brought a swift condemnation from the Panamanian National Legislative Council as a "flagrant violation of the treaty" and was termed the "Great Train Robbery" by one of the leading newspapers.[60] This action clearly indicates the paternalistic attitude of the United States and our insensitivity Panama.

Problems with the implementation legislation, generated in part by congressional attitudes, continued to make the transition to a more equal and partnership-like relationship somewhat less than smooth. In addition, the transition from the Carter administration to the Reagan administration witnessed a shift by the United States from an attitude and stated policy of partnership to one of "cooperation." U.S. domestic politics and an increase in popularity of the conservative internationalist view hindered the achievement of a truly equal partnership.

When the Reagan administration assumed power, the Panamanians expected the worst. They vividly remembered how negotiations were suspended in 1976, due to the campaign rhetoric emanating from the Reagan camp. They were relieved when Reagan did not resurrect the issue of the treaties as a major political question in the 1980 campaign, but instead said that he would abide by the treaties as the law of the land. Incidentally, he has even supported them against the more extremist elements of his own party, since becoming president.

Nevertheless, Reagan's lack of sensitivity and his administration's paternalistic attitudes were revealed by three incidents. In late February 1982, Mexican newspapers reported, and it was later confirmed, that President Reagan and Secretary of State Alexander Haig had sent messages to President Aristides Royo and General Omar Torrijos regarding Panama's relationship with Cuba. These messages reportedly requested that Panama be less friendly with Cuba, and that the relations be significantly cooled. President Royo responded through diplomatic channels rejecting the letter and indicated that it was an infringement on Panamanian sovereignty. General Torrijos returned the notes and suggested that they had been sent to him by mistake and surely they were meant to be sent to Puerto Rico instead.

Panamanians, even more so than other Latin Americans, are very sensitive about foreign intervention. They fear military intervention by the United States on the order of "gunboat diplomacy" which occurred in Panama prior to the 1936 revision of the Hay-Bunau-Varilla Treaty and more recently in 1965 in the Dominican Republic and in Grenada in 1983. Therefore, they have been quite concerned about U.S. policy in El Salvador, Nicaragua, and Grenada. They have not openly worked counter to that policy as has Mexico, but they have been preoccupied with it and have consistently worked for a negotiated settlement as a part of the Contadora group. Our insensitivity to their attitudes was illustrated in the early months of 1981 when U.S. counterinsurgency military units were trained in Panama at the U.S. bases and then, with great fanfare and media coverage, flown out of Panama directly to El Salvador to aid the military government there. It may have been more diplomatic to have had less media coverage and to have sent these U.S. advisors to El Salvador from a base within the United States rather than implicating Panama so directly in this action. This is typical of U.S. paternalism and its use of Panama for its own convenience and illustrates the lack of concern for Panama's political problems, sovereignty, and internal pressures.

The choice of U.S. ambassadors to Panama is another important issue that will continue to affect U.S.-Panmanian relations. In 1982, Senator Jesse Helms (R-NC) suggested that Luis Tambs, who was teaching Latin American history at the University of Arizona, replace Ambassador Ambler Moss. Dr. Tambs was one of the few very outspoken Latin American specialists to strongly oppose the treaties in 1977 and 1978. He was adamant in his opposition testimony before the Senate Foreign Relations Committee, and he suggested that the Panamanians were incapable of running the Canal. He also stated that the Canal would surely end up in the hands of the Communists shortly after treaty ratification.[61] His views were well known in Panama and his suggested appointment caused a great commotion in Panamanian newspapers. To suggest such a strong opponent to the treaties as an ambassador, sent a strong message to Panama that cooperation and compromise in the continuing treaty implementation might be replaced by confrontation. Although Dr. Tamb's name was eventually withdrawn, the perceptual damage had already been done.

All of these actions, like the debate over the treaties and the legislation, had a negative effect on U.S.-Panamanian relations. They all indicate a U.S. presumption of superiority or at least superior national interests, and a lack of sensitivity; and they illustrate that the United States has not yet given up the idea that the former Zone is still U.S. territory, to be used for U.S. policy and programs irrespective of Panamanian sentiment and policy.[62]

Despite the difficulties and the conflicts over PL 96-70, the locomotive incident and the other aforementioned problems, U.S.-Panamanian relations have remained quite positive. There has been important and continuing cooperation and coordination of Canal operations, management, and maintenance. Cooperation and joint operations by the police forces of both nations within the former Zone have been very evident. Both the U.S. Army and the Panamanian National Guard have coordinated their activities. Property exchanges and other joint activities have proceeded smoothly and without major difficulty. By the end of 1983, Panama still remained close to the United States and had become an example of moderate military reform and rule. Panama's stability is in stark contrast to the revolutionary and violent activities of its Central American neighbors. Panama has also continued to work for a negotiated settlement in Central America. Panamanians fear an expansion of the conflict and a possible increase of U.S.

198

interference in their own affairs. Nevertheless, there have been few riots and demonstrations in Panama against the United States, despite the rise of anti-U.S. sentiment in other Central American nations. Panama has remained calm and has continued to be one of our best allies in the region.

Domestic Politics in Panama

One of the most interesting and least known aspects of the whole treaty process was the democratizing effect it had on Panama. Despite claims made in Congress that General Torrijos was a dictator and a traditional Latin American military strongman, he seldom exercised excessive force and was generally quite an effective leader without resorting to violence and intimidation. Alan Riding describes him:

> as a politician, he began as an authoritarian and grew into a conciliator. His power was unchallenged, yet he was rarely repressive; he used acute political instincts to keep his enemies off balance and his supporters divided. He was a poor orator, but he had a charismatic hold over those who followed him.[63]

Panama's ratification of the treaties was more democratic than that of the United States. On October 23, 1977, the entire electorate of Panama had the opportunity to express their sentiment on the treaties. They voted in favor of them by a 2-to-1 margin, after a fairly open period of discussion with numerous demonstrations against them. It was reported by most foreign observers that the election was honest and fair.

Panamanian politics continued to open and "democratize" under Torrijos's leadership. In 1978, elections were held for a constituent assembly designed to amend the constitution and a new president, Aristides Royo, was appointed. General Torrijos stepped out of public office but continued to influence politics from behind the scenes, although, he reduced his input in some of their policy decisions. In 1979, he formed the Democratic Revolutionary party (PRD), which will be very active in the presidential elections scheduled for 1984. Amensty for exiled political opponents was also granted in 1979. Many party leaders and political enemies of Torrijos returned to Panama, including Arnulfo Arias who was deposed by Torrijos and other colonels only ten days after he assumed the of presidency of Panama in 1968. A Freedom House worldwide survey conducted in late 1978 also indicated an improvement in Panama and classified it among three nations where the largest gains in freedom and democracy had occurred during that year.[64]

In 1980, elections for one-third of the National Legislative Council were held. Although Torrijos's faithful supporters, who had previously been appointed by him as members, continued to control the other two-thirds, the election was again fair and honest. The PRD barely won a majority of the open seats; but nevertheless, the movement towards more democracy continued. Elections for another one-third of the National Legislative Council were scheduled for 1982, and presidential elections are to be held in 1984, along with elections for the final one-third of the Legislative Council.

General Torrijos was killed in an airplane accident on July 31, 1981. Had General Torrijos lived, he probably would have run for president in 1984. Without Torrijos, progress towards a more open, democratic state may be slowed or dismantled as as struggle for power develops.

Financial Benefits

Panama began to benefit financially from the treaties in Fiscal Year 1980. In 1979, Panama received a $2.33 million annuity for the use of the Canal. Starting in FY 1980, Panama began to receive a $10 million reimbursement for public services. If the Canal has a profit, a contingency payment may also be made. In FY 1980, just under $77.7 million was budgeted to Panama. However, Panama did not receive the full amount. Approximately $3.8 million were withheld for back debts to the United States.[65] Thus, about $74 million were actually transferred to Panama in 1980. In FY 1982, $81.2 million were paid to Panama.

Although this was a significant increase in revenues for Panama over previous years, it was not the economic windfall that many Panamanians had expected. Therefore, the economic crisis that had plagued Panama for the last few years continued. Of the 1980 budget, these Canal-related monies would increase revenues by about 11.5 percent, from $640 to $714 million. However, Panama, like many other nations, has had the problem of deficit spending, which had helped to create a huge national debt and fueled the continuing economic crisis. Many political leaders had hoped that the additional revenues from the Canal, after passage of the treaties, would resolve this problem. It failed to do so. Even with the additional Canal revenues, 1980 expenditures were still $14 million in the red.[66]

The total benefit to Panama of the additional governmental revenue will be much less than was earlier anticipated, and is therefore quite a disappointment to the political leadership. Panama cannot rely on the Canal for the necessary revenues to solve many of its socioeconomic problems. These additional revenues will help, but other methods of revenue enhancement or expenditure curtailment will also have to be sought.

The National Guard

Politics without Torrijos will develop largely on the basis on leadership of the National Guard and the personalities within the guard.[67] The 9,000 man National Guard has been a political institution in Panama for years; but since 1968, it has been the only institution with any real power. Had Torrijos lived, the guard may have adapted to its new role of joint defender of the Canal with the United States. With Torrijos's involvement with the PRD, the guard may have begun to play less of a role in politics.[68]

The guard is largely a police force. Over three-fourths of the active duty personnel participate in police activities and duties, while the other 2,000 plus make up the infantry and a small navy and air force. The infantry is armed with some artillery, light tanks, and missiles in addition to their standard arms. The air force has mostly helicopters and no fighter aircraft. The navy operates a number of small patrol boats.[69]

The impact of the treaties on the guard could be significant. It will continue to expand, as it already has from 8,000 to over 9,000 since 1978, and its training and mission will have to expand correspondingly. These changes may force its leaders more into the political arena, or they could give access to new sources of graft as more revenues flow into the government, but this will only enhance their political role. Little is likely to alter the guard's political role, however, until after elections of 1984.[70] Torrijos's untimely death probably diminishes the possibility that the guard will develop into less of a political force and will only push the guard to play a more active role, reducing its behind the scenes orientation as the subsequent power struggles impel its leadership on to the center stage.

Who stays and who goes in the civilian leadership of the nation will also depend largely on the guard. This was evident when President Royo was forced out of office in mid-1982. Whether or not elections will be held in 1984 will also depend on the guard.[71]

In July 1982, Royo was replaced by Vice President Ricardo de la Espriella. Although Colonel Florencio Flores Aquilar emerged as head of the guard after Torrijos's death, he retired in March 1982 as did other older leaders in the guard. The new leadership of the guard continues to show that it controls politics through control over the executive and its own organization. Little major political activity will occur without the guard being responsible for it.

To many, the action of the guard in July and August of 1982 seems to indicate that the ''National Guard has taken all power back into its own hands.''[72] Nevertheless there are still power struggles within the National Guard leadership. Torrijos's death has left a vacuum that is yet to be filled and the battles are not yet over.[73]

There are numerous field officers who could emerge from the internal power struggle taking place. Many junior officers have not been promoted for years and a few of the senior officers are very close to the twenty-five year limit on service and should legally retire before 1984. Their continued presence in the military could lead to strong pressures in the lower ranks and a possible barracks rebellion.[74] Whatever happens with regard to the elections in 1984 depends largely, but not entirely, on the guard's leadership and who emerges from the power struggles within it. Whether Panama will have elections or decide its political future by other means also depends on actions by opposition political leaders and groups outside the guard; financial conditions within Panama; Panama's labor organizations, business groups, and government bureaucracy. The Canal will also play a major role. Any significant changes in Canal traffic, operations, and profits could in turn have an impact on domestic politics and definitely will affect the domestic economy. Pressures will also be brought by actions of the United States and its military, by conditions in neighboring countries, and by the reactions of the United States to these conditions and threats.

Conclusions

Whereas the Senate's action on the treaties strengthened, clarified, and improved them, the actions of the House on the implementation legislation created antagonism, controversy, problems, and misunderstandings. They also established a spirit of distrust and misunderstanding between the United States and Panama. The implementation legislation also defeated some of the good will created by the ratification of the treaties.

Recent studies of U.S. foreign policy have emphasized the conflict between the executive and the Congress. Yet an analysis of the treaties, and particularly of the implementation legislation, also reveals the severe competition between the Senate and the House of Representatives. In many instances during the treaty process, the struggles and recriminations between the houses of Congress were greater than those between the Congress and the president.

The main problems created by the implementation legislation revolve around the type and structure of the new Panama Canal Commission and around the economic issues of funding the commission and making treaty-mandated payments to Panama. The commission is highly inflexible and is tied to a complex, dual accounting system that creates a number of administrative difficulties. The commission cannot react quickly to changing traffic conditions, and financial difficulties are much more difficult to resolve. It is less business like and there is less incentive to run the Canal on a cost-effective basis than under the old Panama Canal Company. In addition, after four years of operation, the Congress has yet to pass authorization legislation for the commission. Instead, funding for the commission has been on an ad hoc basis under the overall auspices of the Department of Transportation budget. Therefore, the House has created an unworkable situation. The conflict between the House and the commission reduces the ability of the commission to function more efficiently and effectively. The House demands oversight of the commission but is unwilling to assume that power in a responsible fashion. This, along with restrictions on the service-related payments and the contingency fund payments, created continued friction between the United States and Panama. Thus, many of the major impacts of the implementation legislation have an ongoing negative influence on the bilateral relationship.

Despite these problems, the actual implementation of the treaties and the transfer of the properties and services have occurred without major delays, problems, or disruptions. Most U.S. Canal employees remained on their jobs in Panama in spite of the prediction that the majority would leave if the treaties were ratified. Granted, there are many employee-related difficulties and new stresses in their lives, but they are generally less than were forecast.

Since the treaties took effect, the Canal has continued to operate smoothly and efficiently. Traffic increased through 1982 over earlier years. Improvements have been made on the Canal, and it remains an effective, open waterway for international trade and transportation.

One of the goals of the treaties was to improve U.S.-Panamanian relations, and indeed, they did improve. As a major source of conflict, the 1903 treaty, was removed. Yet, the relationship of equal sovereign powers envisioned in the Kissinger-Tack Agreement and by President Carter did not occur. It was impossible for two nations with such unequal power and historical ties to fundamentally alter this relationship in such a short time.

The Panamanians have generally showed good faith in their attempt to improve their partnership with the United States. They have been mild in their criticisms of the implementation legislation and the problems that it has created. They have underreacted to the verbal attacks of U.S. congressmen and senators. They have remained quiet while the rest of Central America has been caught up in ferment and violence. Generally the United States has not recognized these positive signs, but has only reacted to the friction and the disagreements. Despite this, relations have improved, but the United States still takes Panama for granted and is insensitive to Panama's needs and political requirements.

Domestic conditions in Panama were also changed by the treaties. Panama became more democratic and more politically open. Nevertheless, the National Guard continues to dominate the political scene, despite the move towards more democracy after the treaties. On the other hand, the economic windfall hoped for by Panama did not materialize. The revenues increased by ll.5 percent in 1980 and by approximately the same figure again in 1981.

With all that has occurred, Panama has remained a calm nation in a sea of turmoil and violence in the Central American region. The ratification of the treaties deprived the extremists in Panama of their principal issue and their rallying cry for demonstrations and violence. With the treaties in place, Panama has remained tranquil and is progressing both economically and politically. The Panama Canal, the subject of great fears and dire predictions during the ratification and implementation debates, continues to operate efficiently and effectively, and it is open to all the world to utilize and continues to serve as resource from which each nation, in turn, may benefit.

Endnotes

[1] Some of the problems of ratification are discussed in Chapters 4 and 5.

[2] Interviews.

[3] Ibid.

[4] *Congressional Quarterly Weekly Report*, September 29, 1979, p. 2120 and *U.S. Congressional Record*, 96th Cong. 1st Session, vol. 1979, pp. H3481-H3519.

[5] Carter, *Keeping Faith*, p. 182.

[6] Ibid.

[7] *U.S. Statutes at Large*, Vol. XClll, 96th Congress, lst Session, p. 455.

[8] Comptroller General, *Report to the Congress of the United States*, "Implementing the Panama Canal Treaty of 1977 — Good Planning But Many Issues Remain," No. ID-80-30. Washington, General Accounting Office, May 15, 1980, p. 1.

[9] U.S. *Congressional Record*, 94th Cong., lst Session, Vol. 125, Oct. 19, 1979, p. S-14813.

[10] U.S. General Accounting Office, *Background Information Bearing Upon Panama Canal Treaty Implementation Legislation*, ID-79-33 June 4, 1979, p. 52.

[11] Dennis P. McAuliffe, Testimony Before the Senate Armed Services Committee in Support of Panama Canal Commission Authorization Bill FY 81, Washington, D.C., June 12, 1980, p. 2 (mimeo).

[12] *Mautatino*, 16 of Julio de 1979, pp. 8-A and 9-A, December 7, 1979, p. 7 and January 20, 1980, p. 8, and *The Los Angeles Times*, January 10, 1980. Also, interview with Panama's ambassador to the United States, Juan Josée Amado in Washington, D.C., 8 Sept. 1981.

[13] Interviews.

[14] Michael Blumenfeld, "Testimony Before the Senate Armed Services Committee in Support of Panama Canal Commission Authorization Bill FY 81, Washington, D.C., June 12, 1980, p. 3 (mimeo).

[15] Comptroller General, *Report 1980*, p. i.

[16] U.S. Congress, House, Hearings before the Subcommittee on the Panama Canal/Outer Continental Shelf of the Committee on Merchant Marine and Fisheries, *Panama Canal Commission Authorization, FY 1982, and Oversight*. 97th Congress, 1st Session, Serial No. 97-3, Washington, D.C.: Government Printing Office, 1981, p. 10. Hereafter cited as House Subcommittee on the Panama Canal, *Hearings 1981*.

[17] Ibid., and McAuliffe, Testimony, p. 4 (mimeo).

[18] Ibid.

[19] Interviews.

[20] House Subcommittee on the Panama Canal, *Hearings 1981*, pp. 10-11.

[21] U.S. Congress, House, Hearings before the Subcommittee on the Panama Canal/Outer Continental Shelf of the Committee on Merchant Marine and Fisheries, *Hearing on Panama Canal Commission Authorization, FY 1984, and Oversight*. 98th Congress, 1st Session, March 16, 1983, Washington, D.C.: Government Printing Office, 1983, p. 16.

[22] McAuliffe, Testimony, p. 4 (mimeo).

[23] John Augelli, "The Panama Canal Area in Transition, Part I: The Treaties and the Zonians," *American Universities Field Staff Reports*, North America, No. 3, 1981, p. 10.

[24] Ibid., p. 9-11.

[25] Comptroller General, *Report 1980*, p. 1.

[26] Augelli, "Panama Canal Area in Transition," p. 12.

[27] Comptroller General, *Report 1980*, pp. 15-22.

[28] Ibid., pp. 28-30.

[29] *Panama Proceedings*, vol. 1, No. 3, Spring-Summer 1982, p. 13 (A Benchmarks Publication, Washington D.C.).

[30] Panama Canal Commission, *Annual Report 1980*, pp. 17-18.

[31] Interviews.

[32] Augelli, "Panama Canal, Area in Transition," p. 12.

[33] Ibid.

[34] *Panama Proceedings*, vol. 1, No. 3, Spring-Summer 1982, Supplement, p. A-10.

[35] Interviews.

[36] Comptroller General, *Report 1980*, p. 31-36.

[37] Ibid., p. 21.

[38] Esmeralda Brown, et al., "Panama: For Whom the Canal Tolls?" *NACLA, Report on the Americas*, Vol. XIII No. 5, (Sept-Oct, 1979), p. 31.

[39] *Congressional Quarterly Almanac*, "Panama Canal Implementation Bill Clears," v. 1979, pp. 143, 148; and U.S. Congress, House, *Panama Act 1979*,

Report of the Committee on Merchant Marine and Fisheries, 96th Congress, lst Session, House Report 96-98, Part I (Washington, D.C.: Government Printing Office, April 23, 1979), pp. 145-46.

[40] Comptroller General, *Report to the Congress of the United States*, "Examination of Fiscal Year 1979, Financial Statements of the Panama Canal Organization and Treaty Related Issues," No. ID-81-14 (Washington, D.C., General Accounting Office, January 12, 1981), p. 30. Also see Panama Canal Commission, *Annual Report, 1981*, p. 31.

[41] General Accounting Office, *Background Information Bearing Upon Panama Canal Treaty Implementing Legislation*, No. IE-79-33 (Washington: General Accounting Office), June 4, 1979, pp. 0-41.

[42] Ibid., and Interviews.

[43] Panama Canal Commission, *Annual Report*, 1981, p. 11.

[44] House Subcommittee on the Panama Canal, *Hearings, 1981*, p. 67.

[45] McAuliffe, "Panama Canal Area in Transition," p. 3.

[46] House Subcommittee on the Panama Canal, *Hearings, 1981*, pp. 8-9.

[47] Interview with Michael Rhode, Jr., secretary of the Panama Canal Commission, in Washington D.C., Sept. 9, 1981, and again in April 1983.

[48] Commission Administrator's Report to the Supervisory Board, Jan. 7, 1983 (photocopy).

[49] Ibid.

[50] U.S. Congress, Senate, Committee on Foreign Relations, *Hearings Before the Committee on Foreign Relations on the Panama Canal Treaties*, 95th Congress, lst Session, Part 3, pp. 6-7, GPO Washington, 1977.

[51] Comptroller General, *Report 1980*, pp. 31-36.

[52] U.S. Congress, House, Subcommittee on Panama Canal/Outer Continental Shelf, Committee on Merchant Marine and Fisheries, *Hearing on Vessel Damage Claims*, 98th Congress, lst Session, Feb. 23, 1983.

[53] *Commission Administrators Report to the Supervisory Board*, Jan. 7, 1983 (photocopy).

[54] The Future's Group, *Final Report for the Conference on Future Transportation Alternatives Across the Panamanian Isthmus*, Prepared for the U.S. Department of States, November 15, 1982 (76 Eastern Blvd, Glastonbury, Conn). For a detailed discussion of the technical aspects of the three major canal options, see also, "An Expanded Panama Canal, Lock-Style-Two Plans," *Panama Proceedings*, Washington, D.C., vol. 1,   3, Spring-Summer 1982, pp. 4-8.

[55] Interview with Ely M. Brandes, President of International Research Associates, in Palo Alto, California, June 1983.

[56] The Futures Group, *Report*, p. 7 & p. x.

[57] U.S. Department of State, *Final Environmental Impact Statements for the New Panama Canal Treaties*, Washington: Government Printing Office, Dec. 1977.

[58] Comptroller General, *Report 1980*, pp. 61-73.

[59] Interview with Panama's ambassador to the United States, Juan Josée Amado, Washington, D.C., 8 September 1981.

[60] Frank Gillooly, "Old 299 Returns to Its Birthplace," *New York Times*, June 3, 1979, Section XI, p. 6.

[61] Senate Foreign Relations Committee, *Hearing*, pt III, pp. 154-164.

[62] Interviews.

[63] Alan Riding, "Panama: Troubled Passage for a U.S. Ally," *New York Times Magazine*, November 22, 1981, p. 121.

[64] Michael Goodwin, "Survey Says World's Civil Liberties Have Increased," *New York Times*, Jan. 8, 1979, pp. 4-6.

[65] House Subcommittee on the Panama Canal, *Hearings*, 1981, p. 13.

[66] *The Europa Yearbook*, 1981, A World Survey, Vol. II (London: Europa Publication LTD., 1981).

[67] R. M. Koster, "Panama without Caesar," *New York Times*, Aug. 9, 1981, p. IV-21, and Riding, Troubled Passage for a U.S. Ally," p. 28.

[68] Steve Ropp, *Panamanian Politics: From Guarded Nation to National Guard* (New York: Praeger, 1982), p. 114. See also "The Canal Treaties and the Future Evolution of the Panamanian State," paper presented at the Latin American Studies Association in Pittsburgh, Pennsylvania, April 5-7, 1979 (mimeo).

[69] Ibid., and Alan Riding, p. 81. The International Institute for Strategic Studies (London) in their *Military Balance 1981-1982* list Panama only in a footnote and as having 11,000 paramilitary forces.

[70] Ropp, *Pamanamian Politics*, pp. 113-115.

[71] Koster, "Panama without Caesar," and Riding, "Panama: Troubled Passage for a U.S. Ally."

[72] "Paredes Sneezes, Royo Catches Cold," *Latin American Weekly Report*, WR-82-31, 6 August 1982. See also *Panama Proceedings*, vol. 1 No. 3.

[73] Ibid.

[74] Riding, "Panama: Troubled Passage for a U.S. Ally," p. 128.

CHAPTER 7
EXPLANATIONS, COSTS, AND CONCLUSIONS

We begin our concluding chapter by addressing the question we posed at the beginning: What approach or combination of approaches explains how and why the 1977 Panama Canal Treaties were negotiated and ratified? Throughout our analysis we have employed organizational, bargaining, and ecological perspectives. An integrated approach, based on the eclectic model presented in Chapter 1, was required to investigate particular aspects of the treaties and to keep the different parts of our analysis in perspective.

The content of foreign policy is usually the product of several influences; the process of making foreign policy involves many actors with similar and divergent motives and resources. This generalization holds especially true for the 1977 treaties, which were the product of four years of successful negotiations and of two unsuccessful negotiating attempts that spanned another ten years. Ratification and passage of implementing legislation added two more years to the time the treaties were on the agenda. Time was not the only factor that made the negotiations and approval processes so complex. The Canal issue was highly salient to groups and public opinion, even during the early stages of the negotiations. As negotiations progressed, and during presidential election campaigns, the issue became increasingly politicized. Politicization invited additional entrants into the process, and the volume and variety of interests and motivations that finally emerged made the policy process much more vulnerable to coalition politics, conflict, and stalemate than is typical for most issues in U.S. foreign policy.

The complex nature of the process, and therefore the need for an integrated analytical strategy, can best be demonstrated by reviewing the participants and processes for Canal policy in terms of the conceptual model presented in Chapter 1 (see Figure 7.1) The usual participants in the foreign affairs subpresidency[1] were involved: political and policy advisers to the president; the National Security Council and its staff; and the negotiating team, based in the Department of State, that included the deputy negotiator for the Department of Defense after 1975. Other actors at this level included internal and interdepartmental working groups, such as the Defense Department's Panama Canal Negotiations Working Group and the interagency group of financial experts that "discussed" Panama's last-minute demands for greater economic benefits. In addition to these participants, advice, clearance, and concurrence were occasionally required from the Departments of Treasury, Commerce, Transportation, Labor, Justice, the Federal Aviation Administration, and Civil Service. Of

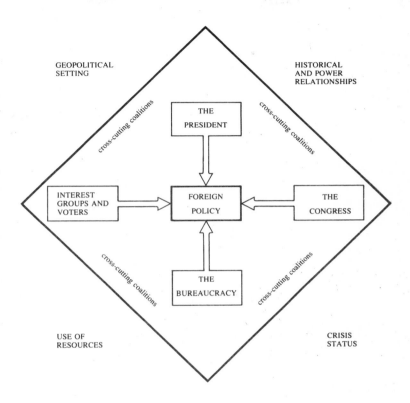

Figure 7.1
Influences on Foreign Policy

GEOPOLITICAL
SETTING

HISTORICAL
AND POWER
RELATIONSHIPS

cross-cutting coalitions

cross-cutting coalitions

THE
PRESIDENT

INTEREST
GROUPS AND
VOTERS

FOREIGN
POLICY

THE
CONGRESS

cross-cutting coalitions

cross-cutting coalitions

THE
BUREAUCRACY

USE OF
RESOURCES

CRISIS
STATUS

these departments, State and later Defense, were most interested in and committed to the success of the negotiations and ratification processes. Once the treaties were signed, and throughout the Senate debate, the White House and executive agencies were remarkably united in strong support for the 1977 treaties. The Committee of Americans for the Canal Treaties (COACT), the bipartisan umbrella group described in Chapters 4 and 5, was established to support and coordinate the activities of unaffiliated groups and individuals as well as protreaty cross-cutting coalitions.

Staff members of executive agencies opposing negotiations combined with vested interests in other agencies and with antitreaty elements within their respective clientele groups. These temporary coalitions had ample

209

opportunity to act against the 1974-77 negotiations and to publicize their viewpoints on the issues. In the Congress, on the other hand, cross-cutting coalitions opposing the treaties and linked to committees and subcommittees in the Senate and House, operated and gained strength after the treaties were signed and throughout the ratification and implementation processes. The participation of eight committees and subcommittees, some with clientele groups strongly interested in or affected by the treaties, created numerous opportunities for cross-cutting coalition building. These coalitions threatened the ratification of the treaties in the Senate. Certain members of the House who were particularly adamant in their opposition to the 1977 treaties acted as both individuals and coalition leaders and were quite effective in shaping and delaying treaty implementation legislation.

Public opinion played several roles during the ratification process.[2] National opinion surveys were commissioned by treaty opponents and supporters and by the Department of State. Statewide surveys, frequently using less than objective questions, were also used to justify positions taken by senators and representatives and by support and opposition groups and by coalitions. All of these participants and the administration tried to influence public opinion; mass media and direct mail campaigns were integral parts of both sides' strategies. The antitreaty ''truth squad'' and the protreaty COACT prepared media packets for their affiliated groups, complete with sample radio spots, letters to the editor, texts for short and long speeches, and fact sheets. The public responded. Senators and Representatives reported receiving hundreds of thousands of postcards, letters, telephone calls, and telegrams. In addition, newspapers throughout the country received letters to the editor and ran editorials on the treaties, and citizens prone to more active participation attended rallys and speeches.

The Canal issue not only had symbolic and emotional appeal, but also personal relevance for many citizens. Many adults remembered being taught in school about Teddy Roosevelt and the Panama Canal and about the valiant struggle against Yellow Fever and other tropical diseases. As a foreign policy issue having public appeal, the 1977 treaties had many advantages over such unfamiliar issues as selling AWACS to Saudi Arabia or a civil war in Chad or even El Salvador. Although many people surveyed did not know a great deal about the provisions of the treaties, they did have some ideas about Panama and the U.S. presence and property there. Most had strong feelings about changing the treaty relationship. Pro- and antitreaty campaigns in the mail and the media addressed these feelings and the symbolic value the Canal had acquired over the years.

The degree of involvement of people, groups, and agencies, as well as congressional and executive actors cannot be explained sufficiently by organizational approaches. Much remains to be explained even after considering and combining the following organizational approaches: the separation of powers approach accounts for institutional vested interests and opportunities for conflict, the bureaucratic politics approach accounts for internal and interdepartmental patterns of involvement, conflict, and cooperation; and cycles of dominance and competition for influence over foreign policy account for conflict between the executive and legislative branches. Organizational approaches and theories about the policy process can explain the actions taken by individuals and groups as well as their resources, strategies, and tactics during the negotiations, ratification, and implementation processes. But what accounts for the degree of involvement by so many participants? What accounts for the depth of commitment to pro- and anti-treaty positions?

A bargaining perspective can be used to analyze the motivations of individuals and groups as well as entire departments and institutions. This perspective also adds an emphasis on beliefs about the merits and means of negotiating compromises to resolve the differences between the United States and Panama. Bargaining theory and the prerequisites for success it specifies help explain the behavior of such individuals as Senate Minority Leader Baker, Senator Allen, Ambassador Linowitz, and President Carter. In many cases, an individual's decision to become an active supporter or opponent of the negotiations and the treaties was strongly affected by his or her beliefs about the fundamental premises that reflected preconditions for successful bargaining:

1. to truly desire a compromise agreement with Panama, recognizing that compromise must be the result when negotiation, rather than force, is used to resolve differences;

2. to see the interests of the United States and Panama as reconcilable;

3. to see the negotiations and the treaties as having positive rather than harmful impacts on U.S. prestige; and

4. to believe that both nations, and especially the United States, have something to gain by negotiating and something to lose by not negotiating.[3]

The degree of consensus on these premises within a committee, bureau, interest group, or institution also helps explain group advocacy or opposition to the treaties. In the Department of Defense, for example, organizational vested interests of the army and SOUTHCOM as well as the Joint Chiefs of Staff and International Security Affairs were naturally predisposed to advocate the status quo in Panama. This institutional proclivity to resist change was displaced, incrementally and disjointedly, by a positive,

211

protreaty consensus concerning these four premises. The Panama Canal Negotiations Working Group was the first unit in the Department to develop strong, shared views about the merit of bargaining with Panama, partly due to the group's close contact with the 1971-72 negotiations, the 1973 Security Council meeting in Panama, and the development of the Kissinger-Tack Agreement on Principles. While a solid protreaty consensus in the Department of Defense finally emerged during 1977, it had not evolved in a linear and progressive fashion. Rather, as we demonstrated in Chapter 4, the process of building shared agreement on these premises and, therefore, on negotiating guidance and specific provisions, involved several major setbacks and conceptual conflicts.

Readiness to accept or reject the four premises listed above is associated with the individual's or group's world view, the set of beliefs and axioms about the United States and international affairs that form a perceptual screen for interpreting specific issues and events.[4] Divergent beliefs associated with the two dominant world views of the 1970s and 1980s, liberal and conservative internationalism, were discussed in Chapters 3 and 4. The conflicting views held by treaty opponents and supporters concerning U.S. interests, Panama, the Canal, the 1977 treaties and related issues were discussed in Chapters 3, 4, and 5. The interrelated views held by participants — about the nature of the world, about bargaining with Panama, and about the 1977 treaties — must be incorporated, along with organizational dynamics, in an integrated explanation of Panama Canal policymaking.

Explanatory concepts from both approaches are presented in Figure 7.2 as determinants arrayed in a "funnel of causality"[5] for support or opposition to the 1977 treaties. While the motives of some participants can be partly attributed to organizational missions, institutional competition, and vested interests, for many others, and especially for principal actors, the degree and intensity of involvement resulted from a combination of organizational predispositions plus, or counteracted by, these interrelated foreign policy views. Prevailing world views and the shape of the foreign policy consensus also had the impact of setting parameters for Canal policy debate within the government, among foreign policy experts, in the media, and with the public. World views and shared beliefs thus affected the setting in which organizational dynamics operated.[6]

The shape and content of the foreign policy consensus have changed during the post World War II period. Timing has been a central theme of our analysis. We have repeatedly argued that the bargaining window was closing just as the 1977 treaties were signed. The resurgence of Cold War themes in debates over U.S. foreign policy demonstrates how fragile the context for initiatives can be, whether the proposed change is conciliatory or confrontational. What influences these views and causes a shift in the

212

Figure 7.2
Funnel of Causalty Applied to Participants' Actions
on 1977 Canal Treaties

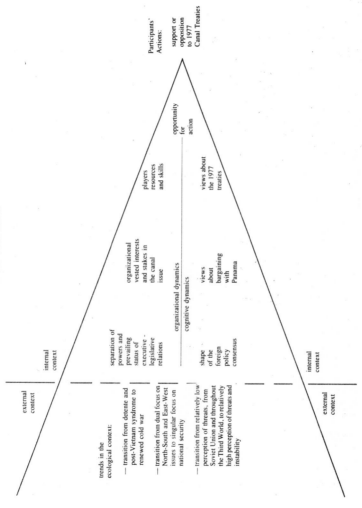

213

shape of the foreign policy consensus? An ecological approach is needed to address this question, and ecological factors are included in the funnel of causality (see Figure 7.2) as distal influences arising in the external context.

Participants' world views and their receptivity to the idea of bargaining with Panama are seen, from an ecological perspective, as a function of the prevailing geopolitical setting, historical and power relationships, and of resource relationships. The elements of these contexts and relationship affecting Panama Canal policy were discussed in Chapters 2 and 3. Two ecological trends affected the negotiation, ratification, and implementation of the 1977 treaties: a moderating trend in the early 1970s and a constricting trend in the late 1970s and early 1980s.

The moderating trend emerged in the hemisphere during the late 1960s and was solidified during the early 1970s. The trend was comprised of several elements: economic and social issues were decoupled from East-West security concerns, a unified Latin American bloc was formed to advocate common positions on North-South issues, and levels of instability and crises associated with leftist movements were reduced. For the United States, reduced perceptions of threats to security and vital interests were instrumental in its adaption to and facilitation of the moderating trend. Moderation in the region was also facilitated and reinforced by reduced tensions elsewhere, in the form of detente with the Soviet Union, rapprochement with the People's Republic of China, and negotiations to end the war in Vietnam. Anti-interventionism became a dominant theme in the post-Vietnam syndrome that affected U.S. foreign policy during the late 1970s. The lesson learned from Vietnam about the difficulty of defending an enclave from a hostile indigenous population also molded military thinking.

Several effects on Canal policy can be directly attributed to this moderating trend, as it enhanced Panama's bargaining position and legitimated claims for an end to U.S. hegemony and for justice and equity in superpower-small power relations. As we noted in Chapter 3, Panama's strategy of internationalizing the Canal issue had the effect, in this context, of providing an opportunity for the Nixon administration to revise its objectives for Canal policy. Ecological changes allowed the Nixon administration to respond positively to Panama's grievances and to agree, as the Kissinger-Tack Agreement suggested, that a superpower could contemplate a true partnership with a small power and establish a cooperative and equitable treaty relationship. Even more amazing, in light of the earlier Cold War period and recent events in the hemisphere, was the fact that the Nixon administration arrived at this conclusion without the eruption of a severe crisis. Granted, the United Nations Security Council meeting in

214

Panama was a minor diplomatic crisis, but this did not pose any type of threat. Despite the fact that there was no actual threat, we noted that the prospect of violence in Panama, against the Canal and U.S. property and citizens was an important consideration for the Nixon, Ford, and Carter administrations. Nonetheless, a confrontation involving the use of force was not the cause of a fundamental change in U.S. Canal policy. Instead, bargaining with Panama seemed to the participants involved, to be a reasonable and prudent course of action. Moreover, bargaining seemed to be a right and just response. Acceptance of the four premises about bargaining with Panama during the 1974-1977 negotiations was compatible with, facilitated by, and reinforced by this moderating ecological trend. That these conclusions could be reached in 1973 and be sustained by three administrations, except for the few notable challenges described in Chapter 4, was largely due to the nature of the ecological context and the related rise of liberal internationalism.

The foreign policy consensus was, however, divided, reflecting an alternative interpretation and perception of the regional and global contexts. As we noted in Chapters 4, 5, and 6, the times were changing, to the detriment of the Carter administration's ratification strategy, the implementation legislation, and the spirit of partnership embodied in the 1974 Kissinger-Tack Agreement. This was the second ecological trend that affected the 1977 treaties: a constricting of previously separated issues into an East-West security dimension and an increase in levels of tension between the United States and Latin American nations. Several elements were associated with this trend: 1) the emergence of perceived threats to U.S. interests and superpower status in the hemisphere and throughout the world; 2) the process of revolutionary change in Central America; and 3) the devaluation of the North-South dialogue and equity issues in favor of national security conceived in narrower, more military terms. These developments made the conservative internationalist world view more appealing and popular. To many participants inside and outside the government and especially in the Congress, the resumption of a Cold War attitude made opposition to the 1977 treaties and the implementation legislation the reasonable and prudent thing to do.

With this background established, we can now address some specific questions and summarize our conclusions about the 1977 Canal treaties. The first two questions are closely related: Why did it take so long for the United States to agree to bargain with Panama? Were new Canal treaties really necessary?

A simple answer can be given to both questions. Panama, which had demanded renegotiation of the original Canal treaty since it was signed in 1903, made its latest demand at a time and in a context that found the

215

United States ready and willing to bargain. From Panama's perspective, as we noted in Chapters 2 and 3, replacing the 1903 treaty with an equitable agreement that recognized and honored its sovereignty had always been a necessity. Treaty revisions in 1936 and 1955 had eliminated the most onerous provisions of the Hay-Buneau-Varilla Treaty, but for Panama, a more equitable treaty was not only necessary, it was long overdue.

Although the U.S. executive branch had grudgingly agreed to negotiate the 1936 and 1955 treaties, the Congress demonstrated even less enthusiasm for redressing Panama's complaints. It took three years to pass legislation implementing the 1936 treaty and two years to pass the 1955 treaty's legislation. Decades later, the 1977 treaties almost failed to obtain Senate approval. As we noted in Chapter 6, the two-year effort to pass legislation implementing the new treaties saw the Carter administration's bill rejected in favor of a House initiative that was much less favorable to Panama and the spirit of the 1977 treaties.

Public opinion during much of the ratification debate reflected only about 30 percent support for the new treaties, although the margin of opposition narrowed by the time the Senate voted on the second treaty. Mail received by members of Congress was overwhelmingly against the treaties. Clearly, the new Canal treaties were unpopular with many people inside and outside of government. Were they really necessary from the U.S. point of view?

Before 1973, administration after administration had answered this question with an adamant "no." Abrogation of the 1903 treaty was not only unnecessary, it was also contrary to U.S. interests. President Kennedy was the first to acknowledge that unilateral U.S. control, in perpetuity, could not and should not be maintained. He was not, however, ready to relinquish control. His administration, the Johnson administration, and initially, the Nixon administration were all unwilling to trade control for partnership. Instead, as we demonstrated in Chapter 3, between 1962 and 1973, the United States was interested in revising the 1903 treaty to suit U.S. needs and interests, not Panama's. Alternative forms of control were considered, including indirect control and token sharing, as the basis for draft treaties proposed by the United States. Throughout these years the United States was willing to maintain the status quo rather than bargain with Panama. At no time prior to the 1973 Security Council meeting in Panama did the United States consider a mutually satisfactory relationship or partnership to be necessary.

The events that led the Nixon administration to launch a new approach to Canal policy were discussed in Chapters 3 and 4. Of particular importance was Panama's internationalization strategy, an initiative that was facilitated by the moderating ecological trend discussed above. Panama's previous attempts to pressure the United States into negotiating a new treaty, made in 1959 and 1964, had failed largely because the regional context and Cold War consensus made these attempts appear to be threats that required a strong affirmation of the status quo. In contrast, Panama's 1973 initiative occurred in local and international environment that facilitated accommodation.

The Senate debate on the 1977 treaties, however, showed the extent to which earlier, Cold War views still prevailed; the divisive process of passing implementation legislation reflected the impact of Cold War and antibargaining views even more clearly. Thus, the time during which the United States behaved as if a new, modern treaty were necessary was quite short, between 1973 and 1978. After 1978, the Carter administration continued to support the 1977 treaties in order to preserve a cooperative relationship with Panama and to enhance U.S.-Latin American relations. Many in Congress, however, were convinced that the treaties were a misguided endeavor and sought to redress the situation by adding to the implementation legislation additional U.S. rights and mechanisms to control Canal finances, administration, and operations.

A question raised frequently during the ratification debate was whether the United States got the best bargain it could. This question is related to another: Were the treaties improved by the Senate during ratification and by the actions of the House of Representatives through the implementation legislation? Our analysis in Chapter 5 and 6 indicates that many members of Congress felt that the treaties should be improved. Even moderate senators who wanted to vote for the treaties believed that certain U.S. rights needed to be clarified, and the leadership amendments incorporating the Carter-Torrijos Statement of Understanding into the Panama Canal Treaty gained widespread support. These amendments opened the door for additional modification of both treaties, including the DeConcini Reservation. By the time both treaties were approved, both strong supporters and committed opponents were disappointed.

From an ideological perspective, both liberal and conservative internationalists were disappointed in the treaties as ratified. For liberal internationalists, acrimonious portions of the debates and modifications like the DeConcini Reservation negated the good will the negotiations had attained and the spirit of partnership the treaties embodied. Senator George McGovern (D-SD) was one of the senators who was so offended by the DeConcini Reservation that he considered withdrawing his support for the treaties. Given the premises of this world view, the implementation legislation was even more damaging and disappointing. For conservative internationalists, on the other hand, the treaties represented an unnecessary relinquishing of U. S. rights and assets. According to this world view, the

217

United States could and should have obtained a better bargain in the form of treaties more favorable to U. S. interests than Panama's.

When a different perspective, an analytical view of the negotiations process, is used to evaluate the treaties, we conclude that the United States did obtain the best bargain it could. The essence of negotiating and bargaining is compromise. This basic fact is what accounts for negative assessments of the treaties and the implementation legislation by both liberal and conservative internationalists. Liberal internationalists resented the fact that the White House compromised with undecided senators in order to win their votes for the treaties. Conservative internationalists resented the idea that the United States, a superpower, should compromise rather than dictate to a small state like Panama. From a negotiations perspective, however, both Panama and the United States made significant concessions and gained significant advantages. The United States traded relatively early termination, the year 2000, of a Canal treaty for neutrality guarantees of unlimited duration. Panama gave up its demand for immediate jurisdiction over the former Zone in return for a relatively short transition period and progressive and significant increases in Canal responsibilities for Panamanians during the treaty period. Panama also gained a greater share of economic benefits. Both the United States and Panama stood firm when essential interests were at stake; both bargained when a compromise was the only way to complete the negotiations successfully. If one assesses the 1977 treaties from a bargaining perspective that takes both parties' fundamental objectives into account, one must conclude that the United States got the best bargain it could with very few exceptions. The 1977 treaties compare positively with the essential U. S. objective of ensuring that the Canal remain open, secure, and effectively operating for the foreseeable future. The United States also sought to safeguard the interests of its citizens and employees in the former Canal Zone; the treaties and the implementation legislation succeeded in accomplishing this goal. The treaties and legislation also succeeded in providing an orderly transition to shared control and the new partnership.

Is the new partnership working and will it last? On balance, as we argued in Chapter 6, the new partnership is working well. The concept of progressively increasing Panamanian participation in Canal administration, operations, and defense, and the concept of shared economic benefits from Canal operations are integral parts of the treaties. These concepts and the detailed provisions that implement them are designed to provide self-reinforcing incentives for Panamanian cooperation. The more the partnership grows, the greater will be Panama's stake in the successful operation administration, and defense of the Canal.

218

Whereas the action of the Senate helped as well as hindered the treaties, the actions of the House on implementation generally complicated the relationship between the United States and Panama. The misunderstandings and antagonism created by the antitreaty sections of the legislation defeated some of the good will created by the ratification to the treaties.

Recent studies on the formulation of U. S. foreign policy have emphasized conflict between the executive and the Congress. Our analysis of the implementation legislation also reveals a high level of competition between the Senate and the House. This competition yielded a significant impact by the House on how the new treaty relationship would actually operate.

Many problems arose between Panama and the United States as a result of the implementation legislation. The most central is the type of organization given to the commission. Other problems include money matters such as payment for public services and the contingency payment when the Canal operations make a profit. Despite these and other lesser difficulties and misunderstandings, the implementation of the treaties has progressed on schedule and without disruptions.

Panama and the United States also have continued to develop an improved relationship. It has not reached a point of equality but it is one of high-level cooperation. The current crisis in Central America forces Panama into a paradoxical situation. They fear that conflict might escalate and somehow draw them into closer involvement. Panama is active in the search for a negotiated settlement to reduce this possibility. On the other hand, Panamanians do not want aggressive Marxist neighbors, while at the same time they speak out against U. S. use of Panama as a forward training and staging area for the conflict. This has created strong opposing attitudes in Panama that could threaten the more open democratic process that has emerged since the signing of the treaties.

The difficulties the 1977 Canal treaties encountered during ratification and implementation raise a broader question: Is the process for making and implementing treaties too complicated and demanding to allow controversial issues to be resolved through negotiations?

The treaty power is shared, under the Constitution, between the executive branch and the Senate. The fact that most treaties are not self-executing, and therefore require implementation legislation, guarantees a role for the House of Representatives as well, as is also the case when appropriations are required to fulfill treaty obligations. Involving the Congress in treaty making has drawbacks as well as advantages.

On the positive side, congressional support can represent public endorsement of a treaty. Public approval, if not full understanding, is important for a republican system of government. When political parties alternate

219

in control of government, public support of treaty commitments registered through the Congress can foster continuity in foreign policy. Similarly, when the foreign policy consensus permits, bipartisan support for treaty commitments can be registered through the advise and consent process and passage of implementation legislation. In a more practical vein, the fact that approval must be obtained from at least two-thirds of the Senate can provide bargaining leverage for the executive branch during negotiations. A U.S. negotiating team can bolster a tough stance by arguing that congressional approval would be contingent upon a particular provision or concession. Administrations have occasionally enhanced the utility of such a strategy by actually including individual senators in negotiating sessions.

These, in principle, are the advantages of having both branches involved in the treaty process. For the 1977 Canal treaties, which were the most controversial treaties to come before Congress in years, few of these advantages were evident. Only the last named, using potential congressional opposition to concessions as bargaining leverage, was evident during the Panama Canal Treaties negotiations. The U.S. negotiating team used this strategy to maintain its bottom line on Canal defense and neutrality provisions and as a justification for holding separate discussions on economic development assistance for Panama.

Our analysis of Canal policy revealed more evidence of drawbacks of congressional involvement in treaty making. Involving the Senate, and possibly the House, adds a third party to the negotiations. Unlike the foreign policy officials representing each government, however, the Congress generally lacks sensitivity to the national interests and self-image of the other country and to the background and substance of the issues under negotiation. This was the case for the 1977 Canal treaties. Moreover, a different motivation tends to guide congressional action as opposed to the behavior of both countries' negotiators. While the actions of some members of Congress many be guided by beliefs about the national interest and issue awareness, domestic political considerations are more frequently the motivating factor. Political motivations may also influence the executive branch's handling of negotiations and ratification; these, however, are usually explained, through diplomatic channels, to representatives of the other government. This occurred when the Canal treaty negotiations were officially suspended during 1976.

Both branches become deeply involved with political considerations during the ratification process, when a two-thirds majority must be mobilized to support a treaty. The political consequences of a senator's vote on the 1977 treaties were emphasized by both treaty supporters and opponents, and both sides tried to influence public opinion in undecided senators' home states.

Members of the House, who face the voters every two years, are more easily subject to political pressure, as they consider a treaty, than are senators. The one-third of the Senate facing re-election soon after a treaty is considered may also feel pressured to act on the basis of political consequences of their vote. Similarly, members of the House, or more likely the Senate, who intend to run for the presidency will consider the short and long-range implications of a treaty vote for their political careers.

In recent years, the negative political consequences for congressmen taking any visible leadership role in foreign affairs seem to have intensified. A number of prominent senators who assumed leadership roles during the ratification of the 1977 Canal treaties, Frank Church (D-Id) Richard Stone (D-Fla), Thomas McIntyre (D-NH), Dick Clark (D-Iowa) and others, lost their bids for re-election partly because of their support of the treaties. These and other senators were targeted by the New Right and the Moral Majority during their re-election campaigns for having voted "to give away the Panama Canal." While the Canal issue was relatively unusual in its saliency to the public and interest groups, the experience of these senators was not. The theme of a recent article by columnist Shirley Christian is that "some congressmen find it best to concentrate on domestic, rather than foreign, policy — if they want to be re-elected.'"[7] Christian relates several cases, including the 1977 Canal treaties, illustrating the role constituency and interest group pressure has played in changing senators' positions and political fortunes. If these cases represent an emerging trend, which is likely, then the legislative branch will become increasingly unable to play the constructive role provided in the Constitution for the treaty power. Moreover, the notable leadership roles taken during the post-World War II period by individual senators such as Fulbright, Vandenberg, Church, and Baker, will become increasingly rare during the very decade when divisive foreign policy issues appear to dominate the agenda.

Another disadvantage of congressional involvement arises from the possibility of modification of a treaty text after its ratification by the other nation. This possibility, and the prospect of failing to obtain majority support for a treaty, account for presidential use of executive agreements rather than treaties. Action by the Senate, in the form of amendments, reservations, and understandings may require additional negotiations or even prevent an exchange of ratifications. Amendments have the strongest effect, altering a treaty text; reservations can also affect the meaning of treaty provisions. If the other government objects to either type of change, the executive branch will need to take corrective action. The DeConcini Reservation to the Panama Canal Treaty did just that. As we demonstrated in Chapters 4 and 5, the DeConcini Reservation severely damaged U.S.-Panamanian relations and required complicated negotiations, involving senate leaders as well as executive officials, to repair this damage and devise a nonintervention reservation for the Neutrality Treaty. In response to changes in a treaty subsequent to its signing, the other government may refuse to exchange instruments of ratification if the U.S. version is unacceptable or substantially different from the signed text. In an era of congressional resurgence, an administration must take care to gauge the modifications that the Senate may make and forewarn the foreign government. Even with the best intentions, however, the executive cannot predict what each senator may do. It would have been impossible, for example, to predict Senator DeConcini's role in the Canal treaty ratification process.

While the case of Canal policy demonstrated the most negative aspects of congressional involvement in the treaty process, especially concerning implementation legislation, one should not conclude that the process itself is a problem. Rather, two nonconstitutional factors — the prevailing status of executive-legislative relations and the prevailing shape of the foreign policy consensus — accounted for the dislocating impacts of congressional involvement in Canal policy. In recent years, a competitive relationship between the executive and legislative branches has replaced bipartisanship in foreign affairs. The 1977 Canal treaties are only one of many issues recently on the agenda for which foreign policy making has been complicated, delayed, and altered by congressional action. The Congress has linked human rights certification to arms sales, acted to prevent covert operations, reduced administration requests for military assistance, and mandated deadlines for the end of deployment of U.S. troops abroad. Even when a majority in both houses agree with an administration's initiative or position, as was the case when an eighteen month limitation under the War Powers Act was applied to the Reagan administration's use of Marines in Lebanon, the need to assert an institutional prerogative or to respond to political pressure may prompt congressional challenges to executive power in foreign affairs.

Institutional competition would not have as great an impact on foreign policy if members of Congress and the administration shared a common set of beliefs about the world and U.S. interests. In the prevailing context, however, the foreign policy consensus remains divided, giving members of Congress who hold opposing beliefs an additional motivation for challenging the merits of executive initiatives. Our analysis of the ratification process and the passage of legislation implementing the 1977 Canal treaties demonstrated the extent to which conflicting beliefs separated members of Congress from the administration and from each other. And, as is always the case, conflicts based on differences in fundamental beliefs are more divisive and bitter than conflicts over strategy, vested interests, and details of substantive issues.

222

What, then, do our analysis and conclusions for the Canal issue suggest about prospects for cooperative solutions to bilateral and regional problems? Would executives have better success in managing bilateral and regional problems if they avoided the treaty process? Or, is the effort of building a majority consensus, in Congress, public opinion, and the media, worth the expenditure of time, resources, and political capital that may be required? Are issues on the foreign policy agenda so divisive and controversial that the executive and legislative branches cannot develop mutually satisfactory policies?

Warren Christopher, who was deputy secretary of state during the years that the Panama Canal Treaties were ratified and their implementation legislation was passed, would answer these questions negatively. He has argued, "On the basis of four years [1977-1981] in the Department of State," that

> the methods of operation now in place leave us poorly equipped to conduct the kind of foreign policy our country requires in a complex, turbulent, dangerous world. We have not yet resolved the dilemma posed by our need to reconcile the imperative of democracy at home with the demands of leadership in the world.[7]

He recommends that the executive and legislative branches form a "compact" on foreign policy making that recognizes a division of labor for each branch and is based on "mutually reinforcing commitments and mutually accepted restraints."[8]

We have reached a similar diagnosis of the procedural problem, namely that separate institutions sharing power must cooperate if that power is to be exercised effectively. We conclude, however, that a more basic ideological problem, namely a lack of consensus, prevents a return to bipartisan cooperation between the branches. An institutional rapproachement would only be effective within a context of foreign policy beliefs that are widely shared, between an administration and the Congress and among foreign policy elites and interest groups. Such a consensus would be based on shared assumptions about U.S. interests and a shared diagnosis of conditions abroad. Given the role played by the ecological context in shaping the foreign policy consensus, external conditions must become either much more or much less threatening for a unified consensus to form.

Endnotes

[1] Thomas E. Cronin, *The State of the Presidency* (Boston: Little, Brown, 2nd ed., 1980), pp. 145-55.

[2] The best summary of linkages between public opinion, groups, and policy is Bernard C. Cohen, *The Influence of Nongovernmental Groups on Foreign Policy Making* (Boston: World Peace Foundation, 1959).

[3] These bargaining conditions, identified by Robert L. Wendzel and Andrew Scott, were discussed in Chapter 1; here, the conditions are phrased in terms of canal policy and bargaining with Panama.

[4] For a discussion of axioms, see Ole R. Holsti and James N. Rosenau, "Cold War Axioms in the Post-Vietnam Era," paper presented at the Annual Conference of the International Studies Association, Washington, D.C., 1978.

[5] Angus Campbell, et. al., *The American Voter* (New York: Wiley, 1960), pp. 24-25.

[6] Shirley Christian, "Washington: Foreign Danger," *Atlantic* (October 1983), p. 36.

[7] Warren Christopher, "Ceasefire between the Branches: A Compact in Foreign Affairs," *Foreign Affairs* Vol. 60 (Summer 1982), p. 997.

[8] Ibid.,p. 998.

SELECTED BIBLIOGRAPHY

Abbott, Willis J. *Panama and the Canal in Picture and Prose*. New York: Syndicate Publishing Co., 1913.

Allison, Graham T. *Essence of Decision*: Explaining the Cuban Missile Crisis. Boston: Little Brown, 1971.

Allison, Graham T. and Peter Szanton. *Remaking Foreign Policy: The Organizational Connection*. New York: Basic Books, 1976.

Aragon, Joseph W. "Public Opinion and the Panama Controversy." Remarks made at Roundtable Discussion. 19th Annual Meeting of the International Studies Association, Washington, D.C., February 23, 1978.

Atlantic-Pacific Interoceanic Canal Study Commission. *Interoceanic Canal Studies 1970*. Washington: GPO, 1971.

Augelli, John. "The Panama Canal Area in Transition, Part I: The Treaties and the Zonians." *American Universities Field Staff Reports*, North America, No. 3 (1981).

————."The Panama Canal Area in Transistion, Part II: The Challenge of Integration and Development," American Universities Field Staff Reports, North America, Part II, No. 4 (1981).

Bailey, Thomas A. *A Diplomatic History of the American People*. 7th ed. New York: Appleton-Century Crafts, 1964.

Baldwin, Hanson W. "Con: The Panama Canal: Sovereignty and Security," *AEI Defense Review*, 4 (August 1977):12-34.

Baltimore Sun. 1975, 1977.

Bax, Frans R. "The Legislative Executive Relationship in Foreign Policy: New Partnership or New Competition?" *Orbis* 20 (Winter 1977):881-904.

Bemis, Samuel Flagg. *The Latin American Policy of the United States*. New York: Harcourt, Brace, 1943.

Bevans, Charles, compilor. *Treaties and Other International Agreements of the United States of America 1776-1949*, Vol. 10 (August 1972). Washington: Department of State.

Bishop, Joseph Bucklin. *The Panama Gateway*. New York: Charles Scribner's Sons, 1913.

Blasier, Cole. *The Hovering Giant*. Pittsburgh: University of Pittsburgh Press, 1976.

Blumenfeld, Michael. "Testimony Before the Senate Armed Services Committee in Support of Panama Canal Commission Authorization Bill FY 81." Washington D.C., 12 June 1980, p. 3. (mimeo).

Brzezinski, Zbigniew. *Power and Principle: Memoirs of the National Security Adviser*. New York: Farrar, Straus, Giroux, 1983.

225

Brown, Esmeralda, et. al. "Panama: For Whom the Canal Tolls?" *NACLA, Report on the Americas* 8, no. 5 (September-October 1979):2-37.

Bunau-Varilla, Philippe. *From Panama to Verdun: My Flight for France.* Philadelphia: Dorrance and Co., 1940.

Byrd, Harry F. "We're Going to Need that Waterway for Many, Many Years." *U.S. News and World Report,* 6 October 1975.

Campbell, Angus et. al. *The American Voter.* New York: Wiley, 1960.

Carter, Jimmy. *Keeping Faith: Memoirs of a President.* New York: Bantam Books, 1982.

Cater, Douglas. *Power in Washington.* New York: Random House, 1964.

Chang M., Moises. *Historia de Panama.* 2nd ed. Bogota, Columbia: Editorial Ltda., 1973.

Christian, Shirley, "Washington: Foreign Danger." *Atlantic* (October 1983): 36-41.

Christopher, Warren. "Ceasefire between the Branches: A Compact in Foreign Affairs." *Foreign Affairs* (Summer 1982):989-1005.

Chuang, Richard Y. "The Enactment of the Implementation Legislation of the Panama Canal Treaties by the United States." *Revue de Droit International* (October/December 1980).

_____. "The Panama Canal Issue." *Diplomatic Observer* (January/March 1978).

_____. "The Process and Politics of the Ratification of the Panama Canal Treaties in the United States." *Revue de Droit International* (April/June 1978):95-113.

_____. "The Ratification of the Neutrality Treaty by the United States." *Revue de Droit International* (July/September 1979):153-165.

Cohen, Bernard C. *The Influence of Nongovernmental Groups on Foreign Policy Making.* Boston: World Peace Foundation, 1959.

Commission Administrator's Report to the Supervisory Board, 7 January 1983 (photocopy).

Commission on United States-Latin American Relations. *The Americas in a Changing World.* New York: Quadrangle, 1975.

Comptroller General. "Implementing the Panama Canal Treaty of 1977—Good Planning But Many Issues Remain," *Report to the Congress of the United States,* no. ID-80-30. Washington: GAO 15 May 1980.

Comptroller General. "Examination of Fiscal Year 1979, Financial Statements of the Panama Canal Organization and Treaty Related Issues," *Report to the Congress of the United States,* no. ID-81-14. Washington: GAO 12 January 1981.

Congressional Quarterly Almanac. Washington, 1975-1977.

Congressional Quarterly Weekly Report. Washington, 1967-1983.

226

Congressional Record. Washington, 1955, 1977-1979.

Corwin, Edward S. *The President*. 4th rev. ed. New York: New York University Press, 1957.

Cox, Robert G. "Choices For Partnership or Bloodshed in Panama," in Commission on United States-Latin American Relations. *The Americas in a Changing World*. New York: Quadrangle, 1975.

Crabb, Jr., Cecil V. and Pat M. Hold. *Invitation to Struggle: Congress, the President and Foreign Policy*. Washington: CQ Press, 1980.

Crane, Philip M. *Surrender in Panama: The Case Against the Treaty*. New York: Dale Books, 1978.

Cronin, Thomas E. *The State of the Presidency*. 2nd ed. Boston: Little, Brown, 1980.

Dennis, Alfred L.D. *Adventures in American Diplomacy*. New York: E.P. Dutton and Co., 1928.

Denver Post. 1975.

Edward v. Carter. 580 F 2d 1055 (D.C. Cir.) 189 U.S. App. D.C., Certiorari denied 436 U.S. 907 (1978).

Eldridge, Albert F. *Images of Conflict*. New York: St Martin's, 1979.

Ford, Gerald R. *A Time to Heal: The Autobiography of Gerald R. Ford*. New York: Harper and Row and Reader's Digest Association, Inc., 1979.

Franck Thomas M. and Edward Weisband. "Panama Paralysis." *Foreign Policy*, 21 (Winter 1975-76):175.

————. *Foreign Policy by Congress*. New York: Oxford Univ. Press, 1979.

Franck, Thomas M. ed. *The Tethered Presidency*. New York: New York University Press, 1981.

Freeman, J. Leiper. *The Political Process*. New York: Random House, 1965.

Gil, Frederico G. *Latin American - United States Relations*. New York: Harcourt, Brace, Jovanovitch, 1970.

Harvard Law Review. "Transfer of the Panama Canal by Treaty Without House Approval," Vol. 29, no. 2 (December 1978):524-35.

Hermann, Charles F. "International Crisis as a Situational Variable," in James N. Rosenau, *International Politics and Foreign Policy*. New York: Free Press, 1969, p. 409-421.

Hilsman, Roger. *To Move a Nation*. New York: Doubleday, 1967.

Holsti, Ole R. and James N. Rosenau. "Cold War Axioms in the Post-Vietnam Era," A paper presented at the Annual Conference of the International Studies Association, Washington, D.C., February 1978.

————. "America's Foreign Policy Agenda: The Post-Vietnam Beliefs of American Leaders," in Charles W. Kegley, Jr., and Patrick J. McGowan, eds., *Challenges to America: United States Foreign Policy in the 1980s*. Beverly Hills, California: Sage, 1979.

227

_____. "Vietnam, Consensus, and the Belief Systems of American Leaders." *World Politics* 32 (October 1979):1-56

Hoover, Robert A. and Lauren H. Holland. *The MX Decision: A New Direction in Weapons Procurement Policy?* Boulder: Westview Press (forthcoming)

Hoover, Robert A. *The Presidency, Congress and the Strategic Arms Limitation Talks* (forthcoming).

Hovey, Graham. "Senators Hopeful on Canal Treaty," *New York Times*, 3 February 1977, p. 8.

_____. "Carter in State of Union Address, Appeals for Canal Pact's Approval," *New York Times*, 20 January 1978, p. A-3.

Hughes, Thomas L. "Carter and the Management of Contradictions." *Foreign Policy* 31 (Summer 1978):34-55.

International Institute for Strategic Studies (London). *MilitaryBalance 1981-1982*. London: Adlard & Son, Ltd, 1982.

Jensen, Lloyd. *Explaining Foreign Policy*. Englewood Cliffs: Prentice-Hall, 1982.

Kegley, Charles W. and Eugene R. Wittkopf. *American Foreign Policy: Pattern and Process*. 2nd ed. New York: St. Martin's Press, 1982.

Kissinger, Henry. "U.S. and Panama Agree on Principles for Negotiation of a New Panama Canal Treaty," [Address by Secretary of State Kissinger, [February 7, 1974]. *Department of State Bulletin*, 70 (25 February 1974):181.

Kohl, Wilfried L. "The Nixon-Kissinger Foreign Policy System and U.S. European Relations: Patterns of Policy Making," *World Politics* 27 (October 1975):1-43.

Koster, R. M. "Panama Without Caesar," *New York Times*, 9 August 1981, p. IV-21.

LaFeber, Walker. "Inevitable Revolutions." *Atlantic Monthly* (June 1982):74-76.

_____. *The Panama Canal*. Expanded Edition. New York: Oxford University Press, 1979.

Lanouette, William J. "The Panama Canal Treaties—Playing in Peoria and in the Senate." *National Journal* 9 (8 October 1977):1556-62.

Lindsay, Forbes. *Panama and the Canal Today*. Revised edition. Boston and Co., 1912, p. 41.

Lockwood, Robert. "The Legislative Veto and Congressional control of Defense Policy." A paper presented as the annual meeting of the American Political Science Association, New York, September 1981.

Los Angeles Times, 1980.

Lovell, John P. *Foreign Policy in Perspective*. New York: Holt, Rinehart, and Winston, 1970.

228

Lowenthal, Abraham F. and Milton Charleton. "Pro: The United States and Panama: Confrontation or Cooperation." *AEI Defense Review*, no. 4 (August 1977):2-11.

Maggiotto, Michael A. and Eugene R. Wittkopf. "American Public Attitudes Toward Foreign Policy," *International Studies Quarterly*, 25 (December 1981):601-631.

Mandelbaum, Michael and William Schneider. "The New Internationalisms: Public Opinion and American Foreign Policy," in Kenneth A. Oye, Donald Rothchild, and Robert J. Lieber, eds. *Eagle Entangled: U.S. Foreign Policy in a Complex World*. New York: Longman, 1979, pp. 34-88.

Matutino (Panamanian Daily Newspaper), 1979.

Mauder, Murray, "Kissinger's Statements Heat Canal Zone Talks," *Washington Post*, 19 September 1975, p. A-2.

McAuliffe, Dennis P. "Testimony Before the Senate Armed Services Committee in Support of Panama Canal Commission Authorization Bill FY 81," Washington: 12 June 1980 (mimeo).

McCain, William D. *The United States and the Republic of Panama*. New York: Russell & Russell, 1965.

McConnell, Grant. *Private Power and American Democracy*. New York: Vintage Books, 1966.

McCullough, David. *The Path Between the Seas*, New York: Simon and Schuster, 1977.

McIntyre, Thomas J. *The Fear Brokers*. New York: The Pilgrim Press, 1979.

Millett, Richard. "Central American Paralysis," *Foreign Policy* 39 (Summer 1980):99-117.

New York Times, 1976-1983.

"Now There's Treaty Trouble in Panama," *U.S. News & World Report*, 17 April 1978, p. 59.

"Panama and the United States: A Design for Partnership." Address by Ellsworth Bunker at Center for Inter-American Relations on March 19, 1974, *Department of State Bulletin*, 70 (29 April 1974):453.

Panama Canal Commission. *Annual Report*, 1980-1981.

"Panama Canal Fight: Senators Feel the Heat," *U.S. News & World Report*, 13 February 1978, pp. 37-38.

Panama Proceedings, Vol. 1, No. 2, (Fall 1981):13.

————., Vol. 1, No. 3, (Spring-Summer 1982):13.

"Paredes Sneezes, Royo Catches Cold," *Latin American Weekly Report*. WR-82-31, 6 August 1982.

Rawls, Wendell. "Senate Panel Opens Hearings on Civiletti," *New York Times*, 22 February 1978.

Riding, Alan. "Central American Quagmire," *Foreign Affairs: America and the World, 1982* Vol. 61, no. 3 (1983):641-59.

_____. "Panama: Troubled Passage for a U.S. Ally," *New York Times*, 22 November 1981, p. 121.

Ripley, Randall B. and Grace A. Franklin. *Congress, The Bureaucracy, and Public Policy*. Rev. ed. Homewood, Illinois: Dorsey, 1980.

Rogers, William D. "The Big Ditch in Panama: Get Out," *Denver Post*, 25 May 1975.

Ropp, Steve. "The Canal Treaties and the Future Evolution of the Panamanian State," paper presented at the Latin American Studies Association in Pittsburgh, Pennsylvania, 5-7 April 1979 (mimeo).

_____. *Panamanian Politics: From Guarded Nation to National Guard*. New York: Praeger, 1982.

Rosenau, James N. *Public Opinion and Foreign Policy*. New York: Random House, 1961.

Rosenfeld, Stephen W. "The Panama Negotiations—A Close-Run Thing," *Foreign Affairs*, 54 (October 1975):1-13.

Roshco, Bernard. "The Polls: Polling on Panama—5, Don't Know; Hell No?" *Public Opinion Quarterly*, 42 (1978):562.

Rowan, Carl T. "Danger Brews in Panama," *Washington Star*, 25 July 1975.

Schelling, Thomas C. *The Strategy of Conflict*. London: Oxford University Press, 1960.

Schlesinger, Jr., Arthur M. *The Imperial Presidency*. New York: Houghton Mifflin, 1973.

_____. "Congress and the Making of American Foreign Policy" in Thomas E. Cronin and Rexford Tugwell, *The Presidency Reappraised*. 2nd ed. New York: Praeger, 1977.

Schneider, William. "Internationalism and Ideology: Foreign Policy Attitudes of the American Public, 1975." A paper prepared for the 19th Annual Conference of the International Studies Association, Washington, D.C., February 1978.

_____. "Behind the Passions of the Canal Treaty Debate: A Matter of Pride and Property," *Washington Post*, 12 February 1978, p. C4.

Scott, Andrew. *The Functioning of the International Political System*. New York: Macmillan, 1967.

Spanier, John and Eric M Uslaner. *How American Foreign Policy Is Made*. 2nd ed. New York: Holt, Rinehart, Winston/Praeger, 1978.

Spanier, John and Joseph Nogee, eds. *Congress, the Presidency and American Foreign Policy*. New York: Pergamon, 1981.

Sprout, Harold and Margaret Sprout. *The Ecological Perspective on Human Affairs*. Princeton: Princeton University Press, 1965.

_____. *Toward a Politics of the Planet Earth*. New York: Van Nostrand, Reinhold, 1971.

Symington, James W. "The Canal: Use Not Territory is the Issue," *Washington Post*, 2 September 1977, p. A-27.

The Europa Yearbook: 1981, A World Survey. Vol II, London: Europa Publication LTD., 1981.

Time. 1977-1978.

Tolchin, Martin. "White House Woos Holdouts on Canal," *New York Times*, 14 March 1978, pp. 1-7.

Tower, John G. "Congress versus the President," *Foreign Affairs*, 60 (Winter 1981/82):229-46.

Turner, Domingo H. *Tratato Fatal!* Panama: Ferguson & Ferguson, 1974.

"U.S. and Panama Agree on Principles for Negotiation of a New Panama Canal Treaty." Address by Secretary of State Kissinger, 7 February 1974, *Department of State Bulletin*, 70 (25 February 1974):181.

U.S. Congress, House of Representatives. Committee on Foreign Affairs and Committee on Merchant Marine andFisheries, *United Nations Security Council Meeting in Panama*, Joint Subcommittee Hearings, 93rd Cong. 2d sess. Washington: GPO, 1973.

––––––. Committee on Foreign Affairs, *United States Relations with Panama*, subcommittee hearings, 86th Cong. 2d session. Washington: GPO, 1960.

––––––. Committee on International Relations, *A New Panama Canal Treaty: A Latin American Imperative*, 94th Cong., 2d sess. H. Res. 315. Washington: GPO, 1976.

––––––. Committee on Merchant Marine and Fisheries, *Panama Canal Briefings*, Committee Hearings, 93rd Cong. 1st sess. Washington: GPO, 1973.

––––––. Committee on Merchant Marine and Fisheries, *Panama Canal Finances*, Committee Hearings, 94th Cong. 2d sess. Washington: GPO, 1976.

––––––. Committee on Merchant Marine and Fisheries. *Panama Canal Miscellaneous: Part I*, Subcommittee on Panama Canal/Outer Continental Shelf Hearings, 98th Cong. 1st sess. Washington: GPO, 1983.

––––––. Committee on Merchant Marine and Fisheries, *Panama Canal Problems*, Subcommittee Hearings, 88th Cong. 1st sess. Washington: GPO, 1963.

––––––. Committee on Merchant Marine and Fisheries, *U.S. Interest in Panama Canal*. Subcommittee on the Panama Canal, 95th Cong. 1st sess. Washington: GPO, 1976.

––––––. Subcommittee on the Panama Canal/Outer Continental Shelf of the Committee on Merchant Marine and Fisheries. *Hearing on Panama Canal Commission Authorization, FY 1984, and Oversight*. 98th Cong. 1st sess. 16 March 1983. Washington: GPO, 1981.

––––––. Subcommittee on Panama Canal/Outer Continental Shelf, Committee on Merchant Marine and Fisheries. *Hearing on Vessel Damage Claims*. 98th Cong. 1st sess., 23 February 1983.

————. Subcommittee on the Panama Canal/Outer Continental Shelf of the Committee on Merchant Marine and Fisheries. *Panama Canal Commission Authorization, FY 1982, and Oversight*. 97th Cong. 1st sess. Serial No. 97-3. Washington: GPO, 1981.

————. *Panama Act 1979*. Report of the Committee on Merchant Marine and Fisheries. 96th Cong. 1st sess. House Report 96-98, pt. 1. Washington: GPO, 23 April 1979.

U.S. Congress, Senate. Committee on Armed Services. *Defense, Maintenance and Operation of the Panama Canal, Including Administration and Government of the Canal Zone*, Committee Hearings, 95th Cong. 2d sess. Washington: GPO, 1978.

————. Committee on Armed Services, *Panama Canal Treaty Implementing Legislation*, 96th Cong., 1st sess., S. 1024. Washington: GPO, 1979.

————. Committee on Foreign Relations and Committee on Merchant Marine and Fisheries. *United Nations Security Council Meeting in Panama*. Joint Subcommittee Hearings. 93rd Cong. 2d sess. Washington: GPO, 1973.

————. Committee on Foreign Relations. *A Chronology of Events Relative to Panama Canal*. 95th Cong. 1st sess. Washington: GPO, 1977.

————. Committee on Foreign Relations. *Background Documents Relating to the Panama Canal*. 95th Cong. 1st sess. Washington: GPO, 1977 (Committee Print).

————. Committee on Foreign Relations. *Hearings Before the Committee on Foreign Relations on the Panama Canal Treaties*. 95th Cong. 1st sess. pts. 1-5. Washington: GPO, 1977.

————. Committee on Foreign Relations. *Panama Canal Treaties Report*. 95th Cong. 2d sess. Executive Report No. 95-12, 3 February 1978. Washington: GPO.

————. Committee on Foreign Relations. *Senate Debate on the Panama Canal Treaties: A Compendium of Major Statements, Documents, Record Votes and Relevant Events*. 96th Cong. 1st sess. February 1979. Washington: GPO.

————. Committee on Foreign Relations. *The Role of the Senate in Treaty Ratification: A Staff Memorandum*, 95th Cong. 1st sess. Washington: GPO, 1977.

————. Committee on the Judiciary, Subcommittee on Separation of Powers. *Panama Canal Treaty (Disposition of United States Territory)*. 95th Cong. 1st sess. Washington: GPO, 1977.

————. Committee on the Judiciary, Subcommittee on Separation of Powers. *Panama Canal Treaties: U.S. Senate Debate 1977-78*. 95th Cong. 1st sess., pts. 1-3. Washington: GPO, 1978.

————. Committee on the Judiciary, Subcommittee on Separartion of Powers. The Proposed Panama Canal Treaties: A Digest of Information, 95th Cong., 2d sess. Washington: GPO, 1978.

————. Special Delegation. *Report of Delegation Studying the Panama Canal Treaties and Other Matters of Interest to the U.S. in Latin America*, 95th Cong. 2d sess. Senate Document No. 95-80. Washington: GPO, 1978.

————. Message from the President of the United States. 95th Cong. 1st sess. Executive Document N. Washington: GPO, 1977.

U.S. Department of State. *Final Environmental Impact Statements for the New Panama Canal Treaties*. Washington: GPO, December 1977.

U.S. General Accounting Office. *Background Information Bearing Upon Panama Canal Treaty Implementation Legislation*, ID-79-33 4 June 1979.

U.S. News & World Report, 27 March 1978, pp. 27-28.

U.S. Statues at Large, Vol XCIII, 96th Cong. 1st sess.

Vance, Cyrus. *Hard Choices: Critical Years in Americas Foreign Policy*. New York: Simon and Schuster, 1983.

Washington Post, 1977-1980.

Washington Star, 1975.

Watts, William and Free, Lloyd A. "Nationalism, Not Isolationism," *Foreign Policy*, 24 (Fall 1976):3-26.

Wendzel, Robert L. *International Relations: A Policymaker Focus*. 2d ed. New York: Wiley, 1980.

Whalen, Jr., Charles W. "Congressional Influence on National Security Policy Making." A paper presented at the annual meeting of the American Political Science Association, New York, September 1981.

————. *The House and Foreign Policy: The Irony of Congressional Reform*. Chapel Hill: University of North Carolina Press, 1982.

Zartman, I. William. *The Analysis of Negotiations*. New York: Anchor, 1975

Zartman, I. William, ed. *The Negotiations Process*. Beverly Hills: Sage, 1978.

APPENDIX A

JOINT STATEMENT BY THE HONORABLE HENRY A. KISSINGER, SECRETARY OF STATE OF THE UNITED STATES OF AMERICA, AND HIS EXCELLENCY JUAN ANTONIO TACK, MINISTER OF FOREIGN AFFAIRS OF THE REPUBLIC OF PANAMA, ON FEBRUARY 7, 1974 AT PANAMA.

The United States of America and the Republic of Panama have been engaged in negotiations to conclude an entirely new treaty respecting the Panama Canal, negotiations which were made possible by the Joint Declaration between the two countries of April 3, 1964, agreed to under the auspices of the Permanent Council of the Organization of American States acting provisionally as the Organ of Consultation. The new treaty would abrogate the treaty existing since 1903 and its subsequent amendments, establishing the necessary conditions for a modern relationship between the two countries based on the most profound mutual respect.

Since the end of the last November, the authorized representatives of the two governments have been holding important conversations which have permitted agreement to be reached on a set of fundamental principles which will serve to guide the negotiators in the effort to conclude a just and equitable treaty eliminating, once and for all, the causes of conflict between the two countries.

The principles to which we have agreed, on behalf of our respective governments, are as follows:

1. The treaty of 1903 and its amendments will be abrogated by the conclusion of an entirely new interoceanic canal treaty.

2. The concept of perpetuity will be eliminated. The new treaty concerning the lock canal shall have a fixed termination date.

3. Termination of United States jurisdiction over Panamanian territory shall take place promptly in accordance with terms specified in the treaty.

4. The Panamanian territory in which the canal is situated shall be returned to the jurisdiction of the Republic of Panama. The Republic of Panama, in its capacity as territorial sovereign, shall grant to the United States of America, for the duration of the new interoceanic canal treaty and in accordance with what that treaty states, the right to use the lands, waters, and airspace which may be necessary for the operation, maintenance, protection and defense of the canal and the transit of ships.

5. The Republic of Panama shall have a just and equitable share of the benefits derived from the operation of the canal in its territory. It is

recognized that the geographic position of its territory constitutes the principal resource of the Republic of Panama.

6. The Republic of Panama shall participate in the administration of the canal, in accordance with a procedure to be agreed upon in the treaty. The treaty shall also provide that Panama will assume total responsibility for the operation of the canal upon the termination of the treaty. The Republic of Panama shall grant to the United States of America the rights necessary to regulate the transit of ships through the canal, to operate, maintain, protect and defend the canal, and to undertake any other specific activity related to those ends, as may be agreed upon in the treaty.

7. The Republic of Panama shall participate with the United States of America in the protection and defense of the canal in accordance with what is agreed upon in the new treaty.

8. The United States of America and the Republic of Panama, recognizing the important services rendered by the interoceanic Panama Canal to international maritime traffic, and bearing in mind the possibility that the present canal could become inadequate for said traffic, shall agree to bilaterally on provisions for new projects which will enlarge canal capacity. Such provisions will be incorporated in the new treaty in accord with the concepts established in principle 2.

APPENDIX B

Texts of Treaties
Relating to the Panama Canal

PANAMA CANAL TREATY

The United States of America and the Republic of Panama,

Acting in the spirit of the Joint Declaration of April 3, 1964, by the Representatives of the Governments of the United States of America and the Republic of Panama, and of the Joint Statement of Principles of February 7, 1974, initialed by the Secretary of State of the United States of America and the Foreign Minister of the Republic of Panama, and

Acknowledging the Republic of Panama's sovereignty over its territory,

Have decided to terminate the prior Treaties pertaining to the Panama Canal and to conclude a new Treaty to serve as the basis for a new relationship between them and, accordingly, have agreed upon the following:

ARTICLE I

ABROGATION OF PRIOR TREATIES AND ESTABLISHMENT OF A NEW RELATIONSHIP

1. Upon its entry into force, this Treaty terminates and supersedes:

(a) The Isthmian Canal Convention between the United States of America and the Republic of Panama, signed at Washington, November 18, 1903;

(b) The Treaty of Friendship and Cooperation signed at Washington, March 2, 1936, and the Treaty of Mutual Understandi g and Cooperation and the related Memorandum of Understandings Reached, signed at Panama,

January 25, 1955, between the United States of America and the Republic of Panama;

(c) All other treaties, conventions, agreements and exchanges of notes between the United States of America and the Republic of Panama concerning the Panama Canal which were in force prior to the entry into force of this Treaty; and

(d) Provisions concerning the Panama Canal which appear in other treaties, conventions, agreements and exchanges of notes between the United States of America and the Republic of Panama which were in force prior to the entry into force of this Treaty.

2. In accordance with the terms of this Treaty and related agreements, the Republic of Panama, as territorial sovereign, grants to the United States of America the rights necessary to regulate the transit of ships through the Panama Canal, and to manage, operate, maintain, improve, protect and defend the Canal. The Republic of Panama guarantees to the United States of America peaceful use of the land and water areas which it has been granted the rights to use for such purposes pursuant to this Treaty and related agreements.

3. The Republic of Panama shall participate increasingly in the management and protection and defense of the Canal, as provided in this Treaty.

4. In view of the special relationship established by this Treaty, the United States of America and the Republic of Panama shall cooperate to assure the uninterrupted and efficient operation of the Panama Canal.

237

Article II

Ratification, Entry Into Force, and Termination

1. This Treaty shall be subject to ratification in accordance with the constitutional procedures of the two Parties. The instruments of ratification of this Treaty shall be exchanged at Panama at the same time as the instruments of ratification of the Treaty Concerning the Permanent Neutrality and Operation of the Panama Canal, signed this date, are exchanged. This Treaty shall enter into force, simultaneously with the Treaty Concerning the Permanent Neutrality and Operation of the Panama Canal, six calendar months from the date of the exchange of the instruments of ratification.

2. This Treaty shall terminate at noon, Panama time, December 31, 1999.

Article III

Canal Operation and Management

1. The Republic of Panama, as territorial sovereign, grants to the United States of America the rights to manage, operate, and maintain the Panama Canal, its complementary works, installations and equipment and to provide for the orderly transit of vessels through the Panama Canal. The United States of America accepts the grant of such rights and undertakes to exercise them in accordance with this Treaty and related agreements.

2. In carrying out the foregoing responsibilities, the United States of America may:

(a) Use for the aforementioned purposes, without cost except as provided in this Treaty, the various installations and areas (including the Panama Canal) and waters, described in the Agreement in Implementation of this Article, signed this date, as well as such other areas and installations as are made available to the United States of America under this Treaty and related agreements, and take the measures necessary to ensure sanitation of such areas;

(b) Make such improvements and alterations to the aforesaid installations and areas as it deems appropriate, consistent with the terms of this Treaty;

(c) Make and enforce all rules pertaining to the passage of vessels through the Canal and other rules with respect to navigation and maritime matters, in accordance with this Treaty and related agreements. The Republic of Panama will lend its cooperation, when necessary, in the enforcement of such rules;

(d) Establish, modify, collect and retain tolls for the use of the Panama Canal, and other charges, and establish and modify methods of their assessment;

(e) Regulate relations with employees of the United States Government;

(f) Provide supporting services to facilitate the performance of its responsibilities under this Article;

(g) Issue and enforce regulations for the effective exercise of the rights and responsibilities of the United States of America under this Treaty and related agreements. The Republic of Panama will lend its cooperation, when necessary, in the enforcement of such rules; and

(h) Exercise any other right granted under this Treaty, or otherwise agreed upon between the two Parties.

3. Pursuant to the foregoing grant of rights, the United States of America shall, in accordance with the terms of this Treaty and the provisions of United States law, carry out its responsibilities by means of a United States Government agency called the Panama Canal Commission, which shall be constituted by and in conformity with the laws of the United States of America.

(a) The Panama Canal Commission shall be supervised by a Board composed of nine members, five of whom shall be nationals of the United States of America, and four of whom shall be Panamanian nationals proposed by the Republic of Panama for appointment to such positions by the United States of America in a timely manner.

(b) Should the Republic of Panama request the United States of America to remove a Panamanian national from membership on the Board, the United States of America shall agree to such request. In that event, the Republic of Panama shall propose another Panamanian national for appointment by the United States of America to such position in a timely manner. In case of removal of a Panamanian member of the Board at the initiative of the United States of America, both Parties will consult in advance in order to reach agreement concerning such removal, and the Republic of

Panama shall propose another Panamanian national for appointment by the United States of America in his stead.

(c) The United States of America shall employ a national of the United States of America as Administrator of the Panama Canal Commission, and a Panamanian national as Deputy Administrator, through December 31, 1989. Beginning January 1, 1990, a Panamanian national shall be employed as the Administrator and a national of the United States of America shall occupy the position of Deputy Administrator. Such Panamanian nationals shall be proposed to the United States of America by the Republic of Panama for appointment to such positions by the United States of America.

(d) Should the United States of America remove the Panamanian national from his position as Deputy Administrator, or Administrator, the Republic of Panama shall propose another Panamanian national for appointment to such position by the United States of America.

4. An illustrative description of the activities the Panama Canal Commission will perform in carrying out the responsibilities and rights of the United States of America under this Article is set forth at the Annex. Also set forth in the Annex are procedures for the discontinuance or transfer of those activities performed prior to the entry into force of this Treaty by the Panama Canal Company or the Canal Zone Government which are not to be carried out by the Panama Canal Commission.

5. The Panama Canal Commission shall reimburse the Republic of Panama for the costs incurred by the Republic of Panama in providing the following public services in the Canal operating areas and in housing areas set forth in the Agreement in Implementation of Article III of this Treaty and occupied by both United States and Panamanian citizen employees of the Panama Canal Commission: police, fire protection, street maintenance, street lighting, street cleaning, traffic management and garbage collection. The Panama Canal Commission shall pay the Republic of Panama the sum of ten million United States dollars ($10,000,-000) per annum for the foregoing services. It is agreed that every three years from the date that this Treaty enters into force, the costs involved in furnishing said services shall be reexamined to determine whether adjustment of the annual payment should be made because of inflation and other relevant factors affecting the cost of such services.

6. The Republic of Panama shall be responsible for providing, in all areas comprising the former Canal Zone, services of a general jurisdictional nature such as customs and immigration, postal services, courts and licensing, in accordance with this Treaty and related agreements.

7. The United States of America and the Republic of Panama shall establish a Panama Canal Consultative Committee, composed of an equal number of high-level representatives of the United States of America and the Republic of Panama, and which may appoint such subcommittees as it may deem appropriate. This Committee shall advise the United States of America and the Republic of Panama on matters of policy affecting the Canal's operation. In view of both Parties' special interest in the continuity and efficiency of the Canal operation in the future, the Committee shall advise on matters such as general tolls policy, employment and training policies to increase the participation of Panamanian nationals in the operation of the Canal, and international policies on matters concerning the Canal. The Committee's recommendations shall be transmitted to the two Governments, which shall give such recommendations full consideration in the formulation of such policy decisions.

8. In addition to the participation of Panamanian nationals at high management levels of the Panama Canal Commission, as provided for in paragraph 3 of this Article, there shall be growing participation of Panamanian nationals at all other levels and areas of employment in the aforesaid commission, with the objective of preparing, in an orderly and efficient fashion, for the assumption by the Republic of Panama of full responsibility for the management, operation and maintenance of the Canal upon the termination of this Treaty.

9. The use of the areas, waters and installations with respect to which the United States of America is granted rights pursuant to this Article, and the rights and legal status of United States Government agencies and employees operating in the Republic of Panama pursuant to this Article, shall be governed by the Agreement in Implementation of this Article, signed this date.

239

10. Upon entry into force of this Treaty, the United States Government agencies known as the Panama Canal Company and the Canal Zone Government shall cease to operate within the territory of the Republic of Panama that formerly constituted the Canal Zone.

ARTICLE IV

PROTECTION AND DEFENSE

1. The United States of America and the Republic of Panama commit themselves to protect and defend the Panama Canal. Each Party shall act, in accordance with its constitutional processes, to meet the danger resulting from an armed attack or other actions which threaten the security of the Panama Canal or of ships transiting it.

2. For the duration of this Treaty, the United States of America shall have primary responsibility to protect and defend the Canal. The rights of the United States of America to station, train, and move military forces within the Republic of Panama are described in the Agreement in Implementation of this Article, signed this date. The use of areas and installations and the legal status of the armed forces of the United States of America in the Republic of Panama shall be governed by the aforesaid Agreement.

3. In order to facilitate the participation and cooperation of the armed forces of both Parties in the protection and defense of the Canal, the United States of America and the Republic of Panama shall establish a Combined Board comprised of an equal number of senior military representatives of each Party. These representatives shall be charged by their respective governments with consulting and cooperating on all matters pertaining to the protection and defense of the Canal, and with planning for actions to be taken in concert for that purpose. Such combined protection and defense arrangements shall not inhibit the identity or lines of authority of the armed forces of the United States of America or the Republic of Panama. The Combined Board shall provide for coordination and cooperation concerning such matters as:

(a) The preparation of contingency plans for the protection and defense of the Canal based upon the cooperative efforts of the armed forces of both Parties;

(b) The planning and conduct of combined military exercises; and

(c) The conduct of United States and Panamanian military operations with respect to the protection and defense of the Canal.

4. The Combined Board shall, at five-year intervals throughout the duration of this Treaty, review the resources being made available by the two Parties for the protection and defense of the Canal. Also, the Combined Board shall make appropriate recommendations to the two Governments respecting projected requirements, the efficient utilization of available resources of the two Parties, and other matters of mutual interest with respect to the protection and defense of the Canal.

5. To the extent possible consistent with its primary responsibility for the protection and defense of the Panama Canal, the United States of America will endeavor to maintain its armed forces in the Republic of Panama in normal times at a level not in excess of that of the armed forces of the United States of America in the territory of the former Canal Zone immediately prior to the entry into force of this Treaty.

ARTICLE V

PRINCIPLE OF NON-INTERVENTION

Employees of the Panama Canal Commission, their dependents and designated contractors of the Panama Canal Commission, who are nationals of the United States of America, shall respect the laws of the Republic of Panama and shall abstain from any activity incompatible with the spirit of this Treaty. Accordingly, they shall abstain from any political activity in the Republic of Panama as well as from any intervention in the internal affairs of the Republic of Panama. The United States of America shall take all measures within its authority to ensure that the provisions of this Article are fulfilled.

ARTICLE VI

PROTECTION OF THE ENVIRONMENT

1. The United States of America and the Republic of Panama commit themselves to implement this Treaty in a manner consistent with the protection of the natural environment of the

Republic of Panama. To this end, they shall consult and cooperate with each other in all appropriate ways to ensure that they shall give due regard to the protection and conservation of the environment.

2. A Joint Commission on the Environment shall be established with equal representation from the United States of America and the Republic of Panama, which shall periodically review the implementation of this Treaty and shall recommend as appropriate to the two Governments ways to avoid or, should this not be possible, to mitigate the adverse environmental impacts which might result from their respective actions pursuant to the Treaty.

3. The United States of America and the Republic of Panama shall furnish the Joint Commission on the Environment complete information on any action taken in accordance with this Treaty which, in the judgment of both, might have a significant effect on the environment. Such information shall be made available to the Commission as far in advance of the contemplated action as possible to facilitate the study by the Commission of any potential environmental problems and to allow for consideration of the recommendation of the Commission before the contemplated action is carried out.

Article VII

Flags

1. The entire territory of the Republic of Panama, including the areas the use of which the Republic of Panama makes available to the United States of America pursuant to this Treaty and related agreements, shall be under the flag of the Republic of Panama, and consequently such flag always shall occupy the position of honor.

2. The flag of the United States of America may be displayed, together with the flag of the Republic of Panama, at the headquarters of the Panama Canal Commission, at the site of the Combined Board, and as provided in the Agreement in Implementation of Article IV of this Treaty.

3. The flag of the United States of America also may be displayed at other places and on some occasions, as agreed by both Parties.

Article VIII

Privileges and Immunities

1. The installations owned or used by the agencies or instrumentalities of the United States of America operating in the Republic of Panama pursuant to this Treaty and related agreements, and their official archives and documents, shall be inviolable. The two Parties shall agree on procedures to be followed in the conduct of any criminal investigation at such locations by the Republic of Panama.

2. Agencies and instrumentalities of the Government of the United States of America operating in the Republic of Panama pursuant to this Treaty and related agreements shall be immune from the jurisdiction of the Republic of Panama.

3. In addition to such other privileges and immunities as are afforded to employees of the United States Government and their dependents pursuant to this Treaty, the United States of America may designate up to twenty officials of the Panama Canal Commission who, along with their dependents, shall enjoy the privileges and immunities accorded to diplomatic agents and their dependents under international law and practice. The United States of America shall furnish to the Republic of Panama a list of the names of said officials and their dependents, identifying the positions they occupy in the Government of the United States of America, and shall keep such list current at all times.

Article IX

Applicable Laws and Law Enforcement

1. In accordance with the provisions of this Treaty and related agreements, the law of the Republic of Panama shall apply in the areas made available for the use of the United States of America pursuant to this Treaty. The law of the Republic of Panama shall be applied to matters or events which occurred in the former Canal Zone prior to the entry into force of this Treaty only to the extent specifically provided in prior treaties and agreements.

2. Natural or juridical persons who, on the date of entry into force of this Treaty, are engaged in business or non-profit activities at locations in the former Canal Zone may continue such business or activities at those locations

under the same terms and conditions prevailing prior to the entry into force of this Treaty for a thirty-month transition period from its entry into force. The Republic of Panama shall maintain the same operating conditions as those applicable to the aforementioned enterprises prior to the entry into force of this Treaty in order that they may receive licenses to do business in the Republic of Panama subject to their compliance with the requirements of its law. Thereafter, such persons shall receive the same treatment under the law of the Republic of Panama as similar enterprises already established in the rest of the territory of the Republic of Panama without discrimination.

3. The rights of ownership, as recognized by the United States of America, enjoyed by natural or juridical private persons in buildings and other improvements to real property located in the former Canal Zone shall be recognized by the Republic of Panama in conformity with its laws.

4. With respect to buildings and other improvements to real property located in the Canal operating areas, housing areas or other areas subject to the licensing procedure established in Article IV of the Agreement in Implementation of Article III of this Treaty, the owners shall be authorized to continue using the land upon which their property is located in accordance with the procedures established in that Article.

5. With respect to buildings and other improvements to real property located in areas of the former Canal Zone to which the aforesaid licensing procedure is not applicable, or may cease to be applicable during the lifetime or upon termination of this Treaty, the owners may continue to use the land upon which their property is located, subject to the payment of a reasonable charge to the Republic of Panama. Should the Republic of Panama decide to sell such land, the owners of the buildings or other improvements located thereon shall be offered a first option to purchase such land at a reasonable cost. In the case of non-profit enterprises, such as churches and fraternal organizations, the cost of purchase will be nominal in accordance with the prevailing practice in the rest of the territory of the Republic of Panama.

6. If any of the aforementioned persons are required by the Republic of Panama to discontinue their activities or vacate their property

for public purposes, they shall be compensated at fair market value by the Republic of Panama.

7. The provisions of paragraphs 2–6 above shall apply to natural or juridical persons who have been engaged in business or non-profit activities at locations in the former Canal Zone for at least six months prior to the date of signature of this Treaty.

8. The Republic of Panama shall not issue, adopt or enforce any law, decree, regulation, or international agreement or take any other action which purports to regulate or would otherwise interfere with the exercise on the part of the United States of America of any right granted under this Treaty or related agreements.

9. Vessels transiting the Canal, and cargo, passengers and crews carried on such vessels shall be exempt from any taxes, fees, or other charges by the Republic of Panama. However, in the event such vessels call at a Panamanian port, they may be assessed charges incident thereto, such as charges for services provided to the vessel. The Republic of Panama may also require the passengers and crew disembarking from such vessels to pay such taxes, fees and charges as are established under Panamanian law for persons entering its territory. Such taxes, fees and charges shall be assessed on a nondiscriminatory basis.

10. The United States of America and the Republic of Panama will cooperate in taking such steps as may from time to time be necessary to guarantee the security of the Panama Canal Commission, its property, its employees and their dependents, and their property, the Forces of the United States of America and the members thereof, the civilian component of the United States Forces, the dependents of members of the Forces and the civilian component, and their property, and the contractors of the Panama Canal Commission and of the United States Forces, their dependents, and their property. The Republic of Panama will seek from its Legislative Branch such legislation as may be needed to carry out the foregoing purposes and to punish any offenders.

11. The Parties shall conclude an agreement whereby nationals of either State, who are sentenced by the courts of the other State, and who are not domiciled therein, may elect to

serve their sentences in their State of nationality.

ARTICLE X

EMPLOYMENT WITH THE PANAMA CANAL COMMISSION

1. In exercising its rights and fulfilling its responsibilities as the employer, the United States of America shall establish employment and labor regulations which shall contain the terms, conditions and prerequisites for all categories of employees of the Panama Canal Commission. These regulations shall be provided to the Republic of Panama prior to their entry into force.

2. (a) The regulations shall establish a system of preference when hiring employees, for Panamanian applicants possessing the skills and qualifications required for employment by the Panama Canal Commission. The United States of America shall endeavor to ensure that the number of Panamanian nationals employed by the Panama Canal Commission in relation to the total number of its employees will conform to the proportion established for foreign enterprises under the law of the Republic of Panama.

(b) The terms and conditions of employment to be established will in general be no less favorable to persons already employed by the Panama Canal Company or Canal Zone Government prior to the entry into force of this Treaty, than those in effect immediately prior to that date.

3. (a) The United States of America shall establish an employment policy for the Panama Canal Commission that shall generally limit the recruitment of personnel outside the Republic of Panama to persons possessing requisite skills and qualifications which are not available in the Republic of Panama.

(b) The United States of America will establish training programs for Panamanian employees and apprentices in order to increase the number of Panamanian nationals qualified to assume positions with the Panama Canal Commission, as positions become available.

(c) Within five years from the entry into force of this Treaty, the number of United States nationals employed by the Panama Canal Commission who were previously employed by the Panama Canal Company shall be at least twenty percent less than the total number of

United States nationals working for the Panama Canal Company immediately prior to the entry into force of this Treaty.

(d) The United States of America shall periodically inform the Republic of Panama, through the Coordinating Committee, established pursuant to the Agreement in Implementation of Article III of this Treaty, of available positions within the Panama Canal Commission. The Republic of Panama shall similarly provide the United States of America any information it may have as to the availability of Panamanian nationals claiming to have skills and qualifications that might be required by the Panama Canal Commission, in order that the United States of America may take this information into account.

4. The United States of America will establish qualification standards for skills, training and experience required by the Panama Canal Commission. In establishing such standards, to the extent they include a requirement for a professional license, the United States of America, without prejudice to its right to require additional professional skills and qualifications, shall recognize the professional licenses issued by the Republic of Panama.

5. The United States of America shall establish a policy for the periodic rotation, at a maximum of every five years, of United States citizen employees and other non-Panamanian employees, hired after the entry into force of this Treaty. It is recognized that certain exceptions to the said policy of rotation may be made for sound administrative reasons, such as in the case of employees holding positions requiring certain non-transferable or non-recruitable skills.

6. With regard to wages and fringe benefits, there shall be no discrimination on the basis of nationality, sex, or race. Payments by the Panama Canal Commission of additional remuneration, or the provision of other benefits, such as home leave benefits, to United States nationals employed prior to entry into force of this Treaty, or to persons of any nationality, including Panamanian nationals who are thereafter recruited outside of the Republic of Panama and who change their place of residence, shall not be considered to be discrimination for the purpose of this paragraph.

7. Persons employed by the Panama Canal Company or Canal Zone Government prior to

243

the entry into force of this Treaty, who are displaced from their employment as a result of the discontinuance by the United States of America of certain activities pursuant to this Treaty, will be placed by the United States of America, to the maximum extent feasible, in other appropriate jobs with the Government of the United States in accordance with United States Civil Service regulations. For such persons who are not United States nationals, placement efforts will be confined to United States Government activities located within the Republic of Panama. Likewise, persons previously employed in activities for which the Republic of Panama assumes responsibility as a result of this Treaty will be continued in their employment to the maximum extent feasible by the Republic of Panama. The Republic of Panama shall, to the maximum extent feasible, ensure that the terms and conditions of employment applicable to personnel employed in the activities for which it assumes responsibility are no less favorable than those in effect immediately prior to the entry into force of this Treaty. Non-United States nationals employed by the Panama Canal Company or Canal Zone Government prior to the entry into force of this Treaty who are involuntarily separated from their positions because of the discontinuance of an activity by reason of this Treaty, who are not entitled to an immediate annuity under the United States Civil Service Retirement System, and for whom continued employment in the Republic of Panama by the Government of the United States of America is not practicable, will be provided special job placement assistance by the Republic of Panama for employment in positions for which they may be qualified by experience and training.

8. The Parties agree to establish a system whereby the Panama Canal Commission may, if deemed mutually convenient or desirable by the two Parties, assign certain employees of the Panama Canal Commission, for a limited period of time, to assist in the operation of activities transferred to the responsibility of the Republic of Panama as a result of this Treaty or related agreements. The salaries and other costs of employment of any such persons assigned to provide such assistance shall be reimbursed to the United States of America by the Republic of Panama.

9. (a) The right of employees to negotiate collective contracts with the Panama Canal Commission is recognized. Labor relations with employees of the Panama Canal Commission shall be conducted in accordance with forms of collective bargaining established by the United States of America after consultation with employee unions.

(b) Employee unions shall have the right to affiliate with international labor organizations.

10. The United States of America will provide an appropriate early optional retirement program for all persons employed by the Panama Canal Company or Canal Zone Government immediately prior to the entry into force of this Treaty. In this regard, taking into account the unique circumstances created by the provisions of this Treaty, including its duration, and their effect upon such employees, the United States of America shall, with respect to them:

(a) determine that conditions exist which invoke applicable United States law permitting early retirement annuities and apply such law for a substantial period of the duration of the Treaty;

(b) seek special legislation to provide more liberal entitlement to, and calculation of, retirement annuities than is currently provided for by law.

ARTICLE XI

PROVISIONS FOR THE TRANSITION PERIOD

1. The Republic of Panama shall reassume plenary jurisdiction over the former Canal Zone upon entry into force of this Treaty and in accordance with its terms. In order to provide for an orderly transition to the full application of the jurisdictional arrangements established by this Treaty and related agreements, the provisions of this Article shall become applicable upon the date this Treaty enters into force, and shall remain in effect for thirty calendar months. The authority granted in this Article to the United States of America for this transition period shall supplement, and is not intended to limit, the full application and effect of the rights and authority granted to the United States of America elsewhere in this Treaty and in related agreements.

2. During this transition period, the criminal and civil laws of the United States of America

shall apply concurrently with those of the Republic of Panama in certain of the areas and installations made available for the use of the United States of America pursuant to this Treaty, in accordance with the following provisions:

(a) The Republic of Panama permits the authorities of the United States of America to have the primary right to exercise criminal jurisdiction over United States citizen employees of the Panama Canal Commission and their dependents, and members of the United States Forces and civilian component and their dependents, in the following cases:

(i) for any offense committed during the transition period within such areas and installations, and

(ii) for any offense committed prior to that period in the former Canal Zone.

The Republic of Panama shall have the primary right to exercise jurisdiction over all other offenses committed by such persons, except as otherwise provided in this Treaty and related agreements or as may be otherwise agreed.

(b) Either Party may waive its primary right to exercise jurisdiction in a specific case or category of cases.

3. The United States of America shall retain the right to exercise jurisdiction in criminal cases relating to offenses committed prior to the entry into force of this Treaty in violation of the laws applicable in the former Canal Zone.

4. For the transition period, the United States of America shall retain police authority and maintain a police force in the aforementioned areas and installations. In such areas, the police authorities of the United States of America may take into custody any person not subject to their primary jurisdiction if such person is believed to have committed or to be committing an offense against applicable laws or regulations, and shall promptly transfer custody to the police authorities of the Republic of Panama. The United States of America and the Republic of Panama shall establish joint police patrols in agreed areas. Any arrests conducted by a joint patrol shall be the responsibility of the patrol member or members representing the Party having primary jurisdiction over the person or persons arrested.

5. The courts of the United States of America and related personnel, functioning in the former Canal Zone immediately prior to the entry into

force of this Treaty, may continue to function during the transition period for the judicial enforcement of the jurisdiction to be exercised by the United States of America in accordance with this Article.

6. In civil cases, the civilian courts of the United States of America in the Republic of Panama shall have no jurisdiction over new cases of a private civil nature, but shall retain full jurisdiction during the transition period to dispose of any civil cases, including admiralty cases, already instituted and pending before the courts prior to the entry into force of this Treaty.

7. The laws, regulations, and administrative authority of the United States of America applicable in the former Canal Zone immediately prior to the entry into force of this Treaty shall, to the extent not inconsistent with this Treaty and related agreements, continue in force for the purpose of the exercise by the United States of America of law enforcement and judicial jurisdiction only during the transition period. The United States of America may amend, repeal or otherwise change such laws, regulations and administrative authority. The two Parties shall consult concerning procedural and substantive matters relative to the implementation of this Article, including the disposition of cases pending at the end of the transition period and, in this respect, may enter into appropriate agreements by an exchange of notes or other instrument.

8. During this transition period, the United States of America may continue to incarcerate individuals in the areas and installations made available for the use of the United States of America by the Republic of Panama pursuant to this Treaty and related agreements, or to transfer them to penal facilities in the United States of America to serve their sentences.

ARTICLE XII

A SEA-LEVEL CANAL OR A THIRD LANE OF LOCKS

1. The United States of America and the Republic of Panama recognize that a sea-level canal may be important for international navigation in the future. Consequently, during the duration of this Treaty, both Parties commit themselves to study jointly the feasibility of a

sea-level canal in the Republic of Panama, and in the event they determine that such a waterway is necessary, they shall negotiate terms, agreeable to both Parties, for its construction.

2. The United States of America and the Republic of Panama agree on the following:

(a) No new interoceanic canal shall be constructed in the territory of the Republic of Panama during the duration of this Treaty, except in accordance with the provisions of this Treaty, or as the two Parties may otherwise agree; and

(b) During the duration of this Treaty, the United States of America shall not negotiate with third States for the right to construct an interoceanic canal on any other route in the Western Hemisphere, except as the two Parties may otherwise agree.

3. The Republic of Panama grants to the United States of America the right to add a third lane of locks to the existing Panama Canal. This right may be exercised at any time during the duration of this Treaty, provided that the United States of America has delivered to the Republic of Panama copies of the plans for such construction.

4. In the event the United States of America exercises the right granted in paragraph 3 above, it may use for that purpose, in addition to the areas otherwise made available to the United States of America pursuant to this Treaty, such other areas as the two Parties may agree upon. The terms and conditions applicable to Canal operating areas made available by the Republic of Panama for the use of the United States of America pursuant to Article III of this Treaty shall apply in a similar manner to such additional areas.

5. In the construction of the aforesaid works, the United States of America shall not use nuclear excavation techniques without the previous consent of the Republic of Panama.

ARTICLE XIII

PROPERTY TRANSFER AND ECONOMIC PARTICIPATION BY THE REPUBLIC OF PANAMA

1. Upon termination of this Treaty, the Republic of Panama shall assume total responsibility for the management, operation, and maintenance of the Panama Canal, which shall be turned over in operating condition and free of liens and debts, except as the two Parties may otherwise agree.

2. The United States of America transfers, without charge, to the Republic of Panama all right, title and interest the United States of America may have with respect to all real property, including non-removable improvements thereon, as set forth below:

(a) Upon the entry into force of this Treaty, the Panama Railroad and such property that was located in the former Canal Zone but that is not within the land and water areas the use of which is made available to the United States of America pursuant to this Treaty. However, it is agreed that the transfer on such date shall not include buildings and other facilities, except housing, the use of which is retained by the United States of America pursuant to this Treaty and related agreements, outside such areas;

(b) Such property located in an area or a portion thereof at such time as the use by the United States of America of such area or portion thereof ceases pursuant to agreement between the two Parties.

(c) Housing units made available for occupancy by members of the Armed Forces of the Republic of Panama in accordance with paragraph 5(b) of Annex B to the Agreement in Implementation of Article IV of this Treaty at such time as such units are made available to the Republic of Panama.

(d) Upon termination of this Treaty, all real property and non-removable improvements that were used by the United States of America for the purposes of this Treaty and related agreements and equipment related to the management, operation and maintenance of the Canal remaining in the Republic of Panama.

3. The Republic of Panama agrees to hold the United States of America harmless with respect to any claims which may be made by third parties relating to rights, title and interest in such property.

4. The Republic of Panama shall receive, in addition, from the Panama Canal Commission a just and equitable return on the national resources which it has dedicated to the efficient management, operation, maintenance, protection and defense of the Panama Canal, in accordance with the following:

(a) An annual amount to be paid out of Canal operating revenues computed at a rate of thirty hundredths of a United States dollar ($0.30) per Panama Canal net ton, or its equivalency, for each vessel transiting the Canal after the entry into force of this Treaty, for which tolls are charged. The rate of thirty hundredths of a United States dollar ($0.30) per Panama Canal net ton, or its equivalency, will be adjusted to reflect changes in the United States wholesale price index for total manufactured goods during biennial periods. The first adjustment shall take place five years after entry into force of this Treaty, taking into account the changes that occurred in such price index during the preceding two years. Thereafter, successive adjustments shall take place at the end of each biennial period. If the United States of America should decide that another indexing method is preferable, such method shall be proposed to the Republic of Panama and applied if mutually agreed.

(b) A fixed annuity of ten million United States dollars ($10,000,000) to be paid out of Canal operating revenues. This amount shall constitute a fixed expense of the Panama Canal Commission.

(c) An annual amount of up to ten million United States dollars ($10,000,000) per year, to be paid out of Canal operating revenues to the extent that such revenues exceed expenditures of the Panama Canal Commission including amounts paid pursuant to this Treaty. In the event Canal operating revenues in any year do not produce a surplus sufficient to cover this payment, the unpaid balance shall be paid from operating surpluses in future years in a manner to be mutually agreed.

ARTICLE XIV

SETTLEMENT OF DISPUTES

In the event that any question should arise between the Parties concerning the interpretation of this Treaty or related agreements, they shall make every effort to resolve the matter through consultation in the appropriate committees established pursuant to this Treaty and related agreements, or, if appropriate, through diplomatic channels. In the event the Parties are unable to resolve a particular matter through such means, they may, in appropriate cases, agree to submit the matter to conciliation, mediation, arbitration, or such other procedure for the peaceful settlement of the dispute as they may mutually deem appropriate.

DONE at Washington, this 7th day of September, 1977, in duplicate, in the English and Spanish languages, both texts being equally authentic.

ANNEX

PROCEDURES FOR THE CESSATION OR TRANSFER OF ACTIVITIES CARRIED OUT BY THE PANAMA CANAL COMPANY AND THE CANAL ZONE GOVERNMENT AND ILLUSTRATIVE LIST OF THE FUNCTIONS THAT MAY BE PERFORMED BY THE PANAMA CANAL COMMISSION

1. The laws of the Republic of Panama shall regulate the exercise of private economic activities within the areas made available by the Republic of Panama for the use of the United States of America pursuant to this Treaty. Natural or juridical persons who, at least six months prior to the date of signature of this Treaty, were legally established and engaged in the exercise of economic activities in the former Canal Zone, may continue such activities in accordance with the provisions of paragraphs 2–7 of Article IX of this Treaty.

2. The Panama Canal Commission shall not perform governmental or commercial functions as stipulated in paragraph 4 of this Annex, provided, however, that this shall not be deemed to limit in any way the right of the United States of America to perform those functions that may be necessary for the efficient management, operation and maintenance of the Canal.

3. It is understood that the Panama Canal Commission, in the exercise of the rights of the United States of America with respect to the management, operation and maintenance of the Canal, may perform functions such as are set forth below by way of illustration:

a. Management of the Canal enterprise.

b. Aids to navigation in Canal waters and in proximity thereto.

c. Control of vessel movement.

d. Operation and maintenance of the locks.

247

e. Tug service for the transit of vessels and dredging for the piers and docks of the Panama Canal Commission.

f. Control of the water levels in Gatun, Alajuela (Madden) and Miraflores Lakes.

g. Non-commercial transportation services in Canal waters.

h. Meteorological and hydrographic services.

i. Admeasurement.

j. Non-commercial motor transport and maintenance.

k. Industrial security through the use of watchmen.

l. Procurement and warehousing.

m. Telecommunications.

n. Protection of the environment by preventing and controlling the spillage of oil and substances harmful to human or animal life and of the ecological equilibrium in areas used in operation of the Canal and the anchorages.

o. Non-commercial vessel repair.

p. Air conditioning services in Canal installations.

q. Industrial sanitation and health services.

r. Engineering design, construction and maintenance of Panama Canal Commission installations.

s. Dredging of the Canal channel, terminal ports and adjacent waters.

t. Control of the banks and stabilizing of the slopes of the Canal.

u. Non-commercial handling of cargo on the piers and docks of the Panama Canal Commission.

v. Maintenance of public areas of the Panama Canal Commission, such as parks and gardens.

w. Generation of electric power.

x. Purification and supply of water.

y. Marine salvage in Canal waters.

z. Such other functions as may be necessary or appropriate to carry out, in conformity with this Treaty and related agreements, the rights and responsibilities of the United States of America with respect to the management, operation and maintenance of the Panama Canal.

4. The following activities and operations carried out by the Panama Canal Company and the Canal Zone Government shall not be carried out by the Panama Canal Commission, effective upon the dates indicated herein:

(a) Upon the date of entry into force of this Treaty:

(i) Wholesale and retail sales, including those through commissaries, food stores, department stores, optical shops and pastry shops;

(ii) The production of food and drink, including milk products and bakery products;

(iii) The operation of public restaurants and cafeterias and the sale of articles through vending machines;

(iv) The operation of movie theaters, bowling alleys, pool rooms and other recreational and amusement facilities for the use of which a charge is payable;

(v) The operation of laundry and dry cleaning plants other than those operated for official use;

(vi) The repair and service of privately owned automobiles or the sale of petroleum or lubricants thereto, including the operation of gasoline stations, repair garages and tire repair and recapping facilities, and the repair and service of other privately owned property, including appliances, electronic devices, boats, motors, and furniture;

(vii) The operation of cold storage and freezer plants other than those operated for official use;

(viii) The operation of freight houses other than those operated for official use;

(ix) The operation of commercial services to and supply of privately owned and operated vessels, including the construction of vessels, the sale of petroleum and lubricants and the provision of water, tug services not related to the Canal or other United States Government operations, and repair of such vessels, except in situations where repairs may be necessary to remove disabled vessels from the Canal;

(x) Printing services other than for official use;

(xi) Maritime transportation for the use of the general public;

(xii) Health and medical services provided to individuals, including hospitals, leprosariums, veterinary, mortuary and cemetery services;

(xiii) Educational services not for professional training, including schools and libraries;

248

(xiv) Postal services;

(xv) Immigration, customs and quarantine controls, except those measures necessary to ensure the sanitation of the Canal;

(xvi) Commercial pier and dock services, such as the handling of cargo and passengers; and

(xvii) Any other commercial activity of a similar nature, not related to the management, operation or maintenance of the Canal.

(b) Within thirty calendar months from the date of entry into force of this Treaty, governmental services such as:

(i) Police;

(ii) Courts; and

(iii) Prison system.

5. (a) With respect to those activities or functions described in paragraph 4 above, or otherwise agreed upon by the two Parties, which are to be assumed by the Government of the Republic of Panama or by private persons subject to its authority, the two Parties shall consult prior to the discontinuance of such activities or functions by the Panama Canal Commission to develop appropriate arrangements for the orderly transfer and continued efficient operation or conduct thereof.

(b) In the event that appropriate arrangements cannot be arrived at to ensure the continued performance of a particular activity or function described in paragraph 4 above which is necessary to the efficient management, operation or maintenance of the Canal, the Panama Canal Commission may, to the extent consistent with the other provisions of this Treaty and related agreements, continue to perform such activity or function until such arrangements can be made.

AGREED MINUTE TO THE
PANAMA CANAL TREATY

1. With reference to paragraph 1(c) of Article I (Abrogation of Prior Treaties and Establishment of a New Relationship), it is understood that the treaties, conventions, agreements and exchanges of notes, or portions thereof, abrogated and superseded thereby include:

(a) The Agreement delimiting the Canal Zone referred to in Article II of the Inter-

oceanic Canal Convention of November 18, 1903 signed at Panama on June 15, 1904.

(b) The Boundary Convention signed at Panama on September 2, 1914.

(c) The Convention regarding the Colon Corridor and certain other corridors through the Canal Zone signed at Panama on May 24, 1950.

(d) The Trans-Isthmian Highway Convention signed at Washington on March 2, 1936, the Agreement supplementing that Convention entered into through an exchange of notes signed at Washington on August 31 and September 6, 1940, and the arrangement between the United States of America and Panama respecting the Trans-Isthmian Joint Highway Board, entered into through an exchange of notes at Panama on October 19 and 23, 1939.

(e) The Highway Convention between the United States and Panama signed at Panama on September 14, 1950.

(f) The Convention regulating the transit of alcoholic liquors through the Canal Zone signed at Panama on March 14, 1932.

(g) The Protocol of an Agreement restricting use of Panama and Canal Zone waters by belligerents signed at Washington on October 10, 1914.

(h) The Agreement providing for the reciprocal recognition of motor vehicle license plates in Panama and the Canal Zone entered into through an exchange of notes at Panama on December 7 and December 12, 1950, and the Agreement establishing procedures for the reciprocal recognition of motor vehicle operator's licenses in the Canal Zone and Panama entered into through an exchange of notes at Panama on October 31, 1960.

(i) The General Relations Agreement entered into through an exchange of notes at Washington on May 18, 1942.

(j) Any other treaty, convention, agreement or exchange of notes between the United States and the Republic of Panama, or portions thereof, concerning the Panama Canal which was entered into prior to the entry into force of the Panama Canal Treaty.

2. It is further understood that the following treaties, conventions, agreements and exchanges of notes between the two Parties are not affected by paragraph 1 of Article I of the Panama Canal Treaty:

(a) The Agreement confirming the cooperative agreement between the Panamanian Ministry of Agriculture and Livestock and the United States Department of Agriculture for the prevention of foot-and-mouth disease and rinderpest in Panama, entered into by an exchange of notes signed at Panama on June 21 and October 5, 1972, and amended May 28 and June 12, 1974.

(b) The Loan Agreement to assist Panama in executing public marketing programs in basic grains and perishables, with annex, signed at Panama on September 10, 1975.

(c) The Agreement concerning the regulation of commercial aviation in the Republic of Panama, entered into by an exchange of notes signed at Panama on April 22, 1929.

(d) The Air Transport Agreement signed at Panama on March 31, 1949, and amended May 29 and June 3, 1952, June 5, 1967, December 23, 1974, and March 6, 1975.

(e) The Agreement relating to the establishment of headquarters in Panama for a civil aviation technical assistance group for the Latin American area, entered into by an exchange of notes signed at Panama on August 8, 1952.

(f) The Agreement relating to the furnishing by the Federal Aviation Agency of certain services and materials for air navigation aids, entered into by an exchange of notes signed at Panama on December 5, 1967 and February 22, 1968.

(g) The Declaration permitting consuls to take note in person, or by authorized representatives, of declarations of values of exports made by shippers before customs officers, entered into by an exchange of notes signed at Washington on April 17, 1913.

(h) The Agreement relating to customs privileges for consular officers, entered into by an exchange of notes signed at Panama on January 7 and 31, 1935.

(i) The Agreement relating to the sale of military equipment, materials, and services to Panama, entered into by an exchange of notes signed at Panama on May 20, 1959.

(j) The Agreement relating to the furnishing of defense articles and services to Panama for the purpose of contributing to its internal security, entered into by an exchange of notes signed at Panama on March 26 and May 23, 1962.

(k) The Agreement relating to the deposit by Panama of ten percent of the value of grant military assistance and excess defense articles furnished by the United States, entered into by an exchange of notes signed at Panama on April 4 and May 9, 1972.

(l) The Agreement concerning payment to the United States of net proceeds from the sale of defense articles furnished under the military assistance program, entered into by an exchange of notes signed at Panama on May 20 and December 6, 1974.

(m) The General Agreement for Technical and Economic Cooperation, signed at Panama on December 11, 1961.

(n) The Loan Agreement relating to the Panama City water supply system, with annex, signed at Panama on May 6, 1969, and amended September 30, 1971.

(o) The Loan Agreement for rural municipal development in Panama, signed at Panama on November 28, 1975.

(p) The Loan Agreement relating to a project for the modernization, restructuring and reorientation of Panama's educational programs, signed at Panama on November 19, 1975.

(q) The Treaty providing for the extradition of criminals, signed at Panama on May 25, 1904.

(r) The Agreement relating to legal tender and fractional silver coinage by Panama, entered into by an exchange of notes signed at Washington and New York on June 20, 1904, and amended March 26 and April 2, 1930, May 28 and June 6, 1931, March 2, 1936, June 17, 1946, May 9 and 24, 1950, September 11 and October 22, 1953, August 23 and October 25, 1961, and September 26 and October 23, 1962.

(s) The Agreement for enlargement and use by Canal Zone of sewerage facilities in Colon Free Zone Area, entered into by an exchange of notes signed at Panama on March 8 and 25, 1954.

(t) The Agreement relating to the construction of the inter-American highway, entered into by an exchange of notes signed at Panama on May 15 and June 7, 1943.

(u) The Agreement for cooperation in the construction of the Panama segment of the Darien Gap highway, signed at Washington on May 6, 1971.

(v) The Agreement relating to investment

guaranties under sec. 413(b)(4) of the Mutual Security Act of 1954, as amended, entered into by an exchange of notes signed at Washington on January 23, 1961.

(w) The Informal Arrangement relating to cooperation between the American Embassy, or Consulate, and Panamanian authorities when American merchant seamen or tourists are brought before a magistrate's court, entered into by an exchange of notes signed at Panama on September 18 and October 15, 1947.

(x) The Agreement relating to the mutual recognition of ship measurement certificates, entered into by an exchange of notes signed at Washington on August 17, 1937.

(y) The Agreement relating to the detail of a military officer to serve as adviser to the Minister of Foreign Affairs of Panama, signed at Washington on July 7, 1942, and extended and amended February 17, March 23, September 22 and November 6, 1959, March 26 and July 6, 1962, and September 20 and October 8, 1962.

(z) The Agreement relating to the exchange of official publications, entered into by an exchange of notes signed at Panama on November 27, 1941 and March 7, 1942.

(aa) The Convention for the Prevention of Smuggling of Intoxicating Liquors, signed at Washington on June 6, 1924.

(bb) The Arrangement providing for relief from double income tax on shipping profits, entered into by an exchange of notes signed at Washington on January 15, February 8, and March 28, 1941.

(cc) The Agreement for withholding of Panamanian income tax from compensation paid to Panamanians employed within Canal Zone by the canal, railroad, or auxiliary works, entered into by an exchange of notes signed at Panama on August 12 and 30, 1963.

(dd) The Agreement relating to the withholding of contributions for educational insurance from salaries paid to certain Canal Zone employees, entered into by an exchange of notes signed at Panama on September 8 and October 13, 1972.

(ee) The Agreement for radio communications between amateur stations on behalf of third parties, entered into by an exchange of notes signed at Panama on July 19 and August 1, 1956.

(ff) The Agreement relating to the granting of reciprocal authorizations to permit licensed amateur radio operators of either country to operate their stations in the other country, entered into by an exchange of notes signed at Panama on November 16, 1966.

(gg) The Convention facilitating the work of traveling salesmen, signed at Washington on February 8, 1919.

(hh) The Reciprocal Agreement for gratis nonimmigrant visas, entered into by an exchange of notes signed at Panama on March 27 and May 22 and 25, 1956.

(ii) The Agreement modifying the Agreement of March 27 and May 22 and 25, 1956 for gratis nonimmigrant visas, entered into by an exchange of notes signed at Panama on June 14 and 17, 1971.

(jj) Any other treaty, convention, agreement or exchange of notes, or portions thereof, which does not concern the Panama Canal and which is in force immediately prior to the entry into force of the Panama Canal Treaty.

3. With reference to paragraph 2 of Article X (Employment with the Panama Canal Commission), concerning the endeavor to ensure that the number of Panamanian nationals employed in relation to the total number of employees will conform to the proportion established under Panamanian law for foreign business enterprises, it is recognized that progress in this regard may require an extended period in consonance with the concept of a growing and orderly Panamanian participation, through training programs and otherwise, and that progress may be affected from time to time by such actions as the transfer or discontinuance of functions and activities.

4. With reference to paragraph 10(a) of Article X, it is understood that the currently applicable United States law is that contained in Section 8336 of Title 5, United States Code.

5. With reference to paragraph 2 of Article XI (Transitional Provisions), the areas and installations in which the jurisdictional arrangements therein described shall apply during the transition period are as follows:

(a) The Canal operating areas and housing areas described in Annex A to the Agreement in Implementation of Article III of the Panama Canal Treaty.

(b) The Defense Sites and Areas of Military Coordination described in the Agreement in

Implementation of Article IV of the Panama Canal Treaty.

(c) The Ports of Balboa and Cristobal described in Annex B of the Agreement in Implementation of Article III of the Panama Canal Treaty.

6. With reference to paragraph 4 of Article XI, the areas in which the police authorities of the Republic of Panama may conduct joint police patrols with the police authorities of the United States of America during the transition period are as follows:

(a) Those portions of the Canal operating areas open to the general public, the housing areas and the Ports of Balboa and Cristobal.

(b) Those areas of military coordination in which joint police patrols are established pursuant to the provisions of the Agreement in Implementation of Article IV of this Treaty, signed this date. The two police authorities shall develop appropriate administrative arrangements for the scheduling and conduct of such joint police patrol.

TREATY CONCERNING THE PERMANENT NEUTRALITY AND OPERATION OF THE PANAMA CANAL

The United States of America and the Republic of Panama have agreed upon the following:

ARTICLE I

The Republic of Panama declares that the Canal, as an international transit waterway, shall be permanently neutral in accordance with the regime established in this Treaty. The same regime of neutrality shall apply to any other international waterway that may be built either partially or wholly in the territory of the Republic of Panama.

ARTICLE II

The Republic of Panama declares the neutrality of the Canal in order that both in time of peace and in time of war it shall remain secure and open to peaceful transit by the vessels of all nations on terms of entire equality, so that there will be no discrimination against any nation, or its citizens or subjects, concerning the conditions or charges of transit, or for any other reason, and so that the Canal, and therefore the Isthmus of Panama, shall not be the target of reprisals in any armed conflict between other

nations of the world. The foregoing shall be subject to the following requirements:

(a) Payment of tolls and other charges for transit and ancillary services, provided they have been fixed in conformity with the provisions of Article III(c);

(b) Compliance with applicable rules and regulations, provided such rules and regulations are applied in conformity with the provisions of Article III;

(c) The requirement that transiting vessels commit no acts of hostility while in the Canal; and

(d) Such other conditions and restrictions as are established by this Treaty.

ARTICLE III

1. For purposes of the security, efficiency and proper maintenance of the Canal the following rules shall apply:

(a) The Canal shall be operated efficiently in accordance with conditions of transit through the Canal, and rules and regulations that shall be just, equitable and reasonable, and limited to those necessary for safe navigation and efficient, sanitary operation of the Canal;

(b) Ancillary services necessary for transit through the Canal shall be provided;

(c) Tolls and other charges for transit and ancillary services shall be just, reasonable, equi-

252

table and consistent with the principles of international law;

(d) As a pre-condition of transit, vessels may be required to establish clearly the financial responsibility and guarantees for payment of reasonable and adequate indemnification, consistent with international practice and standards, for damages resulting from acts or omissions of such vessels when passing through the Canal. In the case of vessels owned or operated by a State or for which it has acknowledged responsibility, a certification by that State that it shall observe its obligations under international law to pay for damages resulting from the act or omission of such vessels when passing through the Canal shall be deemed sufficient to establish such financial responsibility;

(e) Vessels of war and auxiliary vessels of all nations shall at all times be entitled to transit the Canal, irrespective of their internal operation, means of propulsion, origin, destination or armament, without being subjected, as a condition of transit, to inspection, search or surveillance. However, such vessels may be required to certify that they have complied with all applicable health, sanitation and quarantine regulations. In addition, such vessels shall be entitled to refuse to disclose their internal operation, origin, armament, cargo or destination. However, auxiliary vessels may be required to present written assurances, certified by an official at a high level of the government of the State requesting the exemption, that they are owned or operated by that government and in this case are being used only on government non-commercial service.

2. For the purposes of this Treaty, the terms "Canal," "vessel of war," "auxiliary vessel," "internal operation," "armament" and "inspection" shall have the meanings assigned them in Annex A to this Treaty.

ARTICLE IV

The United States of America and the Republic of Panama agree to maintain the regime of neutrality established in this Treaty, which shall be maintained in order that the Canal shall remain permanently neutral, notwithstanding the termination of any other treaties entered into by the two Contracting Parties.

ARTICLE V

After the termination of the Panama Canal Treaty, only the Republic of Panama shall operate the Canal and maintain military forces, defense sites and military installations within its national territory.

ARTICLE VI

1. In recognition of the important contributions of the United States of America and of the Republic of Panama to the construction, maintenance, and protection and defense of the Canal, vessels of war and auxiliary vessels of those nations shall, notwithstanding any other provisions of this Treaty, be entitled to transit the Canal irrespective of their internal operation, means of propulsion, origin, destination, armament or cargo carried. Such vessels of war and auxiliary vessels will be entitled to transit the Canal expeditiously.

2. The United States of America, so long as it has responsibility for the operation of the Canal, may continue to provide the Republic of Colombia toll-free transit through the Canal for its troops, vessels and materials of war. Thereafter, the Republic of Panama may provide the Republic of Colombia and the Republic of Costa Rica with the right of toll-free transit.

ARTICLE VII

1. The United States of America and the Republic of Panama shall jointly sponsor a resolution in the Organization of American States opening to accession by all nations of the world the Protocol to this Treaty whereby all the signatories will adhere to the objectives of this Treaty, agreeing to respect the regime of neutrality set forth herein.

2. The Organization of American States shall act as the depositary for this Treaty and related instruments.

ARTICLE VIII

This Treaty shall be subject to ratification in accordance with the constitutional procedures of the two Parties. The instruments of ratification of this Treaty shall be exchanged at Panama at the same time as the instruments of ratification of the Panama Canal Treaty, signed this date, are exchanged. This Treaty shall enter into force, simultaneously with the Panama Canal Treaty, six calendar months from the date of the exchange of the instruments of ratification.

DONE at Washington, this 7th day of September, 1977, in the English and Spanish languages, both texts being equally authentic.

ANNEX A

1. "Canal" includes the existing Panama Canal, the entrances thereto and the territorial seas of the Republic of Panama adjacent thereto, as defined on the map annexed hereto (Annex B), and any other interoceanic waterway in which the United States of America is a participant or in which the United States of America has participated in connection with the construction or financing, that may be operated wholly or partially within the territory of the Republic of Panama, the entrances thereto and the territorial seas adjacent thereto.

2. "Vessel of war" means a ship belonging to the naval forces of a State, and bearing the external marks distinguishing warships of its nationality, under the command of an officer duly commissioned by the government and whose name appears in the Navy List, and manned by a crew which is under regular naval discipline.

3. "Auxiliary vessel" means any ship, not a vessel of war, that is owned or operated by a State and used, for the time being, exclusively on government non-commercial service.

4. "Internal operation" encompasses all machinery and propulsion systems, as well as the management and control of the vessel, including its crew. It does not include the measures necessary to transit vessels under the control of pilots while such vessels are in the Canal.

5. "Armament" means arms, ammunitions, implements of war and other equipment of a vessel which possesses characteristics appropriate for use for warlike purposes.

6. "Inspection" includes on-board examination of vessel structure, cargo, armament and internal operation. It does not include those measures strictly necessary for admeasurement, nor those measures strictly necessary to assure safe, sanitary transit and navigation, including examination of deck and visual navigation equipment, nor in the case of live cargoes, such as cattle or other livestock, that may carry communicable diseases, those measures necessary to assure that health and sanitation requirements are satisfied.

254

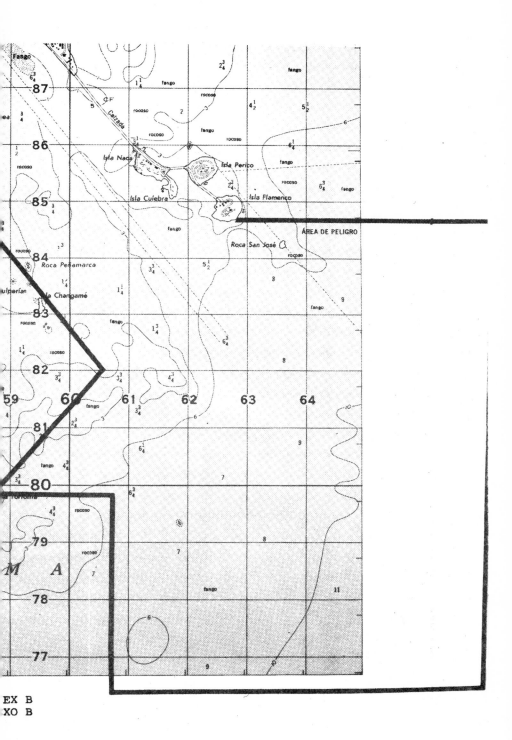

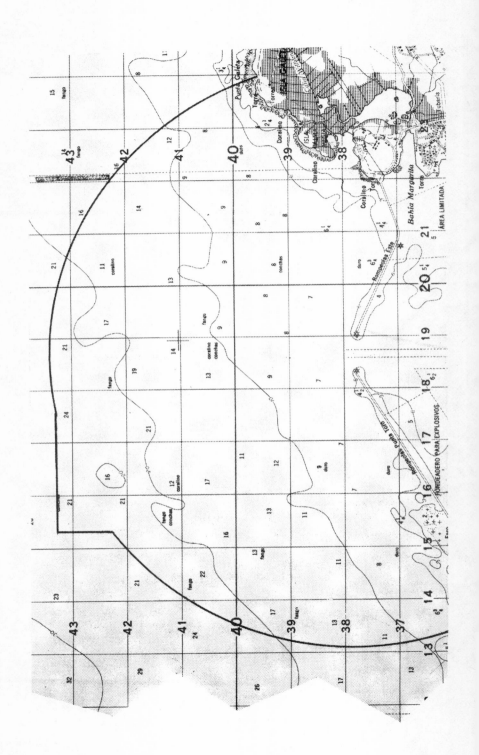

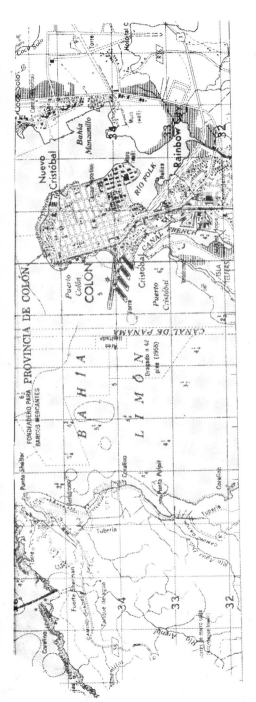

MAP ATTACHMENT TO ANNEX "A" OF
TREATY CONCERNING THE PERMANENT
NEUTRALITY AND OPERATION OF THE
PANAMA CANAL.

MAPA ADJUNTO AL ANEXO A DEL
TRATADO CONCERNIENTE A LA
NEUTRALIDAD PERMANENTE DEL
CANAL Y AL FUNCIONAMIENTO DEL
CANAL DE PANAMA

[ANNEX B]
[ANEXO B]

PROTOCOL TO THE TREATY CONCERNING THE
PERMANENT NEUTRALITY AND OPERATION
OF THE PANAMA CANAL

Whereas the maintenance of the neutrality of the Panama Canal is important not only to the commerce and security of the United States of America and the Republic of Panama, but to the peace and security of the Western Hemisphere and to the interests of world commerce as well;

Whereas the regime of neutrality which the United States of America and the Republic of Panama have agreed to maintain will ensure permanent access to the Canal by vessels of all nations on the basis of entire equality; and

Whereas the said regime of effective neutrality shall constitute the best protection for the Canal and shall ensure the absence of any hostile act against it;

The Contracting Parties to this Protocol have agreed upon the following:

ARTICLE I

The Contracting Parties hereby acknowledge the regime of permanent neutrality for the Canal established in the Treaty Concerning the Permanent Neutrality and Operation of the Panama Canal and associate themselves with its objectives.

ARTICLE II

The Contracting Parties agree to observe and respect the regime of permanent neutrality of the Canal in time of war as in time of peace, and to ensure that vessels of their registry strictly observe the applicable rules.

ARTICLE III

This Protocol shall be open to accession by all States of the world, and shall enter into force for each State at the time of deposit of its instrument of accession with the Secretary General of the Organization of American States.

DEPARTMENT OF STATE PUBLICATION 8912

Inter-American Series 112

Bureau of Public Affairs
Office of Media Services

Released September 1977

INDEX

259

87, 88-89, 131-133, 145, 149, 154, 155, 183-184, 190
Duration and Termination 72-74, 87, 88
Economic issues and costs 38, 87, 90-91, 133-134, 149, 158, 174, 178, 187-189 190, 194, 200
Lands and waters 83, 190-191
Neutrality 70, 73, 74, 87, 88, 149, 155, 175
Personnel 87, 133, 158-159, 175, 179-181, 203
Property transfers 38, 68-69, 71-72, 136, 155, 160, 175, 184-187, 196
Public services 38, 70, 133, 149, 175, 181-184, 187
Sovereignty issue 26, 28, 32, 35, 44, 45, 131
Unresolved issues 193-196
Treaty negotiations (*See also* Foreign Policy Analysis, Negotiations Perspective) 1-2, 10, 37
and Dual track strategy 68-69
and Dual-duration formula 79
and First Negotiating Round (1973-1975) 68-72
and Nixon Administration (1971-1972) 212
and Internationalization of the Canal issue 214, 216-217
and Negotiating Style 69
and Second Negotiating Round (1975-1976) 80-83
and Third Negotiating Round (1977) 83-92
and Two-treaty Formula 88-89, 116
Truth squad 155-156
U.S. Army Corps of Engineers 29
U.S. Army Southern Command 31
U.S. Central American Relations 12-13, 29-30, 31, 40, 197, 198-199, 204
U.S. Comptroller General 182-188
U.S. Department of Defense 7, 31, 33-34, 35, 40, 45, 49, 51, 67, 72-74,

76, 79, 81, 98, 111-113, 116, 130, 132, 142, 144, 156, 174, 175, 176, 181, 183, 188, 191, 193, 211
and Panama Canal Negotiations Working Group 80, 113, 211
U.S. Department of State 7, 33-34, 40, 45, 49, 51, 67, 73-74, 76-77, 80, 81, 95, 98, 111-113, 133, 135, 141, 145-147, 152, 173, 174, 175, 193
U.S. Department of Transportation 193, 202
U.S. Navy 29, 31
U.S.-Panamanian relations 10-12, 30, 31-32, 34, 47, 65-66, 110-111, 118, 174, 179, 195-199, 221-222
and Flag Riots (1964) 31, 32, 45, 47, 66, 84
and Engine 299 196
United Nations 88, 148
Security Council meeting in Panama (1973) 49-51, 65, 109, 212, 214-215, 216
United Brands Fruit Company 134
Vance, Cyrus 37, 83-84, 86-87, 88, 89, 90, 91, 93-94, 100, 119, 137
Viguerie, Richard 99
Walker Commission 23
War Powers Act of 1973 5
Wayne, John 153
Wright, James (D. Tex) 162
Zorinsky, Edward (D-Neb) 154